EXTRAORDINARY ORDINARY LIVES

VOCATION STORIES
OF MINNESOTA VISITATION SISTERS

Elsa Thompson Hofmeister — 2009

ELSA THOMPSON HOFMEISTER

First Edition • March 2009

13 12 11 10 09   1 2 3 4 5

ISBN 13: 978-0-9821405-1-2
ISBN 10: 0-9821405-1-7

Library of Congress Catalog Number: 2009924257

Manufactured in the United States of America.
Printed and bound by Sentinel Printing Company
Designed by James Monroe Design, LLC.

James Monroe Publishing, LLC.
7236 Bald Eagle Lane
Willow River, Minnesota 55795
www.jamesmonroedesign.com

To order, visit: www.visitationsisters.com

To Margaret MacNeil,
who interpreted Sister Mary Regina's message
as a charge to write this book.

And to my husband, Don,
who believed that I could do it
and bore me up every step of the way,
lest I dash my foot against a stone.

UNDERWRITERS

We, the Sisters of the Visitation, wish to express our heartfelt gratitude to the generous friends who made the publication of this book possible.

Anonymous

Catherine A. &
David F. DeSutter

Helen L. &
Thomas P. Flynn, M.D.

Frances C. &
Michael J. Galvin, Jr.

Julie K. & Thomas P. Hurley

Jacqueline C. Breher &
William Jackson

Patricia A. & F. Craig Jilk

Jessie McClintock Kelly

F. Alexandra &
Robert C. Klas Sr.

Barbara G. & David A. Koch

Rajah H. & John L. Kolb

George D. McClintock

Andrea &
Lawrence J. McGough

Harry G. McNeely, Jr.

Brenna M. Murphy

Angela M. Nichols

Cynthia M. &
John D. O'Halloran

Mary Ann &
Thomas L. Okner, M.D.

Vivian W. Piasecki

Sandra &
Thomas S. Schreier, Jr.

Dr. Sandra Smith-Hanen &
Dr. Mike F. Hanen-Smith

Barbara D. &
Thomas F. Votel

43 / 200

Sister Mary Dorothy

Sister Personne Marie

Sister Jane de Chantal

Sister Maria Thérèse

Sister Katherine

S. Brigid Marie

Sister Mary Denise

Sister Mary Paula

Sister Mary Frances

Sr. Mary Frances

CONTENTS

ACKNOWLEDGEMENTS

I wish to acknowledge the many people who have helped me bring this book to life. Clearly, I am most deeply grateful to the fourteen Sisters of the Visitation who were so generous and honest in sharing with me the stories of their private and precious vocational calls. They are Sisters Frances Betterman, Mary Immaculata Binzel, Marie Thérèse Conaty, Carol Ann DePresca, Margaret Agnes Doyle, Marie Antoinette Hynes, Brigid Marie Keefe, Mary Paula McCarthy, Katherine Mullin, Mary Frances Reis, Jane de Chantal Smisek, Péronne Marie Thibert, Mary Denise Villaume and Mary Dorothy Yegge, VHM. Although Sister Mary Regina McCabe has gone on to her heavenly home and was not available to be included, it was her spirit that inspired me to write the vocation histories of her sisters. Their voices speak for her and for the untold numbers of Visitation Sisters who preceded her during the last four hundred years.

Next, my gratitude goes to the members of the Book Advisory Board. They guided the process of the book's development, reading and suggesting revisions, aiding in the selection of a publisher, working in small groups on cover design, layout and choice of photographs to be included, securing financial underwriting, promotion and distribution and finally giving their blessing. Their energy and encouragement provided great support to me during the lengthy period of writing. They are Cathy Edwards, Marilou Eldred, Annamarie Ettel, Patricia Hampl, Judy MacMahon Leahy, Margaret MacNeill, Sister Mary Margaret McKenzie, VHM, Joseph S. Micallef, Dawn Nichols, Maureen O'Connor, Mary Ann Okner, Sister Mary Denise Villaume, VHM, Father Terry Weber, Helen Wilkie, Anne Williams and Jane McClintock Wyatt.

I thank the members of my talented, creative writing group, B. J. Carpenter, Betty Christiansen, Sherry Derus, Mary Henrickson, Maggie DeGennaro Lauer and Elaine Voboril. They have met faithfully with me every week at The Loft Literary Center to support, comfort, advise and suggest revisions. And I am grateful to the Loft's writing teacher, Mary Jean Port, whose inspired instruction caused us to form a group that gives continued life to the enthusiasm she engendered in us.

James (Jay) Monroe not only published *Extraordinary Ordinary Lives*, he designed the front and back covers and interior layout while providing me with invaluable clues to untangling the complex world of the book business. I thank him, and thank my friend, Joseph M. Shuster, author of *Beyond Fossil Fuels*, who highly recommended Jay, his publishing advisor, to me. My two discriminating and meticulous editors, Leif Fedje and Maureen O'Connor, may not realize how extremely helpful they were in polishing and shaping my text, but I know and I will always be grateful to them for their transformative work.

Finally, I must thank the family members who contributed so much to assist the progress of the book. My husband, Don, was the tireless driver, both literally and figuratively, who brought me where I needed to go and lifted me up every time my energy or courage faltered. Sons Franz and Joe spent many hours patiently helping me with organizational and business procedures, and my granddaughter, Cecilia Hofmeister, listened, critiqued and encouraged the entire adventure. To all of you, and to all the dear people mentioned above, I express my gratitude and love for helping me present a picture of Salesian Spirituality in human form, alive and extending its blessings in the world.

—Elsa Thompson Hofmeister
March, 2009

PROLOGUE

Nuns. Creatures of mystery. Who are they, and what drives them to live apart from their families and friends? Vows of poverty, chastity and obedience don't play well on the twenty-first century stage; they weren't all that popular in most of the twentieth, either. Do nuns in essence take a sabbatical from society and live outside its norms to avoid engaging with life? Is it fear that drives them to renounce life as most of us know it?

Or are the reasons more complex? Could it be that nuns have chosen a path unfamiliar to those less attuned to the spiritual world? Stranger still, is it possible that they have not made a choice, but instead have heard a call and been *chosen*?

I hadn't known that the secular world considered nuns to be mysterious until after I graduated from the Convent of the Visitation High School in 1956. People like me are known as Cradle Catholics, born and baptized into a faith shared by nearly everyone around us. Veiled and robed nuns weren't unusual in our world. They were the sisters who nurtured our childhoods and were counted among the beloved members of our tribes—feminine elders like our mothers, grandmothers and aunts.

It was not until I left my sheltered compound for the larger world that I learned that "non-Catholics" considered nuns to be peculiar people. Back then, in our innocent arrogance, we Catholics called everyone but ourselves "non-Catholics." I was surprised to hear my associates in our secular workplace question the lives led by the consecrated women who had played such a large part in my development into personhood, womanhood.

It was hard to explain to others how they did this; at the time I didn't fully realize how important their example was to me. The sisters who nurtured my faith were among my role models, women who were daily living out their devotion to God through the service of prayer and teaching. Their steady awareness of the presence of God provided a foundation of faith that could guide me in bringing my life to fulfillment. They provided me with the instruments to meet the challenges of growing up—it was up to me to use them. If I persevered and grew in the virtues they practiced, the crescent that represented my girlhood would configure into a circle: symbol of both womanhood and the wheel of life's journey.

That was the promise the sisters made to the students at our school. Give each action each day to God, and we would become the women we were meant to be. The Visitation Sisters presented each graduating senior with an actual gold crescent as a reminder of our incompleteness. Though the crescent's meaning was figurative, its hard, metallic contour grounded it in reality.

I did my best to describe the sisters to those who were not Catholics and to tell them what a religious vocation meant, but I was aware that I didn't express it very well. I was not one of those who had heard the silent summons. It wasn't until years later that my invitation arrived, and then it was not to enter a monastery, but to become involved in a deeper understanding of religious life through writing about it. Now I could finally answer my friends' questions and pay tribute to the women we honor with the title *Sister*.

On May 22, 2004, Sister Mary Regina McCabe, VHM, died at age ninety-eight. The VHM stands for Visitation of Holy Mary, the religious order that embraced her and informed her consciousness for eighty years. Hers was a life spent in joyful witness to her vocation, and I silently wept at her funeral Mass, realizing that her radiant spirit would no longer shine upon us. At least not from where we could see it. I believed that her spirit would continue to influence us from her home in heaven.

I first met Sister Mary Regina when I was a student at Visitation Convent, a highly respected school for girls in Saint Paul, Minnesota. She was witty and fun to be with, a tiny woman, barely five feet tall, but indomitable in intellect and will. She stood for no nonsense in her classroom, demanding and accepting only the best that each of us could be and do. Expert at discerning each girl's strengths, she graciously received the sometimes flawed efforts of the less gifted, but scorned slovenly work from those of us she knew to be talented in English. One questioning arch of that dark eyebrow sent us scurrying back to our desks, determined to live up to her challenges.

She charged the air around her with such energy and humor that I nearly always was surprised when the class period ended. It was impossible to be restless or bored as we delved ever more deeply into literature. We loved her for telling us that *Hamlet's* Ophelia was a ninny. She could not understand why such a ridiculous creature was romanticized in literary criticism: "She was an absolute ninny, allowing herself to be victimized by that brooding boy. She should have given up on him the minute he started acting like an idiot. Don't you girls go thinking she was some great, tragic figure. I'm telling you, she was a ninny."

Standing before us, our copies of Thackeray's *Vanity Fair* open on our desks, she would say, "Look for the *meaning* behind the words, girls. Don't take every sentence literally; what do you think the author is *saying?*" Her love of great writing was apparent in her voice and eyes as she guided us to a greater appreciation of excellence.

She and I remained friends over the years; my husband of just a few hours knew how much I loved her and didn't protest when I insisted that the first stop on our honeymoon be Visitation Convent. I wanted our marriage to receive the blessing of all the nuns, but especially that of Sister Mary Regina.

Years later, in 1993, when I accepted an administrative position at Visitation Convent School, I saw her nearly every day as she worked and hummed in the kitchen. In her eighties by then and no longer teaching, she had lost none of her old spark and was still interested in the affairs of the school and the world beyond it. We talked frequently as the dough rose in the pans, our conversations often turning to God and the Church she loved so dearly, though she was very aware of its foibles and mistakes.

We also discussed the shrinking numbers of women aspiring to become nuns and wondered what it portended for the future. Although the world seems to be entering a phase of awakened interest in spiritual life, many religious orders are diminishing in numbers, and even dying out entirely. Some Visitation monasteries throughout the world, while perhaps not flourishing, are holding their own, but Sister Mary Regina's community, relocated now from Saint Paul to Mendota Heights, was definitely aging and shrinking.

Sitting in the chapel at her funeral, I observed sadly how small the ranks of her sisters had become. Her death had reduced their numbers to twelve. As her sisters tenderly closed the lid of her coffin and draped the burial pall over it, I pictured her tiny frame standing erect before the angelic host, filled with awe, but probably not fear. Her God was one of love, not wrath; her trust in His promises secure.

While imagining her in heaven, I sensed she glanced in my direction, much as she used to in class if she detected anyone's attention wandering. I seemed to hear her say to me, "Don't just sit there feeling mournful; *do* something." She didn't want me to be a ninny like Ophelia, drowning myself uselessly in grief.

I smiled as I remembered her impatience with moping girls. When she noticed that one of her students seemed moody or unhappy, she would draw her aside privately for a gentle probe. A plan of some kind to address the problem would usually emerge; she thought that time spent feeling sorry for oneself was time wasted. It would be better spent in prayer, action or both.

During the summer days after her death, my conviction grew that I was to do something with the sisters. But what? I had taken early retirement several years before and was deeply involved in a writing project that would be hard to abandon. I could see that my help was not needed in the school; it was staffed with excellent lay teachers and administrators committed to continuing the Visitation spirit. Enrollment was high, the graduates were actively involved and a contribution campaign was solidly in place. Each night I quietly prayed that Sister Mary Regina would enlighten me, but she was up to her old classroom tricks. She preferred that her students use their minds and hearts to resolve questions instead of getting direct answers from her.

I finally went to see two administrators of the school, and it was from one of them that direction came. Margie MacNeill, at that time the director of the upper school, knew that the sisters were concerned about their dwindling numbers. There was no specific written history of their monastery or of the religious vocations that had been fulfilled there.

Margie said, "These sisters should have their stories written and preserved." She paused and then looked at me with a direct gaze for which she is well-known. "You're a writer, Elsa; *you* should interview the community members and write about them for posterity."

Was *this* what Sister Mary Regina had asked of me that day in May? Hardly in the habit of receiving revelations from beyond, I cautioned myself against being dramatic, but Margie's words felt valid. I decided I should pay a visit to the current Mother Superior, Sister Mary Denise Villaume, who found the idea worth considering. She took it to her advisory council and, within a few months, I met with the monastic community and was enthusiastically commissioned to undertake this project.

We discussed the matter of how to tell the story. Should it be a broad overview from the time of the sisters' arrival in Saint Paul with a cameo view of each one? Their descriptions would be based on items gleaned from the brief biographies composed at the times of their deaths, with the current sisters adding material from their memories.

It didn't feel right. The unique spirit of the Visitation is *relational*. It is found in the hidden corridors of the heart, in the open expression of giving and receiving love, not just in written exposition.

No, the story must come from the hearts of the sisters living in community today. They continue to live the legacy of those who preceded them, not just in the last one hundred years in Saint Paul, but also in the nearly three hundred years before that. They represent the charism of their Holy Founders and of the Visitation Order down the centuries.

As I interviewed the sisters, seeking the stories that led to their commitment, I began to feel the heartbeat, the pulse, of the dedicated, contemplative life that runs through all nuns. I also realized what a great honor it was for me to receive the confidences of these beautiful women. They placed their trust in me, allowing me into the most intimate, precious part of their lives: their calling and their answer to that call.

In the following pages I attempt to capture the unique spirit of the Order of the Visitation of Holy Mary. This distinctive spirit is called *Salesian*, named after Saint Francis de Sales, one of the Order's founders. The other founder was Saint Jane de Chantal, a devout widow who shared Francis' dream of creating an order of women whose ordinary lives would become extraordinary through the embodiment of the "little virtues" of humility and gentleness.

I have arranged the following chapters in the order in which I interviewed the sisters so their stories will unfold to you the same way they did to me. But first, I briefly describe the historical context that frames the vocation stories of the Saint Paul/ Mendota Heights Sisters.

THE JOURNEY BEGINS

The Sisters of the Visitation of Holy Mary have been a spiritual force in the world for nearly four hundred years. Their order was established in 1610 by Francis de Sales and Jane de Chantal, two religious luminaries of the seventeenth century, who were formally canonized as saints by the Catholic Church not long after their deaths in 1622 and 1641, respectively.

Both came from noble families. Francis de Sales, Bishop of Savoy, was a gentle soul, very unlike his fiery and famous near-contemporary, John Calvin. During his lifetime, Calvin had entreated Catholics to throw off the shackles of adherence to human rules and embrace Protestantism. He emphasized salvation of the elect through the Lord's grace alone. De Sales, entering the arena of the Reformation a few years later, eloquently persuaded the newly converted to return to the Mother Church by reminding them of the traditions that celebrated God's abiding mercy, love and forgiveness. The two men never met, but their writings strongly influenced the development of Western Christian belief with its dissensions and divisions.

Francis was born in 1567 to parents who were members of the old Savoyard aristocracy. He attended the best schools of the time, studying rhetoric, humanities, law and theology. While still a very young man, he came into contact with the Calvinist doctrine of predestination and suffered a severe crisis of faith, believing himself to be damned eternally to hell. Praying incessantly to the Blessed Virgin, he begged her to release him from despair. When his prayers were answered and he returned to a state of belief in a loving God, he took a vow of chastity and resolved to become a priest.

He prevailed in this in spite of resistance from his father, François de Boisy, who wished him to become a magistrate. François had already obtained several important positions for his brilliant son and had selected a wealthy heiress to be his bride. The Bishop of Geneva, who had learned of Francis' extraordinary holiness, intervened on his behalf to help him defy his father's wishes. The bishop found for him a high office in the diocese under the patronage of the pope himself, and his father finally gave in.

As an ordained priest and, later, bishop, Francis quickly drew a following among nobles and peasants alike. He loved the poor, emulating them in his manner of living, and became famous for his goodness, patience and gentleness. As a bishop and member of the nobility, he could have adorned himself in rich robes and precious stones. Instead, he dressed plainly and simply, preaching throughout the countryside on what he called the "little virtues" of gentleness, kindness, humility, cheerfulness and graciousness. His message was that it is within reach of all to lead lives of holiness in spite of the cares of everyday life. He has been called the

Saint of Common Sense, for he did not set impossible goals for ordinary men and women in their search for the devout life. In fact, he wrote the first book of spiritual instructions for the laity, *Introduction to the Devout Life.*

Francis also wrote letters of spiritual direction, many of them to a woman named Jane de Chantal, who was to become his companion in establishing a religious order based on the "little virtues."

Jane Frémyot was born in 1572 into a fervently Catholic family. As a child she was unusually observant of religious practices, growing up in a household that encouraged and nourished her faith. She witnessed her father's many courageous acts in defiance of the Protestantism that was threatening to prevail in France. During a particularly adversarial period, her thirteen-year-old brother was kidnapped by a faction that threatened to return his head in a sack if her father persisted in denouncing them. Her father sent his son's captors a letter stating that he would rather his son "die honourably now than let him live to know that his father had turned traitor, acting against his honour and duty as a Christian gentleman." The kidnappers were so impressed by his integrity that they returned the boy unharmed. The letter itself is in the municipal archives of the city of Dijon.

When Henry the Fourth ascended the throne and proclaimed France a Catholic country, he offered Jane's father a position in his court as a reward for his loyalty, but the pious man turned it down. He told the king that after his civic and family duties were behind him, he wished to become a priest and retire to contemplative life.

Little wonder that in such an atmosphere young Jane grew strong in her faith. At age twenty she married the Baron de Chantal and, though it was an arranged union, as was the custom of the time, the couple loved each other dearly. They lived in the de Chantal family's feudal chateau, where they had four children: a son and three daughters. Jane was happy with her husband and children, bringing the old castle into orderliness and prosperity, while treating the tenants in her care with great kindness. When her husband was away at the king's court in Paris, she dressed as plainly as the peasants she served. Other ladies of the area criticized her for dressing beneath her station, but they could not dissuade her. She answered them by saying that the only eyes she needed to please were a hundred miles away. She became known throughout the countryside for her many acts of charity as well as her prayers on behalf of the poor. They called her *la bonne dame* (the good woman) for her extraordinary kindnesses to those in need.

This idyllic existence was suddenly and cruelly interrupted by the death of her husband in a hunting accident. Jane was only twenty-eight years old. Broken-hearted, she was forced to move into her father-in-law's house to protect her children's inheritance. This was a most unhappy situation for the young widow. The household was run by her father-in-law's mistress, who considered Jane little more than a servant and subjected her to humiliating treatment for the next seven years. It grieved Jane to live in a place in which the virtue of purity was so flagrantly ignored. She took a vow of chastity and prayed that God would send a spiritual guide to direct her.

Her prayer was answered when, in a vision, she saw the man who would be this guide. Later, while visiting her father in Dijon during the Lenten season, she saw Francis de Sales preaching. She immediately recognized him as the man God had shown her. Legend has it that Francis too experienced a shock of recognition, for he had prayed to meet a person who would help him in his work, and had seen Jane's face in a dream. She stood now before him, asking him to place her under his tutelage. He became her spiritual advisor and mentor, and they began the correspondence that led to their founding of the first Visitation Monastery in the town of Annecy, near Dijon. (Annecy had become the seat of the Catholic bishops of Geneva, as at the time Geneva was under the control of the Protestants.)

Jane arranged for the futures of her oldest children and took the two youngest with her to Annecy. There, she and Francis established their new monastic order of women, an order that was grounded in humility, gentleness and simplicity. When writing guidelines for the new community, Francis urged Jane to concentrate on the virtues of humility and kindness, rather than making mortifications and penances a focus for the sisters. This was a huge turning point in the history of religious life. The significance of this enormous change in customs and behavior should not be underestimated.

Monasticism in the seventeenth century and before that, in medieval times, was arduous and demanding. Many women who sought to embrace their vocations were sent home because they were not physically strong enough to follow the penitential rules. They were required to spend long hours at prayer on their knees in cold chapels, fasting from meat and sleeping little. The prevailing belief was that suffering was good for the soul.

Francis and Jane believed that the intention to be virtuous in all words and actions would lead souls to God without the necessity of harsh physical deprivations. Moderation and simplicity were their watchwords as they set up a dwelling in which ordinary women, even those beyond their youth or in poor health, could follow God's call to His service.

Theirs was a revolutionary vision, and it appealed greatly to women of the time. Disenchanted with the extravagances and moral dissolution of court life, but discouraged by the stringent demands of regular convent customs, women of high birth came eagerly to be mentored into religious life under the gentle tutelage of Jane de Chantal. She graciously received these women, who were to become the first Sisters of the Visitation of Holy Mary, and the new community, which started with three, grew to ten within the first year. Women of low birth were welcomed too; they acted as serving women to the others, following the practices of the times. Europe was generations away from becoming a classless society.

The name chosen by Francis and Jane for the new order comes from the gospel story of Mary's visit to her cousin, Elizabeth, mother of John the Baptist. Each was carrying within her a child who would become a bringer of good news to humankind; each manifested the reality of a woman giving and receiving love.

From the beginning, the Sisters of the Visitation have sought to live with their attention fixed on the words chosen as the foundation stone of their order from Matthew 11: 29, "Learn from me, for I am gentle and humble of heart."

Gentleness is a quality that turns away the forces of violence. In Francis' words, "There is nothing so strong as gentleness and nothing so gentle as real strength." He understood the difference between force and power. Force, which is violent, compels obedience through fear and intimidation. Power, which is gentle, ennobles and strengthens through example and guidance. Francis de Sales emerges as a grand figure of non-violence in a time of savage religious turmoil.

He encouraged the sisters to embrace the belief that souls are drawn to God, not through constraint, but through love; it was he who coined the well-known phrase: "You can catch more flies with a spoonful of honey than with a barrel of vinegar." The honey bee is a well-loved symbol of Saint Francis.

The Visitation motto, *Vive Jésus*, "Live Jesus," means that every thought and action is to be performed with the love of Jesus and His will in mind. To be virtuous one need only seek God in each moment, turn to the business at hand—whatever it may be—and do it well. Saint Francis taught that the most ordinary act becomes extraordinary when performed to the best of one's ability and for the love of God.

Under this loving and tender interpretation of the devout life, the new religious congregation flourished and blossomed. The honeyed words of Francis were carried like pollen from sister to sister, led by Jane as she traveled through France establishing new houses. When Francis died in 1622, there were thirteen Visitation Monasteries in France, and by the time Jane died in 1641 there were eighty-six.

The communities followed the constitution written by Saint Francis, which Raphael Pernin in *The Catholic Encyclopedia* calls "admirable for wisdom, discretion and sweetness." Until it was modified in the 1970s, following the directives of the Second Vatican Council, the order had not been found in need of any reform, so well did it suit the purposes for which it was designed.

While rules of extreme austerity, such as sleep deprivation and periods of long fasting, were not dictated, the *interior* discipline of each sister was emphasized. Obedience and poverty were stressed; no order was stricter than the Visitation when it came to the owning of property. The sisters own nothing in person, everything in common. Even the large silver crosses worn around their necks are exchanged every year, to further emphasize that principle.

Another distinguishing feature of the order's spirit is found in their governance. Each Visitation community is autonomous and independent of the other houses. They have no central authority or Superior General. Each community elects its Mother Superior by secret ballot, an office that is never sought nor lobbied for. The Holy Spirit guides their choice. After serving three years, the superior may be elected for another three by the same secret ballot, but then is ineligible for the next term. The charism of the order eschews any exercise of power of one over another; their system of leadership protects them from succumbing to such temptation.

Francis de Sales is often depicted with bees surrounding him, an apt metaphor for the saint whose words traveled as though on small, persistent wings, bringing new life to those who heard. Visitation communities continued to grow, crossing over barriers of nationality and language, as though fertilized by those little carriers of good news. By the middle of the eighteenth century the order had extended into Switzerland, Italy, Spain, Germany, the Low Countries and Poland.

Even the storms of the French Revolution did not quench the fires of Salesian Spirituality. Though the government closed all the convents within its reach during this turbulent period, the flame of the Visitation spirit was kept alive in the foreign houses. After the revolution, when civil order was restored in France, the monasteries began to return. They flowered there again, and even crossed the Atlantic to America in a single leap via the book Saint Francis had written for the laity.

In 1799, three women in Georgetown who were seeking a religious order had been living under the Jesuit rule, but were profoundly moved after reading Francis de Sales' *Introduction to the Devout Life*. The Visitation charism, grounded as it is in simplicity, moderation, optimism and flexibility, greatly appealed to them. They asked for, and received, permission from their bishop to establish a Visitation Monastery. From the seed of this first convent in Georgetown, others spread: first to Mobile, then Saint Louis, Baltimore, Frederick, Philadelphia and beyond.

In 1872, a Catholic businessman, John Stoughtenberg Prince, was the former mayor of Saint Paul and the father of several daughters. He had sent his eldest girl to the Visitation Convent in Saint Louis for high school and had been deeply impressed by the quality of her education. He and his wife observed that their daughter was not only making excellent progress academically, she was also growing more gentle and gracious in her demeanor. Eager to have a Visitation Convent School in

Saint Paul, he gathered a group of wealthy Catholic businessmen to whom he extolled the quality of a Visitation education. They put up money to buy a property for the sisters and approached Archbishop Thomas Grace for his support in their venture. The archbishop responded with enthusiasm and extended an invitation to the Saint Louis Visitation Monastery.

One year later, six sisters left their monastery in Saint Louis and traveled by steamboat to Saint Paul. On the weeklong journey, they stayed on land for one night in Dubuque, Iowa, where they had a joyful reunion with sisters they never thought they'd see again. Those sisters had left Saint Louis some years earlier to establish a monastery in Dubuque and, because their order was cloistered, all had assumed their separation would be permanent. Instead, they shared an evening filled with reminiscence, offering thanks to God for this unexpected opportunity to re-connect.

The journey was an adventure for the little group. The oldest member, Mother Agatha Russell, was about sixty years old and had come from Ireland to visit relatives in Saint Louis in 1830. While there, she felt called to religious life, and she never returned to Ireland, instead entering the Visitation Monastery, where she remained for forty-three years until answering a new call to Saint Paul.

The world had changed radically during her years in the cloister, and she marveled at all the new things she saw. She was especially excited by her first sight of a train noisily chuffing along its tracks, its shrill whistle blasting, its stack blowing black smoke into the air. She spent hours on deck watching the iron horses as they followed the course of the Mississippi River up and down, paralleling the journeys of the steamboats.

Mirrors had been invented well before steam engines, but they were perceived as an unnecessary vanity, and were not found in the convent. These first Saint Paul sisters enjoyed recounting their surprise when, on the first day of their trip, they had come to the deck to take the air and seen another group of sisters seated across from them. They had not been informed that other nuns besides themselves would be aboard. Mother Agatha indicated to her sisters that they should bow to the other group, and they were pleased to see them bow back. This dictated that they rise and cross the deck to greet each other. As they did so, they saw the others rise and start to approach them too. They were almost upon each other before realizing they had been seeing themselves in the reflection of the ship's large looking glass. They were the only nuns on board.

Their journey up the river was peaceful, but they were eager to embrace their new life and were ready to leave the boat when it arrived at Saint Paul's Landing. By 1873 Saint Paul was a railroad hub and had many industries in operation, as well as some beautiful residential areas near the river and Lowertown. The sisters were escorted in an open carriage by Mr. Prince and his sons for a tour of the city. They wanted to impress the citizens with the new sisters Mr. Prince had recruited, and also wanted the sisters to be aware of St. Paul's size and grandeur.

He neglected, however, to inform them that they were on a sight-seeing tour, and they became quite alarmed at the distance they were covering. As they traversed block after block, they worried that this new home of theirs was in a place far larger than they had been led to believe. Would their prospective students be able to travel so far from their homes to attend the school? They didn't realize that they were simply going around neighborhoods and backtracking the distances they had already covered. They were relieved later to learn that their convent at 5 Somerset Street was not far from the river and the landing where they had debarked.

The make-up of the group was typical for members of a community setting out to establish a new foundation. There would be a seasoned nun—Mother Agatha—and a young sister of great promise who would likely grow into a position of leadership. This nun was twenty-two-year-old Sister Clementine Shepherd. She did, indeed, fulfill her potential, becoming in time a Mother Superior beloved not only by her community, but by generations of students and their grateful parents.

Accompanying Sisters Agatha and Clementine was another nun of middle age, and two "lay" sisters and an "out" sister. The lay sisters were women who were not fully professed, having taken only "simple" vows. They did most of the domestic work of cooking and laundry. In spite of the egalitarianism of the order, these sisters functioned rather like servants to the fully professed sisters. Although the sisters were American-born, this was a carry-over from European customs, where every lady had a lady's maid; the sisters from upper-class families were attended by sisters from serving-class families. They followed the same vocational call, but had different roles within their monasteries.

The out sister literally went out to shop for food and supplies, since the cloistered sisters did not leave the monastery grounds. The lay and out sisters were usually uneducated and came from the serving classes, and the situation did not seem unusual to them until several years later, when Archbishop John Ireland, who succeeded Archbishop Grace, pointed out the discrepancy.

When Archbishop Ireland paid his first pastoral call to the Visitation Monastery, he was startled to see the out sister in a bonnet and the two lay sisters in white veils. He wondered why they didn't all wear the same habit. Mother Agatha explained the system to him, but he would have none of it.

"This is America," he exclaimed. "Your practice is not democratic. It won't do." He went on to deplore Europe's lamentable class distinctions. He thought it was poor policy for any society to acknowledge social classes based on birth, education or wealth.

Those artificial barriers had no place in a convent; all the sisters should be equally professed.

Archbishop Ireland wanted them to change their rule. His reasoning made sense to the sisters and they proceeded to make the adjustments he wanted. They quickly came to see that he had done them a great service so early in their establishment. The other Visitation Monasteries in the United States eventually came to the same conclusion and did away with any rankings among their sisters, but it took them longer to see the injustice that had been so obvious to Archbishop Ireland.

Mother Agatha's entourage arrived in Saint Paul on August 12, 1873, and by September 1 she had put an ad in the local paper describing the type of education they offered young ladies:

> *The Academy occupies a healthy and pleasing site in the most desirable part of the city, its location being only one block from the Street Railway. The house will be ready for the reception of pupils on the first Monday of September. A limited number of boarders will be received. The course of instruction pursued at this institution furnishes all the branches of a thorough English education, also such accomplishments as languages, music, drawing, painting and needle work. The study of music is particularly attended to, and a special care is taken to instruct the pupils thoroughly in each department. (qtd. in McCarthy 10)*

The academy opened on September 7 with fourteen students. By the end of the year there were twenty-nine.

The young ladies who attended the convent on Somerset Street in 1873 studied not at desks in orderly rows, but on easy chairs and sofas in informal groupings. It was considered desirable for each girl to be able to draw and play an instrument, do fine needlework and, of course, improve her skills in reading, writing and arithmetic.

Religion was an important subject; the mission of the school then, as today, was to produce strong, Christian women who would live in the world practicing devotion to God and service to their communities. They would uphold high moral standards and exhibit refined behavior. The qualities that constitute "refined behavior" have changed considerably in over one hundred years, but the virtues of gentleness and humility remain timeless and are still stressed and emphasized in the Visitation schools today.

The sisters and their students soon outgrew their first little home, and they had it moved to a property on Robert Street and Aurora Avenue, where they attached it to a larger house already there. Before long, even this property was too small. Steady growth dictated several more moves, but the facilities were still more like large Victorian homes than institutional buildings. In 1913, Clara Hill, James J. Hill's daughter, paid out of her own pocket to build a real school and monastery building at 720 Fairmount. Though she had attended Visitation, she had not graduated, which was not unusual at the time. Many girls attended high school only until they and their parents felt they had mastered appropriate skills and learned how to handle themselves well in society. The Alumni Association was so grateful for Clara's financial donation that they made her an honorary alumna, and in 1914 added her photograph to their collection. It still hangs on the wall of the current school in Mendota Heights, between two depictions of the Fairmont building.

It wasn't until the school was established on Fairmont Avenue in 1913 that formal classrooms with desks and chalkboards made their appearance. The building at 720 Fairmount was dark red brick, four stories high and dominated on the corner by a square bell tower. A wall eight feet high of the same dark brick surrounded the monastery and its grounds on all sides. To the uninitiated it looked forbidding, a completely enclosed dwelling walled to keep those inside from escaping. We knew better. A cloister wall is not erected to keep the sisters in; it is to keep the world out. The sisters are there by choice, not coercion. The contemplative life requires separation from the distractions of the world; the assurance that the times of prayer will be free from interruption.

In her memoir, *Virgin Time*, Patricia Hampl, a graduate of the Visitation Class of 1964, captures the spiritual environment at 720 Fairmount, its impact on the students and our view of the nuns who taught us. "Teaching was a profession, and we were a job. We did not provide life's meaning. This was a refreshing wind to have gusting through what was otherwise an oppressively protective environment" (29).

It was good for us to understand this. Adolescents tend to believe that nothing matters more than their own concerns. The sisters' devotion to us was unquestioned, but we knew that the most significant part of their lives was celebrated in the chapel, not the classroom. They fit us into the flow of their days, accommodating our lessons around the hours at which the Divine Office was to be said, not the other way around. When they disappeared through the doors leading to their cloister, we knew we were not to follow. We had our world, and they had theirs.

After fifty-three years, the Fairmont location was considered inadequate to serve the ever growing student population, as well as the increasing number of sisters. The community purchased land in Mendota Heights to construct a new monastery and school. The timing coincided with the emergence of the ideas of Vatican II, the Church Council that initiated so many changes in the way Catholics conduct their affairs.

Nuns who had not ventured beyond their walls for years now found themselves moving from quarters where they had expected to spend their entire lives. They traveled by airplane to distant states to further their educations, attend Salesian conferences and even visit their parents and brothers and sisters. They were urged to look at their customs and to purge rules that had been established in distant centuries, rules that may have outlived their original intent and were being retained mostly from habit. Just as when Archbishop Ireland, so many years earlier, had advised them to embrace democratic principles in their governance, the Vatican was now telling religious orders to examine their customs and reshape those that were outmoded.

When the Visitation Order in the United States was established in 1799, the sisters looked to Annecy for the regulations to govern them and define the pattern of their days. The customs they adopted had been developed while France was still a monarchy, and desirable behavior was modeled after courtly conduct. For certain ceremonies, a sister would genuflect before approaching her Mother Superior, just as ladies of the court once genuflected before their queen. By the time Vatican II was convened, customs such as these had long been considered archaic by most of society, but they still were practiced in monasteries as part of their inherited rituals.

It was a time of great upheaval, not only for Visitation Sisters, but for Catholics the world over. When the Saint Paul community moved to Mendota Heights, they were even unsure of how extensively to divide their cloistered space from the areas open to the public. The contemplative life was not to be discontinued, of course, but in a foundation that had the active ministry of a school, more openness with the laity was encouraged.

The new building in Mendota Heights opened in 1966. Paradoxically, as the school continued to wax, the monastery began to wane. A home that had been built for fifty sisters proved too large, while the school was stretched beyond capacity with the start of each new term. When the wide-scale exodus of religious from their monasteries swept the Church in the seventies after Vatican II, Visitation was less affected than many of the larger orders, but still lost members of its community. Perhaps more significantly, few young women were seeking to embrace monasticism as a way of life.

When I began interviewing the sisters, there were fourteen members in their community. One, Sister Mary Carmelita, had developed Alzheimer's and could not participate in the process. She has since died, as has Sister Mary Immaculata, whose story is included here. The future of the community is uncertain. As death takes its natural toll, the monastery numbers continue to dwindle.

Under these circumstances, one might expect to find an air of despondency among the sisters. But no. The future is a cause for worry only for those who believe that the future is in their hands and under their control. As you will see in the ensuing stories, each sister expresses her confidence in the Holy Spirit to guide and enlighten the future, whatever it may be.

SISTER BRIGID MARIE

From the start, this project was in the hands of the Holy Spirit, and I was willing to follow where I was led. I had had no plan or design for arranging the sisters' stories, so, as I said earlier, I decided to present them in pretty much the same order in which they were given to me.

The sisters arranged for the sessions to be held in a parlor adjacent to the cloistered quarters, directly across the hall from the chapel. As I laid out my recording equipment on a small table covered with a dainty lace doily, I felt a quiver from the adventure that was starting.

Nothing in the room suggested that business was to be conducted here. The straight-backed chairs had seats softly clothed in rose-colored silk; the sofa was patterned in stripes of ivory and pink, shot through with gold thread. Portraits of saints and popes looked down at me, neither friendly nor hostile—they were waiting. Suspended over the sofa was a large, ornately framed print of Raphael's *Madonna of the Chair*, the chubby legs of the Christ Child glowing pink and gold in the subdued light. He appeared to be waiting too.

Sister Brigid entered from the cloister side, smiling as she greeted me in her soft, musical voice. It was March 7, 2005, and although Sister Brigid was sixty-three years old, her voice still retained the childlike quality of the timid girl once known to the world as Kathleen Keefe. The shyness that marked, and marred, her childhood is evidenced now only by blushes that sometimes suffuse her light Irish skin when she is addressed. Prayer and practice have, over the years, conquered most of her fear of speaking to others.

Born in 1942 in Minneapolis, she was the eldest child of John and Bernice Keefe. John's work required the family move to New York when Kathleen was two years old; they stayed until she was six. During these war years, housing was nearly impossible to find in New York. They had to settle for a home in a tough neighborhood in Flushing. Kathleen started kindergarten in a large, noisy New York Public School, an environment that was terrifying to the shy little girl.

She had always been frightened of meeting new people, fumbling miserably when urged by her mother to speak up to grown-ups and look them in the face. Each time she tried, she became more self-conscious, and the rate of her mother's criticism increased. The chaotic atmosphere of her schoolroom did nothing to assuage her fears of being with people she didn't know, but her mother was not sympathetic. She believed that her daughter found school difficult only because she didn't want to mingle, but Kathleen knew better. She still remembers how wild the other kids were, running from one end of the classroom to the other, screaming and throwing things. Eventually the inexperienced teacher got them settled down, but it was well into the school year by then, and it was too late for Kathleen to feel secure in that environment. She was very relieved when the family was told they could return to Minneapolis before the end of that year.

Her little sister, Mary Jo, was born while the Keefes were in New York, and she seemed to have absorbed the sass and élan of that bold city. She was out-going and happy-go-lucky, suffering none of the timidity that made Mrs. Keefe so impatient with Kathleen. Another child, a boy named John, was also born just before the family returned to Minneapolis.

When Kathleen started first grade she was relieved to discover that the children at Christ the King School in Minneapolis were better behaved than her New York kindergarten classmates had been. She began to make friends and not feel like so much of a failure, but her shyness persisted, as did her mother's irritation with her.

Kathleen's paternal grandmother tried to get Kathleen's mother to be less critical and demanding, because she could see that pushing the little girl was a mistake. Grandma Keefe was a comfort to Kathleen, as she seemed sensitive to the child's feelings. She had lost her husband at a young age and brought up six children during the Great Depression on her own, and Kathleen loved her and admired her strength.

Sister Brigid sees now that her mother thought she was doing the right thing by prodding her daughter to be more assertive. Self-help books on child rearing were almost non-existent at that time, and parents relied on the only methods they knew even though they are now seen as coercive. She also recognizes that the pain of inadequacy she felt as a child helped her become a better teacher. From her own experience she understood that shy children in the classroom need to be left alone until they gain their own sense of the environment. Urging them to mingle and speak up only drives them further into their fear. Time and gentle approval nearly always results in their learning to join in and become willing students.

"Maybe that innate shyness of yours explains why I didn't get to know you better when I came back to Visitation to work in the upper school," I offered. "I often caught a glimpse of you working quietly in the business office, and I remember that you always smiled at me, but we never really conversed."

"That's probably true," she answered. "It's no longer hard for me to be around people, but until I get to know them I tend not to be chatty. You and I had different roles and never really worked together."

She smiled. "For all my shyness, I was never shy when I was with my sister, Mary Jo. When we were left alone we would play for hours cutting out clothes for our paper dolls and creating animated families with the stiff cardboard figures. Sometimes we pretended to be dogs for an entire day, and had to bark or whine and paw to communicate with each other. We played school, lining up the dining room chairs in rows and placing our dolls and teddy bears on the seats as pupils. Then, as teachers, we instructed the group and corrected their imaginary papers. My childhood had its difficult times, but there was much happiness as well. I don't want to give the impression that my mother's scolding made it totally bleak."

The quiet, feminine pursuits she and Mary Jo enjoyed together in the home changed as their world expanded to include the children in their neighborhood in Minneapolis. The Keefes had a vacant lot next door to their house, and nearly every summer morning kids would gather to play baseball from seven o'clock until noon. In the evenings they rode their bikes around the block and played games in the street and in the alley. It was fun, and she felt natural and relaxed with the kids. The last thing on her mind was her future, let alone her future as a nun.

And then one night, when she was nine, she had her first spiritual experience. The neighborhood kids had been playing kick the can until it got too dark to see each other, and friends were drifting away and going home. Kathleen, instead of going into her house, lay down on the soft grass in the yard to be alone for a moment. Slowly, she became aware of the starry sky above her. She had seen the stars a thousand times before, of course, but never like this. They seemed to be speaking to her in the silence, conveying a wordless message that there was *more* out there than she had ever known. A sense of something that transcended human experience, something big and nameless and powerful beyond comprehension, came over her. She began to feel the immensity of God and His eternal presence. If only she could stay out there forever, drinking in the beauty of the night sky, dazzled by the canopy above her! The science of the stars, the constellations and positions, held no interest for her this night. Only the cosmic ballet held her rapt attention. When her father called her to come in, she felt as if she were returning from another world into one that should have been familiar, but now was strangely different.

The memory of that magical night stayed with her, but she didn't relate it in any way to her Catholic faith. She was already beginning to perceive the difference between religion as a belief system and spirituality as awareness of the presence of God. Knowing that she had experienced something wonderful, she spoke to no one about it. Her normal life resumed with school and friends, but she was aware of a new intensity about religious teachings.

Once, in first grade, she was mesmerized by the way her teacher explained the passion of Christ and the events leading to the crucifixion. To her horror, a boy raised his hand and asked if he could get a drink of water. How could he *do* such a thing? What irreverence! The teacher said maybe everyone needed a break, but the experience was ruined for Kathleen. It was like a shocking interruption to a meditation. She never forgot it.

"I remember those spiritual experiences very clearly, but at that age they didn't last long, even though they were very intense. They were quickly erased by other sensations—absorptions in a game or my schoolwork or my friends."

In fifth grade she acquired a boyfriend, which made her mother frantic. The nagging she had directed at her daughter to be more outgoing and friendly wasn't meant to result in this! He was a boy named Stephen who came to the house to play with her younger brothers, but it was clear he had his eye on Kathleen. Mother was terrified this would set a terrible precedent for the younger children; there shouldn't be any kind of this nonsense going on in children so young!

"That winter our classroom won a fire prevention contest of some kind, and our reward was a free trip to the Ice Capades. My boyfriend asked me to go with him, which meant sitting with him on the bus and at the show. This pushed Mother beyond her limit and her concern accelerated. Two ten-year-olds behaving as if they were on a date! I thought I'd never hear the end of it!"

"Did you get to go to the show?"

"I went all right, but with the other girls, and I didn't sit with him or any of the boys. That was the sad end to my first romance. Mother was relieved, of course, but I felt pretty bad. Shortly after that, Stephen lost interest in me and found another girlfriend. I was really wounded. From a discreet distance, I followed his progress through the rest of elementary school and noticed that he was never without a girlfriend. To him, it was just a way of life, but to me it had been a hurtful experience. I had been flattered by his attentions and was confused when he broke off with me so abruptly. You can imagine it didn't do anything for my confidence when I was actually old enough to start dating! I managed to transfer the timidity I felt with most grown-ups to the high school boys I met."

High school was troublesome for Kathleen. She and her mother clashed on the matter of which school she should attend. Virtually every girl from Christ the King was planning to go to Holy Angels, an academy for girls in Richfield. Kathleen was determined to go there too; she wanted to stay with her friends. But Mrs. Keefe, ever suspicious that outside forces could hurt her family, had heard a rumor that the Holy Angels girls brought vodka to school in their purses and used it to spike their orange juice.

In vain, Kathleen asked her where she had heard such a thing; the other girls and their mothers thought it was ridiculous and were not deterred by the rumor. Kathleen was usually too timid to be defiant, but this time she argued and cried. Her mother was adamant and insisted that her daughter would be safer at Visitation Convent School in Saint Paul, a much smaller high school for girls.

Besides, the family had ties there. Grandma Keefe had been a girlhood friend, in fact the *best* friend, of Sister Jane Margaret, a nun at Visitation. When Mr. Keefe was a little boy, his mother had often brought him and his twin brother over to the convent to show them off to Jane Margaret. Also, when Kathleen's mother was a student at the College of Saint Catherine, she had a friend who had graduated from Visitation. When the friend married, Mrs. Keefe was a bridesmaid and had gone to the convent with the wedding party. It was then a custom for Visitation graduates to introduce their bridegrooms to the nuns by visiting on the wedding day. Mrs. Keefe had been very impressed by the sisters that day; their gracious and warm reception of the wedding party stayed in her head. She had a feeling that her young daughter would be safer with these sisters than anywhere else.

The arguing and pleading continued until late spring. Then her mother surprisingly took a more conciliatory tone, and asked

Kathleen if she would please just consider visiting the school once to see what it was like. She didn't say Kathleen wouldn't have to go there if she didn't like it, but still, the door had opened a crack and, sensing a possible weakening, Kathleen agreed to spend an afternoon at the school. An appointment was made and she took an afternoon off from school to accompany her mother to the dreaded Visitation Convent.

Mrs. Keefe picked her up at Christ the King and drove her to Visitation in Saint Paul. As Kathleen came reluctantly into the parlor with her mother, she was welcomed by the kind face of Sister Jane Margaret, the lady who had once been a childhood playmate of the grandmother she loved. Sister took Mrs. Keefe off to a room where they could speak privately and sent Kathleen on a tour of the school with a student named Kathy Mullin. Kathy was pretty and vivacious, enthusiastic about how much she liked the school. She showed Kathleen the classrooms, the chapel, the dining room and the gym, chattering away about how nice the girls and sisters were.

Kathleen couldn't believe what was happening to her. It was as though her resistance thawed and flowed out of her heart during the little tour. After weeks and months of fighting with her mother, she couldn't understand how she could have a change of heart so quickly. She wasn't really listening to Kathy very carefully; she was experiencing a strange sensation that this place was *right* for her, and that she would be coming here! She had no premonition at the time that her stay at Visitation was to be much longer than the usual four years. (Nor did either girl realize that the choice of her tour guide was prophetic: Kathy Mullin later became not only a Visitation Sister, but spent years as admissions director, giving school tours to countless numbers of girls.)

When Kathleen rejoined Mrs. Keefe and Sister Jane Margaret in the parlor, she amazed her mother by saying she would like to be a Visitation student. Sister was probably less amazed. She had witnessed this type of transformation before. Kathleen's girlfriends back at Christ the King were surprised too, and disappointed, but she did not waver from her decision.

"What do you think caused you to change your mind?" I asked her.

"I still can't put a finger on it. It wasn't any one person or thing, but there was an overall feeling to the place that just melted my opposition and softened my resentment of my mother. Given our relationship, it was very hard for me to give in to her, but this time I didn't hesitate to admit that she had been right." The mysticism of the place was speaking to the mysticism that she had not yet recognized in herself.

There is a magic here at Visitation that many acknowledge and respond to. I too have wondered about it for years. So many of us who have entered its doors have chosen to remain, if not literally as professed sisters, at least in our hearts and in our memories. When I came back in 1994 to become upper school director, it was like slipping back into the beauty and security of my girlhood. The day I reported for work, the first sound that greeted my ears was the singing of the Divine Office, echoing down the hall from the chapel. That singing has been repeated five times a day in unbroken continuity since I graduated in 1956, and for nearly four hundred years before I arrived.

Kathleen started at Visitation in September of 1956 and stayed there for four happy years, even though she had to board at the school for the first two. It was just too far from her home to make the long bus ride every day, so she boarded at school during the week and went home on Fridays. By junior year she had a driver's license and could commute daily, now joined by her younger sister, Mary Jo.

During those first two years she missed Mary Jo and her family, but still was happy to be a boarder. Girls in boarding schools often develop a special closeness to each other and to their teachers because they see so much of them. Day girls attended classes and went home, but boarders made fudge and popcorn together and cajoled the sisters into joining their games. Part of the school's yard was transformed into an ice rink during the winters, and the sisters and girls skated together. The convent began to feel like another home.

Sister Brigid remembers especially loving a young science teacher named Sister Anne Countryman. One day during a history class, Kathleen started talking to a friend when she should have been studying, and Sister Mary Patricia sent her to the hall as punishment. While standing there, she saw Sister Anne approaching and was embarrassed to be seen by her favorite teacher being disciplined for misbehavior. Sister Anne neither questioned nor reprimanded her. Instead, she waved at her as she approached.

"Why, Kathleen," she smiled, "how lucky to find you here. I've been worrying that you haven't seemed very well-prepared for the big biology test coming up. Would you like to use this time to review with me?"

"Oh, thank you, Sister," Kathleen answered, blushing. "I've been worried about it too, because biology is really hard for me." Sister Anne held out her book, and the two spent the rest of the period in the hall together, going over the concepts that were difficult for Kathleen.

The girls in her class recognized Kathleen's timidity, and often arranged dates for her with boys they thought would be sensitive to her. Unfortunately, their idea of sensitivity applied to boys who were as bashful and frightened of dating as Kathleen, and she remembers many miserable dances and parties, stumbling and mumbling to boys with cold, sweaty hands, each of them tongue-tied with terror. One potential swain was so overcome with anxiety he disappeared and called his mother to come get him, and Kathleen had to go home with another girl and her date.

"I'll never forget that—I was so mortified. It was my worst date ever out of many bad dates."

In spite of these romantic disasters, Kathleen assumed she would marry and have children. She just figured she'd have to wait until she was thirty or so, because she thought by then she would have outgrown her shyness. The possibility of becoming a nun didn't enter her mind.

"It was in my junior year that I began to come into my own more, to feel less like a child and more like an older person. I started to become more aware of myself and others, and I began to have more spiritual experiences and to pay attention to them. When receiving Communion, I often felt a curious sensation of warmth, a feeling I can only describe as being loved, though it is hard for me to define it precisely, even today. I didn't connect it to a vocation or consider speaking to a sister or a priest. What I learned in religion classes in school was one thing; this was something else."

Kathleen could not have explained it at the time, but, once again, as on the starry night when she was still a child, she was seeing the difference between the linear structure of religion and the timelessness of the Divine Presence, eternally indwelling. She was hearing the first whisper of a call to spiritual life, a gentle murmur that would grow in volume until finally manifesting itself as the voice of God.

No longer boarding at school, she began attending the early morning Communion services offered by her parish church during Lent, seeking the warmth and love she experienced even when there was no Mass. She developed a life-long love of hard-boiled eggs that year, because the time it took to run down to church, receive Communion at the short service, and return home before leaving for school was exactly the time needed to hard boil an egg.

Nearly every family in her neighborhood was Catholic, and attending Lenten devotions and Holy Week services were not unusual practices. There was no questioning it; it was just something everyone did, just as every family had a container of palm branches displayed somewhere in the house. They had been handed out at Mass on Palm Sunday, and each parishioner walked home carrying a branch or an armful of palms, not feeling a bit out of place as they might have in a mixed neighborhood. The kids walked to church in a group and walked home again together after following the Stations of the Cross, Benediction, celebrating the joy of Holy Thursday and the sorrow of Good Friday, as they had been doing for years.

But now it was different for Kathleen. She was often quiet on those walks home, silently meditating on the meaning of the passion and redemption. She was developing a habit of prayer.

Sister Anne Countryman gave her a book about Beatrice and Dante; its spiritual content touched her, and she asked for more reading of this type. Sister Anne began providing her with titles of other books; *Gifts from the Sea*, by Anne Morrow Lindberg, was a special favorite, and Sister Anne mentored her through it. Still, Kathleen did not relate it to her future, continuing to assume she would someday be a wife and mother.

Others noticed, however, that she seemed different from most other girls her age, and they began to ask her about it. There was a convent of Sisters of Divine Providence in her neighborhood, and Kathleen saw the nuns there frequently when she delivered packages to them from her parents. These sisters began to ask her about her plans after high school, and she knew they were fishing to see if she were considering becoming a nun. This annoyed her and she began to dodge their questions. She wondered if they thought she was some kind of weird person, an unpopular type that no man would ever want to marry. Why in the world would anyone think she might want to be a nun, of all things? One day, when a particularly pointed question was put to her, Kathleen answered angrily that she had *never* considered being a nun, but that *if* she ever did, she would be a Visitation sister. Her own words surprised her, but she didn't reflect on why she had said them. She preferred to ignore the subject, even to herself.

The sisters at Visitation were gentler in their approach, but several of them hinted that Kathleen seemed especially attracted to things religious. Sister Mary Regina was famous among the convent girls for what they called her "library talks." At some point during nearly every girl's senior year, Sister Mary Regina invited her into the library for a little chat.

Kathleen did not look forward to her library talk when the invitation came; she was sure she would be questioned about whether she might have a religious vocation. But Sister Mary Regina did not raise the subject. They talked about life in general and the need to remember that Saint Francis stressed the holiness of ordinary actions. Kathleen should remember that the smallest act is sanctified when done willingly and for the glory of God. Sister also emphasized that real strength lies in gentleness, and real power in surrendering one's will to God. Only when conceits are relinquished can the Holy Spirit work freely through humans.

"I've always been thankful that Sister Mary Regina did not discuss religious vocations with me that day. I suspect I might then have thought the idea to become a sister was not really my own; that the seed had been planted by Sister Mary Regina instead."

Kathleen's first revelation came on a snowy Saturday in the parking lot of Saint Mary's Home for the Elderly. The senior girls had been asked if they would like to volunteer to help out at the home on Saturdays. A Franciscan sister from the home came to Visitation to speak about helping out, and she made clear that volunteering was a real commitment and they should not commit to if they were half-hearted about it. "These people count on your presence and are more disappointed than you might believe if you don't show up."

The girls who volunteered took their jobs very seriously and were faithful in going to Saint Mary's every Saturday morning. Then, one wintry day, there was a huge snowstorm. Kathleen's little group, who drove together from Minneapolis, debated over the phone about attempting the drive. They decided the commitment was too important to break, so they braved the snowy streets and drove into Saint Paul.

To their surprise, they were the only girls who showed up that day. The Saint Paul students felt the drive was too dangerous. The Franciscans and their residents were delighted, of course, and praised the girls highly for being so dedicated. After they worked their hours, one of the sisters invited them to come downstairs for a little talk before they left.

"Uh-oh, here it comes," thought Kathleen. She figured that because they had answered the call of duty so seriously, the sister would probably think they had some extraordinary virtues and should probably be nuns. She whispered to her friends that that's why they were being invited, but they laughed and said she couldn't be serious.

"Well if she does ask," Kathleen said before they followed the nun into the dining room, "just tell her if you ever *were* going to join a convent, it would only be Visitation. That will get her off your back."

Her prediction was correct. After telling them again what a heroic thing they had done, Sister asked them if they had ever thought of becoming nuns. The other girls just laughed and said no, but, once again, it made Kathleen angry. She delivered her little speech about *only* being a Visitation nun, and said they'd better get going as the drive home would be difficult.

Out in the parking lot she told the other girls how annoyed she was that anyone would have her pegged as a nun type. To her surprise, both girls said, almost together, "We think you would be a very good nun." They were no longer laughing; they were serious.

"No!" Kathleen answered loudly. "I don't want to be a nun. I don't want anything to do with it. How could you say such a thing?" Now even her friends were turning against her.

But as she struggled with the wheel to get out of the parking lot, a curiously powerful feeling washed over her. It was the same warmth that came to her when she received Communion, the sensation she had experienced years before, looking at the stars and feeling the immensity of God's universe. Suddenly, it all came together for her; her private spiritual realities and the daily lives of the sisters. Was that what being a religious was about? She had never thought of it that way before.

She said nothing to her friends, but began to think about it. She wondered where all her previous resistance had come from. In spite of loving the sisters at Visitation and admiring them greatly, she somehow considered being a nun something undesirable, as if the only reason they were there was because they couldn't get husbands. Now she saw how ludicrous that was. They were there because they were answering the call God had issued to them.

Sister Mary Regina invited her into the library for a second talk, and this time she did ask her if she had ever considered religious life. Kathleen didn't say much to her, but she assented that the idea had been on her mind. Sister said, "I think it would be very good if you would go to college and while you're there, think about it. See if God is calling you. Then come back to see me and we'll talk about it."

Kathleen started at the University of Minnesota and attended one year but did not do well there. The difference between her high school class of thirty-six and the big classes at the "U" was overwhelming to her. It felt like kindergarten in New York all over again.

Instead of returning to school she worked for the next year in sales at Powers Department Store in Minneapolis, often visiting the sisters at Visitation but not discussing her possible vocation. She was reluctant to face her feelings directly, although she knew they were still present, waiting to be released. Then her sister, Mary Jo, graduated from Visitation and, at the reception following the ceremony, Kathleen dropped her wallet somewhere on the convent grounds. She got a call later that day saying it had been turned in to the office. The next morning when she went to collect it, it was Sister Mary Regina who came out to the parlor to give it to her.

"I'll bet that was no coincidence," I said. Sister Mary Regina was one of the most intuitive women I had ever known.

"I'm sure it wasn't. This time the subject of my vocation was not skirted around and Sister asked me openly what my intentions were. I told her that I hoped to enter the convent, but not yet. Because I had thought to delay marriage until I was in my late twenties or early thirties, I thought I would accept my vocation at that age, too. Sister Mary Regina thought it made more sense to stop delaying and give it a try. There would be a year as a postulant and another in the novitiate before even temporary vows were made, and by then she said I would have a clearer sense of the genuineness of my calling."

Kathleen decided she was right. She was young—only twenty—but she thought that if God were truly calling her, she could grow up and mature as well in the convent as living at home. She dreaded telling her parents, because she was sure they wouldn't be happy with her.

Mr. Keefe was the more accepting of the two. He loved his daughter and didn't want to lose her to a cloister where he would only see her a few times a year, but he didn't actively discourage her. Mrs. Keefe was both skeptical and disapproving.

"You're only doing this because you can't face life, Kathleen," she said sourly. "You've always been shy and you think if you lock yourself up in a convent you won't have to meet new people. You're just avoiding life."

Neither parent asked Kathleen why she had made this choice; they proceeded from their own assumptions. She never felt that she was hiding from anything, but didn't see any point in trying to explain it to them. Once she saw the connection between what was happening within her and what the sisters were living for, she knew what was drawing her to embrace that same life. She understood that it was the most mature part of herself that had made the decision to leave everything behind and follow her longing for a deeper, more spiritually attentive life.

Only her Grandma Keefe seemed to understand, and it felt good to Kathleen to be hugged and congratulated by her. This was the grandmother who had consoled her as a child and told her that accepting difficulties could make her strong.

She intended to enter in October, but the Mother Superior suggested she come in August, on the Feast of Saint Jane de Chantal. Kathleen had already read enough to believe that the Holy Spirit worked through an order's superior, so her first act of obedience was to follow her request. In August of 1962, at age twenty, she renounced the world as she had known it and entered the enclosure of the monastery.

There she donned a black skirt and stockings, a black blouse, black oxford shoes and a short veil for chapel. The clothing was not a surprise, but she was completely unprepared for the customs the sisters followed within their cloister. It was like entering another culture.

She was interested in learning the meaning behind the rituals, but found them unsettling and strange nonetheless. For instance, when a woman entered the convent at that time, she was asked to bring an item from home to present to the Mother Superior as a symbolic gesture of the life she was leaving behind. Kathleen brought a cup and Sister Mary Denise went with her to show her how to make her presentation. Sister demonstrated the correct manner. To properly present the object, she had to kneel down and kiss the superior's hand. Kathleen was stunned. All she could think of was the court of King Arthur. Visions of knights in armor and ladies in courtly dress appeared before her eyes.

"Where are we?" she wondered to herself. "What century is this?" The courtly customs observed by Saints Francis and Jane in the seventeenth century were based on their everyday behavior and were the norm for them, but in 1962 such actions were only seen in the movies.

Other monastic regulations were equally foreign to Kathleen. She saw the sisters lowering their veils to cover their eyes when receiving communion to signify humility, and they kept silent for long periods of each day, even at meals. She was instructed in the proper ways to sit and stand and to enter and exit doorways. The sisters encouraged all aspirants to walk and use the stairs with dignity; there were to be no exhibitions of boisterous activity. They were also to keep their voices gently modulated and ladylike. This last, at least, was easy for Kathleen. Speaking softly came naturally to her.

These experiences felt strange and awkward at first, but as she adjusted to convent life, she could see that for the older sisters, following the rituals was a way of expressing their relationship with God. Their ceremonies were beautiful and elegant, comprising a devout and dignified orchestral arrangement that had been playing for nearly four hundred years. None of them realized that half a world away, variations on the theme of their symphony were being composed in Rome.

Kathleen didn't waver in her desire to become a sister, but her first two years in the novitiate felt long. She was lonely. There was only one other girl there and, not only was she was a year ahead of her, she was also a talented cook. She helped in the kitchen nearly every day, leaving Kathleen alone.

The novices and fully professed sisters did not associate with each other except at prayer and mealtimes, and neither of those occasions included conversation. She understood it was her duty to develop a deeper interior life and learn to pray with concentration, but she was still lonely.

The convent dog at that time was a big Saint Bernard named Martin who quickly became Kathleen's friend. One of her tasks was to walk him, and they developed a game together they loved to play. The monastery had a beautiful cloister walk framed by arches down its entire length. On one side was the red brick of the building and on the other the garden, visible through the archways. She and Martin would start at one end and race each other down the long passage. The dog always waited eagerly for her command, "On your mark, get set, go!" never bounding out until the "Go!" They ran together daily back and forth until they were both panting and out of breath. Exhausted, they collapsed in a heap of furry paws and black-stocking legs: two free spirits wordlessly communicating the joy they felt in each other's presence. Kathleen remembered the fun she had with her sister when they pretended to be dogs, so adopting a canine personality came naturally to her.

As a child she had yearned for a dog. Lying on the living room floor, she would spread *The Big Book of Knowledge* out before her. Every imaginable breed of dog was represented and she slowly turned the pages, dreaming of having one to love and be loved by in return. Her mother wouldn't allow it, though; there were enough children to manage without having an animal to trip over and take care of. Now her hope of owning a dog was finally realized in big, clumsy Martin.

Kathleen's connection to animal life went well beyond her

memories of childhood longing. She said she has often pondered the depth of her attachment to animals, especially dogs, seeing the natural wonders of all creation manifested in their innocence and unconditional love.

"Have you heard of *thin places*, Elsa?" she asked me. "It is an Irish term for those moments when the barrier between heaven and earth seems very thin. Without warning, ordinary experiences will open up and there is a sudden encounter with God. It happens in nature for me and beckons me to little glimpses of what lies beyond the apparent. It happens when I am most sensitive to the beauty of the natural world and the animals God created. That is characteristic of the Irish, I have heard. Saint Brigid has few statues to honor her in Ireland; instead the Irish have named streams, springs and hills for her. I can relate to that. Because of this bond I feel with nature, I loved Martin and have since become the caretaker of many of the convent dogs, including the two mischievous terriers we have today."

At the end of her year as a postulant she shed her schoolgirlish clothes and received her habit, identical to that of the professed sisters but with a white veil. She chuckled now as she remembered the awkwardness of the ceremony. The usually solemn ritual was marred by mistakes, and Kathleen could sense her mother's impatience out in the part of the chapel reserved for the laity.

"What happened that was so awkward?" I asked.

"First, I was mortified by my appearance. At that time a novice was received wearing a wedding dress to symbolize that she has become 'the bride of Christ,' and I borrowed my aunt's. It didn't fit very well and the veil had pretty well disintegrated over the years. Sister Jane Margaret tried to shorten it and cut the rattiest parts off, but I thought it still looked ridiculous. There were no mirrors in the monastery so I couldn't verify it, but at best I figured I looked like a most unlikely bride of anyone, let alone Christ.

"It was Sister Mary Regina's first acceptance of a novice since her election as Mother Superior, so she was nervous and that increased my nervousness. The presiding archbishop was Leo Binz, and while he was no amateur, he was not at the top of his game that day. First he forgot my name. When I approached the opening in the cloister grille to face him, he pronounced in a sonorous voice, 'You will no longer be called…' and then he looked embarrassed.

"Sister Mary Regina whispered, 'Kathleen.'

"He tried again, '…Kathleen, but you will be called…' Once again, he was stymied. He shuffled through the book he was reading from and then went to the two priests who were assisting in the sanctuary, but neither of them had it either. From inside our enclosure we could hear the rustling of the congregation.

"He was red-faced when he returned to the grate and Sister Mary Regina hissed, 'Brigid Marie.'

"…'you will be called Brigid Marie.' Thank God that part was finally over!"

Kathleen realized she was not Kathleen any more. She was led away by one of the sisters who helped her out of the unsightly bridal dress and into the graceful habit of a sister of the Visitation of Holy Mary. There was no doubt in her mind that she would continue on this journey to her final profession of vows. She would be Sister Brigid Marie Keefe, VHM, for eternity.

The ceremony was finally over, and the community went with her to the convent garden to receive her family and friends. Mrs. Keefe was still unhappy with the life her daughter had chosen, and was stiff and uncomfortable at the reception. Her father and brothers and sisters were more gracious, wishing her joy, although they still didn't understand. Happily, her grandmother attended, too, and her good wishes and hugs felt genuine.

After that, life in the novitiate became easier for Sister

Brigid. She and the other novice started college classes at Saint Catherine's, although at first Brigid was worried about going to college. She had not been successful at the university. Sister Jane Margaret was wonderfully comforting to her. "We'll just start you very slowly, my dear," she reassured in her kind voice. "You can take your time to get acclimated. You don't have to take a full load. When you were in high school here, you were a very good student, and there's no reason to think you won't be again."

Sister Brigid has remained grateful to Sister Jane Margaret throughout her life for getting her past that fear of failure. In some ways she found it hard to relate to Sister Jane Margaret as there was a sixty-year age difference between them, but, in this case, the older woman knew just what to say to give confidence to the timid novice.

At Saint Catherine's she enjoyed getting to know sisters from other orders who were attending there. The veiled and black-gowned girls were a little sorority unto themselves, meeting and chatting. A frequent topic was Vatican II and its implications. Most of the young sisters were in favor of the changes, which allowed for a less restrictive climate among religious.

Many of the old customs, such as kissing one's superior's hand, were seen as an anachronism and not essential to religious life. Sister Brigid could happily embrace changes to practices that were mainly symbolic, but found it harder to deal with the ideas sometimes presented in the classroom.

Because so much in the Catholic Church was being questioned, the theology teachers felt freer to express their personal beliefs than they had earlier. It was difficult to hear directly such statements as, "There is no longer any validity to the contemplative life." This was a harsh judgment and Sister Brigid did not agree with it. She was afraid if she told Sister Jane Margaret what was being said, the college might be regarded as a dangerous place and she would be pulled out. That she did not want, but she did wish she could talk to her eighty-year old formation director about it. Instead, she had to struggle with it and work it out for herself.

"How did you do that?" I asked her. "You were so young and so new in your vocation, not yet a fully professed sister."

"It was very hard," she answered, "but I did do it, and I felt good in coming to my own conclusions. You see, I knew, deep inside, that there was something to my vocation that was not out of date and never would be. I had a sense that what was in me, the reason I had for entering the convent in the first place, was something spiritual that was strong enough and true enough that it wouldn't disappear"

"Did this process take you long?" I asked.

"Oh yes, that is, the actual processing. I'm telling you this now in words but what I felt then was more intuitive. I knew that God had invited me to this life, but because I was young and a student, I thought everything had to be solved in my head. I had to be able to reason it out then." She smiled at me. "I was much more of a head person in those days. Now I know that real meaning lies in the heart."

Sister Brigid stayed at Saint Catherine's studying to be a teacher, while also learning how to be a nun. It was almost time for her final profession of vows when suddenly the community became concerned that she had not spent enough time in the monastery for them to know her well. She was among the first of the sisters to go out to college full-time for classes instead of staying at Visitation and having the professors come to her. Without warning, the decision was made to pull her from school and have her enter more visibly into community life.

This was a startling test of obedience: since entering the convent, most of her time had been spent at Saint Catherine's and it was the life she was accustomed to. She was given kitchen and garden work in the morning, and it took a while for her to adjust to the big change in routine. To her surprise, she found she liked the kitchen work and had to admit that it did result in her mingling more with the other sisters. She began to develop a sense of community. Perhaps her struggle to keep believing in the worth of contemplative life would no longer feel so lonely.

Afternoons she was assigned to teaching religion to the sixth graders and she loved her students and their interaction with her. She used the Socratic Method, which employs questions and exploration rather than answers, so they had lively discussions. But what she loved most was the informal communication with the girls outside of class. Those were the times when she felt their spirits connecting. She supervised the students during play practice when they had to wait for their turn on stage, listening to them chattering about their daily lives. Joining their conversations, she came to know and understand them well. In these informal settings, Socrates quietly disappeared, taking his great brain with him. He was not missed, as the conversations of the mind were replaced by the feelings of the heart.

Sister Katherine, the friendly girl who had given her the school tour ten years earlier, was teaching the fourth grade, and a layperson named Irma Johnston had the fifth. The three women devised ways to get all three grades together, setting up activities before and after school and providing group prayer opportunities. They formed a tight little community, enjoyed equally by students and teachers. Salesian charism flourished and flowered as the girls and women celebrated a sense of community forming among themselves.

As the time for final profession approached and it became apparent that she would receive the community's approval to proceed, her students tried to talk her out of it. In the manner of many youngsters, they thought a religious life was a waste and told her she should leave and get married. Sister Brigid just laughed and told them she remembered having felt exactly that way about nuns when she was a schoolgirl.

She still sees many of her former students and teases them about their opposition to her vocation. She said to me, "You know how Saint Paul is. We keep running into everyone we know at wakes and funerals. I love reminding my old students that they tried their best to get me to leave."

1966 was the year that the sisters moved to their new home and school in Mendota Heights, so Sister Brigid was extremely busy, helping with the move, teaching her classes and preparing to make her final vows. Because the whole community had to work together to accomplish the packing and organizing, her final year in the novitiate was spent associating more fully with all the other sisters than any time previously.

They received her into the order officially as a professed nun in 1967 and, to her delight, her entire sixth-grade class attended the ceremony. By then her family had become more accepting of her choice, although her mother remained unconvinced.

She returned to Saint Catherine's and completed her interrupted education while continuing to teach in the middle grades. After several years she felt it was time to try her hand in the upper school but believed she would be more confident doing that if she had more theology. She enrolled in the graduate program at Saint John's University near Saint Cloud, a move that necessitated her living away from Visitation Convent for several months at a time during the summers. This would have been impossible before Vatican II, but now more and more of the sisters were venturing out to colleges and even to some family and community events.

Studying at Saint John's was exhilarating for Sister Brigid. Except for that brief period at the University of Minnesota, she had always been a good student, and Saint John's had a faculty of brilliant theologians. After receiving a master's degree in Religious Education she returned to Visitation and the senior classes with enthusiasm.

"In spite of my interest in teaching, it did not come naturally to my personality. I learned the technical names for my type of person from the Meyers-Briggs Type Indicator. I am intuitive and imaginative rather than concrete and sequential, but I understood that students need a logical and orderly presentation of material. I was good at inspiring them, but I realized they needed solid ground under their feet if the inspirations were to take root.

"I didn't dislike my classes, but I realized how draining they were. Getting organized and prepared cost me a lot of energy. I was swimming upstream against the flow of my nature. I liked the religion electives best, as there I could design my own lessons and only the girls who really wanted those specific classes signed up for them. In spite of feeling overstretched, I had volunteered to interview freshmen to make sure they were happy with their classes and friends and generally adjusting to the school. This was work I especially loved as one-to-one counseling is one of my gifts, but I was busier than was good for me."

Sister Brigid's teaching load got bigger, as did the demands made upon teachers everywhere. Evaluation became more complex if a school wanted to keep its accreditation, and the number of faculty committee meetings and amounts of paperwork increased dramatically. Parents became more demanding as colleges tightened their entrance requirements; some were apt to challenge the necessity of religion classes at the expense of more academic subjects, even though they had enrolled their daughters in a convent school.

Teaching is much like performing on stage; it demands that one be on-time and fully present, prepared and ready to interact. The curtain goes up when the bell rings, and the audience expects the actors to know their lines and deliver what was promised.

None of the sisters had the luxury of doing only what they

most desired, especially as the community was smaller than before, and Sister Brigid also had the responsibility of caring for the dogs. Her love of animals had never lessened, but the demands of walking and feeding them regularly took time. She was well aware that dogs become unhappy and confused if not fed and exercised at appointed times, so neglecting their needs when she had other work to do was not an option.

And it was determined her help was needed in the business office. At that time the school business was handled by the sisters, and Sister Brigid was asked to take care of accounts receivable and payroll. The combination of teaching, counseling, dog care and office work became more than she could handle and still have any kind of interior spiritual life. None of those obligations could be postponed, let alone put off, except possibly the freshmen, but that was part she loved best and it would be hard to let go.

"A responsible person doesn't let down the freshmen, tell students to wait a few minutes while the teacher gets organized, tell clients to wait for their money or make dogs wait for their dinner. Because I was a responsible person I found myself taking care of my duties but neglecting myself."

In 1988 she finally expressed her concerns to Sister Péronne Marie, who was the Mother Superior at the time. Her vocation had called her to a life of prayer and service, but the service was overshadowing the prayer. She was hoping she might be relieved of the business office, but Sister told her she had no one else with her particular skills who could take over. Instead, she suggested that Sister Brigid give up teaching for a while to see if that would relieve the pressure.

It was a relief to her to return to a more fulfilling life of prayer. She missed the students, but her spiritual needs were nurtured and, though the business office job grew bigger, it didn't become more than she could handle.

In 2002 she left the business office entirely to take over as Formation Director, as the Mistress of Novices is now called. Because there are fewer women entering convents these days, she has only had two applicants to work with, but it has been the most rewarding work of her life. With these two candidates she joined a group of sisters and novices from several orders in the area. The exchange of ideas was enlightening and uplifting, and she found herself learning as much as she was teaching. It enabled her to see herself and her community through the eyes of others. She found it to be life-sustaining and the best use of her gifts since she had entered the convent.

Since that time she has once again perceived the finger of God beckoning her to a new calling. Some thirty years ago a survey was put out by the Visitation Federation President asking what the sisters would do if they didn't have a school. She remembers answering, "Counseling or some kind of spiritual directing." Now, in discussions with her own spiritual director, she has discerned that she will become a spiritual director during this next phase of her life. She is enrolled at the Sacred Ground Center for Spirituality, taking classes to earn certification in spiritual direction.

"I worried when I first applied that I might be too old to start on such a venture," she admitted. "I was delighted to hear them say that one might be too young to be a spiritual director, but one could *never* be too old."

As our final interview came to a close, she leaned toward me and said in her soft voice, "The words that passed between Francis and Jane still make me feel a sense of closeness to them. I feel the way I did when I first walked into Visitation as a reluctant eighth-grader—I had such a sense of *place*. They had so much love between them and they brought that to a higher level of consciousness of God's love. It permeates their writing;

it's beautiful and it's also common sense. Their spirituality is not beyond the grasp of ordinary human beings."

As Sister Brigid looks back on her forty-five years in the convent, she believes that the inspiration that started Visitation will never die. Whatever form their charism will take is in the hands of God, but their legacy of heart speaking to heart will continue to influence human experience for the better.

SISTER MARY PAULA

In Revelation 2, John tells us that when we enter heaven God will reveal to each of us our real name, His true name for us, written on a white stone. Sister Mary Paula McCarthy is looking forward to this particular revelation—she'd like to ditch the litany of names she's been carrying around all her life.

Her baptismal name was Catherine Anne, but until she learned to spell, she thought it was Cather Nan. Her brothers and sisters often called her Annie, while in the neighborhood all the children had nicknames and hers was Tillie. When she went to college she decided to get rid of the pet names and use Catherine, so her friends there called her Cathy. The convent gave her a new identity as Sister Mary Paul, but after Vatican II she changed Paul to Paula, preferring the more feminine tone.

Old friends still call her either Tillie or Cathy, but she remains Annie to her siblings. She eagerly awaits the news from the white stone as she's ready to ditch the litany of names she's been carting around these seventy and more years.

"That *is* a surprising number of aliases to possess," I said. "It's a good thing you've behaved yourself all these years and never wound up on a Wanted poster. What would they have called you?"

She laughed. "I suppose by whatever name I was using at the time I committed the crime."

She grew up in Saint Paul in a well-heeled Catholic neighborhood, halfway between Saint Thomas College and the Town and Country Club. It was a friendly little enclave, one where everyone knew everyone else. All the kids walked in a group to and from Saint Mark's Catholic School during the school year and played together in the summer. Her older brothers and other teen-aged boys organized activities for all the neighborhood children; there was a game of kick the can nearly every evening at seven o'clock. Anyone who wanted could play, from the littlest kids to the oldest. The older boys also organized treasure hunts and fox and goose chases, forming teams with a variety of ages competing against one another. They were like camp leaders, assigning nicknames to all the kids.

It was a good thing for little Catherine Anne McCarthy that the neighborhood was such a warm and friendly place because the atmosphere within her household was often charged with anger.

Sister Mary Paula said, "My father's stepmother came to live with us when I was a baby. When his father, my Grandfather McCarthy, knew he was dying, he asked my dad to take care of his wife, Bamie. I don't think he could have known how much his request would distress my already troubled mother or perhaps he wouldn't have asked it. Bamie was Grandpa's second wife, and she was quite close in age to my mother. The only way my dad could afford to take care of her was to move her in with us. I was the seventh of eight children so you know Mother already had plenty to do and she was not happy with my dad's decision.

"The two women fought constantly, and the arguing exacerbated my mother's already difficult nature. I realize now that it's quite likely that she suffered from undiagnosed clinical depression, but I didn't understand that as a child. I only knew the pain of the emotional distance between my mother and myself."

Sister Mary Paula looked sad, thinking of her mother. She said, "I think she was in many ways a product of her culture. She had a bright intellect and was a gifted artist, but when her first child was born she put away her paint brushes and canvases to devote her life entirely to her family. She played dumb to my dad's smart; she thought that was the role of a good wife. The resentment that bubbled beneath her exterior was not acknowledged, but we children felt its presence. We lived with it daily, wondering if there was something wrong with us that made our mother so angry and disapproving.

"Not that our home life was all bad," she hastened to add. "My mother's nagging and the poor relationship with Bamie were always there, but that was not the only reality. Our home was noisy, warm, competitive, argumentative, active, busy with children and adults in and out—it was secure, but it could also be difficult."

The step-grandmother, Bamie, was consistently warm to the children so they gravitated naturally to her, causing their mother to be jealous as well as unhappy. Florence McCarthy had come from a wealthy family and was cultured and well-educated, having graduated from the Minneapolis School of Art. Bamie was from a working-class German neighborhood in the parish of the Sacred Heart. With only an eighth-grade education, she could see that her step-daughter-in-law not only disliked her but regarded her as inferior.

Frederic McCarthy was warm and loving, but he had a volatile temper that exploded into frightening rages when he felt pushed too far, which was often in his divided household. The children idolized him, but they also lived in the shadow of his sometimes unpredictable wrath.

Upon graduating from Saint Mark's at the end of eighth grade, Catherine Anne looked forward to attending Visitation Convent School in the fall. Her older sisters had gone there and she was happy to follow them. It was a welcoming environment; the sisters treated the girls respectfully and affectionately. The students were encouraged to be gracious and courteous to each other and, above all, to remember daily that their smallest actions were sanctified if done for the love of God. The spirit of Saints Francis de Sales and Jane de Chantal permeated the place with their admonition to do ordinary things extraordinarily well.

It was well that, once again, her school provided stability, for during her junior year, in 1945, her home life changed drastically. Only fifty-five, her father was diagnosed with cancer and died after a short illness. It was a devastating occurrence for the young girl; she had loved him deeply. Mourning her father, she felt that she was at the lowest point of her life, but it was shortly to grow even worse.

While her father was alive, he could patch up the fights between his wife and stepmother, but when he died there was no one to intervene. During the first fight they had after his death, the widow ordered Bamie out, and Catherine Anne was deprived of both her surrogate mother and her father within the space of a few months.

Bamie went to live with a cousin of Catherine Anne's father, but Mrs. McCarthy was so angry she cut off all contact with her, and the children were not allowed to see her. She eventually moved to Florida, and nothing was heard from her again. Catherine Anne's grief sent out an arc of pain from her heart that seemed to have no end. It was not to be closed into a circle of resolution for nearly thirty-five years. Jumping ahead in her narrative, Sister Mary Paula told me how she finally reached that closure.

"In 1980, after Mother entered a care facility, the family house was cleaned out for sale while I was away studying for the summer. When I arrived home, I went to see it one last time. It was completely vacant as I made my way through the empty rooms, saying good-bye to my childhood memories. Then, in an upstairs room, I spotted a cardboard box sitting alone in a corner. When I opened it, I was amazed to see that it was the unfinished bedspread that Bamie had made especially for me.

"I was the baby of the family when Bamie first came to live with us, and she had said she would like to crochet a special gift for the baby. Evening after evening, she patiently worked the long threads into little hexagons, with popcorn stitches in the middle of each for embellishment. I would often sit in her room with her and listen as she crocheted, telling me that the spread would be for my marriage bed. Now and then she would gather up a few medallions, sew them together and then begin on another.

"'Catherine Anne,' she would say, smiling down at me, sitting on the floor. 'When you marry you must get a four-poster bed for this spread. This kind of cover should never go on an ordinary bed. Only a four-poster will show it off as it is meant to be shown.'

"Now the unfinished gift was in my hands. It felt like a miracle to touch it again and to remember the loving hands that created it while I watched. I kept thinking, 'This is mine. This is what Bamie made just for me, and now here it is.' I traced my fingers over it and wondered, 'Why wasn't it sold with the other things? It's the only piece left in the entire house. How did this happen to be preserved just for me?'"

Sister Mary Paula took it back to the convent with her and sewed the pieces together, facing them with a blue backing that showed off the intricate hook work. Unfinished, it was too small for that bridal four-poster Bamie had pictured for her, but now, with its backing, it was just the right size for the narrow bed of a nun. Lying under it at night, she finally feels at peace with her grandmother and the losses they both sustained during her sixteenth year. She hadn't realized how hurt she had been through all those long years until she felt the pain go. When she receives her true name on that white stone in heaven, she hopes to be reunited with her beloved Bamie and learn *her* true name, too.

As a senior in high school, Catherine Anne won the Pepsi-Cola scholarship prize, the precursor to the Merit Scholarship program. Only one boy and one girl from each of the (then) forty-eight states were selected, so it was indeed an honor. The full–tuition scholarship to the college of her choice included ten dollars a month spending money. During the months between taking the test and learning she had won, Annie prayed very hard. For the first two weeks or so, she prayed that she would get it. Each night she would implore God to let her be the one selected.

But over time, something seemed wrong with her prayer. The selfishness of it became apparent to her, and she began to pray instead that of the six girl finalists in Minnesota, the one who won would be the one who used it to best glorify God. When she was announced the winner, the full import of what she had prayed for came to her. She could see the responsibility she had taken on and the weight of its burden. Her triumphant happiness was tempered by this realization. That was probably the first step leading to her call to religious life. She had moved beyond herself and would have to discern the ways in which she could serve God best.

"Was your mother happy for you when you won?" I asked.

"She was happy in the only way she knew how to be. She bragged to her friends about me, saying how thrilled she was that her smart daughter had won this honor. But I knew that it really wasn't about me. It reflected well on *her*; it brought honor to *her*. I finally couldn't stand to hear about it any longer. We had a huge argument when I told her to stop boasting about me."

"Was she happy you wouldn't be an expense to her?" I asked.

"I don't know. The one thing the scholarship didn't cover was room and board, which was three hundred dollars a semester. She complained about it in every letter she wrote to me."

Having won the scholarship, she now had to choose a school. Her older brothers were attending Saint Thomas College in Saint Paul, so they asked their teachers for recommendations of a school for their younger sister. She wanted a good education with a major in English or journalism. When the boys brought all the recommendations home, the only name on every list was Trinity College, an all-women's school in Washington DC. Catherine Anne was given two pieces of advice to heed. Her brothers told her, "Annie, go to a Catholic college. It isn't just for what you'll learn there, but for the friends you will make. The people you meet in college are most apt to be your friends for life and it will be a richer life for you as a Catholic." The other advice came from one of her brother's advisors. He said that it would be good for her to go away from the Midwest, as it was the only culture she had ever known and it would be well to experience life elsewhere.

All signs pointed to Trinity so she mailed in her application, was immediately accepted and left home. She was filled with the expectations all young women have when stepping out into the world to discover themselves, but there was more. Her mission went beyond herself. She was to discern how to best serve God with the gifts given her.

At Trinity College she met her intellectual equals for the first time; her little class of twenty-five girls at Visitation had not challenged her with the mental stimulation she was capable of absorbing. She did well in her studies, but decided as a freshman that she would enter as many activities as possible and be content with a B average. Friends were important to her, and she made many good ones during her four years at Trinity. Still, she wondered constantly what it was that God wanted her to do.

In the Advent Season of her junior year, a copy of a prayer made its way around the campus, and many of the girls took it up. One was supposed to say the prayer fifteen times a day from the Feast of Saint Andrew on November 30 until Christmas, and ask for a special favor. The prayer went like this:

> *Hail and blessed be the hour and the moment in which the Son of God was born of the most pure Virgin Mary in Bethlehem at midnight in piercing cold. In that hour, vouchsafe, oh my God, to hear my prayers and grant my desires through the merits of Jesus Christ and his Virgin Mother. Amen.*

She began saying the prayer. The favor she hoped to have granted was the answer to how she was supposed to spend her life. Like her earlier prayer, which went from asking for the scholarship for herself to asking for it to go to the most worthy girl, this prayer began to evolve. She said, "You know, Jesus, this is really superstitious. Do I think I'm supposed to get an answer at the very moment in which you came into this world? I've had enough theology and history to know that you probably weren't born on December 25, it wasn't cold in Bethlehem and it probably wasn't the year Zero. It was most likely 4 BC."

In the study of scripture and theology she didn't confuse history with fairy tales. She knew that thinking she would get an answer to her life's purpose at exactly that moment in time that Christ supposedly was born was childish and even silly. So she tried to talk it out sensibly with God, saying "OK, God. I know it's ridiculous of me to expect an answer that follows some formula. I'll say the prayer, but I won't believe that the answer to it will somehow materialize at some special, magical moment. But God, I *am* begging you to give me an answer in any way you see fit. I feel like I'm hanging here not knowing which direction to take. I want to serve you, but I don't know how. Please, God, show me the way."

Christmas vacation started and she went home for the holidays. The family went to Midnight Mass on Christmas Eve and, as always, arrived about an hour early so they would be sure to get seats. In her pew waiting for Mass to start while the organist played preludes and the choir tuned up, she took out her rosary and began to say its prayers.

A rosary is divided into five groups of ten beads, or decades, called mysteries. Each decade stands for a joyful, sorrowful or glorious mystery surrounding the events in the life of Jesus Christ. The prayer known as The Hail Mary is said on each bead while the devotee meditates on the meaning of the particular mystery. She began to think about the first joyful mystery, the Annunciation, in which an angel comes to Mary and tells her she has been chosen to be the mother of God. Mary cannot understand how this could be, but she acquiesces completely to God saying, "Not my will, but Thine, be done."

A light flickered in Catherine Anne's mind. "Hmm," she thought. "I am to surrender my will and listen to the voice of God. All right, God. I will do that." Then she moved on to the second mystery, the Visitation. This refers to the visit Mary made to her cousin, Elizabeth, the mother of John the Baptist. The light flickered again. "This is not just about being connected up with God; it must be taken to others. It must be shared in some way. How am I to share my life with others? I'll listen, God. Please tell me."

Then she started the third joyful mystery, the Nativity, which celebrates the birth of the Messiah. Now the light was glowing, not flickering. She felt a great lifting of her spirits as she realized the message she was receiving. Mary had to withdraw from the world and enter into a private space to nurture the Christ within her and give birth. "Oh my God," she thought. "This is clear. I am being called to do those things. Yes Lord, I can see what you want. I will go to religious life." God, who so often worked through His mother, had seen fit to give His answer while Catherine Anne was meditating on the mysteries of Mary's life. She, like Mary, would withdraw to a private place where she could nourish her spirit's growth and learn how to serve God.

When she looked at her watch, it was one minute to twelve. She started to smile. "Dear God," she thought. "You do have a sense of humor. I laughed at the words 'the hour and the moment,' and here You are." She could hardly sit still in the pew, so delightful was the irony of getting her answer at one minute to midnight.

She also found it ironic that she was being called to convent life. When she was a freshman in high school, Sister Mary Rose had told the class that God would not call anyone to religious life who would not be happy.

"That was a relief," she said to me now. "I remember thinking, 'Good. I am off the hook. I would never be happy as a nun.' But God had other plans for me."

Now that the question of *how* she was to live her life was answered, she had to find out *where* and in *which* order of religious. There were so many religious orders to consider. The Carmelites seemed like an obvious choice; they were the strictest, the purest, the holiest of women. But she didn't feel a strong attraction to them. She couldn't see how her talents would be used there, given her education and inquisitive intellect.

While at college, she volunteered as a religion teacher on weekends, working with black children in a poverty-afflicted parish. Loving her students, she devised special teaching materials for them, because the textbooks of the times pictured only white children. Her interest in this work caused her to wonder if her call might be to serve the poor, especially within the black population.

Once again, she received direct help in coming to a decision, this time from a Dominican priest who taught a theology class the semester after she returned from her dramatic Christmas vacation. Toward the end of the semester they studied Saint Thomas Aquinas and the subject of life choices. Saint Thomas believed the ideal life was neither wholly active nor wholly contemplative. He called it the *mixed* life, which encompasses both contemplation and activity. One's prayer life is the fountain that feeds the activity.

The priest asked the class, "If you're considering religious life, how do you make a decision? What do you do? First of all, consider where and when this feeling first arose. Perhaps it was the influence of the religious group that taught you or a group you've been working with." She felt as though he were speaking directly to her, though she hadn't told anyone of her Christmas Eve experience.

He continued. "If you haven't had much contact with religious groups, get to know them. Visit them, talk to them, listen to and observe them. Especially, pay attention and pin down what *they* say is their motto, their single sentence that expresses who they are and what they stand for, what they believe in. Study them enough to see if they actually *live* that motto."

Praying in the college chapel that evening, she remembered the stained glass windows in the chapel at Visitation Convent.

On the window depicting Saint Francis de Sales were the words, "All through love; nothing through constraint." It was clear to her that those words were Visitation's motto, and she began to reflect on how well the sisters lived up to the declaration. She reviewed her four years in their high school and thought, "Never once, in all that time was I coerced into doing anything out of fear or restraint. Everything I experienced, ever, in those four years, was done through love."

She discerned that she had received her reply. Her first answer had come in December and this was now May. Feeling confident that God's plan for her had been revealed, she saw that the Visitation Convent of Saint Paul was to be her home for life.

When summer arrived, she returned home and went straight to the convent to talk with Sister Mary Regina. She wanted to speak with her in particular rather than one of the other sisters, because she had learned during her senior year at Visitation that Sister Mary Regina had not been happy during her first year in the novitiate. She confessed that she had cried every night.

"But Sister," the girls had protested, "Why did you stay? If you were so homesick and unhappy, what made you continue?"

Sister Mary Regina thought a while before answering them. "Because," she began, "because there was something *more*, something beyond my unhappiness. Even before I entered the convent I was aware of an emptiness in my life. I might be at a party and having a good time, and then that feeling would come over me, the feeling that this was somehow not enough… that there was something else I was meant to do."

"Didn't you have that empty feeling when you were in the novitiate? When you were crying?"

"No. Not there," she answered. "I had a sense that I would get over my unhappiness. God wanted me to be there and I knew that He would help me. And He did."

Now the young woman faced her former mentor, this time

speaking to her in the formality of the parlor, not the intimacy of her old classroom. Sister Mary Regina advised her to return to Trinity and finish college.

"You knew Sister Mary Regina," Sister Mary Paula smiled at me. "She said I would 'be of more use' to them if I came in with my college education completed."

Catherine Anne graduated from Trinity College in May of 1951 and entered Visitation Convent in July. It was not as she had hoped. She appeared destined to repeat Sister Mary Regina's experience—and then some. Nearly every night she cried, not just during her first year, but through all three years of formation.

It was very difficult to find herself working in the kitchen, sewing and tending the garden instead of employing her mind in intellectual pursuits. Was this why she had received such accolades in scholarship? Did becoming holy mean becoming a drudge? She had come to Visitation from one of the best colleges in the country where she had not only done well, but had put out a yearbook, written articles for the student newspaper and directed plays. Now she was told to weed the garden—she who didn't know a weed from a flower. She had to sew an apron and embroider her laundry number on her handkerchiefs. There was not one task she was asked to perform that she could do well. She broke dishes, pulled up flowers instead of weeds and stabbed her fingers on the embroidery needles. It was a time of great discouragement, of feeling totally inadequate.

Every day, after a night of crying, she thought of returning home, but then she would walk down a hall and see a crucifix and think, "I can't go home. I belong here. Christ suffered more than I am suffering." Another, less edifying, image also served to keep her there. When she entered the convent, she gave her good winter coat to her sister, and had only a shabby old coat that she wore in the cloistered yard. Although her mistress of novices, Sister Mary Helen, assured her she would give her a token and that home was only a streetcar ride away, she thought, "I can't ride the streetcar in this ratty coat—I'd be too embarrassed." Reminiscing now, she laughs to think that two such extremes— devotion to God and girlish vanity—worked together to establish her in religious life.

Also helping to get her through bouts of discouragement was the clear memory of the night she received her message from the mother of God. Many passages from Saint Francis de Sales were included in the novitiate readings. In one he had written, "Our Lady, by a secret visitation which she has made to their hearts, has joined and united them [the Visitation sisters] together." She believed her "secret visitation" had come from Mary while she prayed the rosary on that Christmas Eve, hoping for an answer.

Her solitary tears continued, and Sister Mary Helen told her she must come and tell her each night that she couldn't stop. She hated to disturb the poor woman's sleep, but she often wound up there. Sister would listen to her in sympathy, but she didn't urge her either to stay or go; she knew this was a struggle that her young charge would have to work out with God.

Her misery increased when over-crowding in the monastery resulted in the need to share bedrooms. Another young woman was put into her room with nothing separating them but a curtain hanging from a rod down the center of the room.

It was the custom in all monasteries of that era to observe the Great Silence, the dictum going back to Saint Benedict that required religious to speak only to God during the hours between final night and first morning prayers. The young nun-to-be obeyed her mistress of novices and spoke to her during those silent hours, but she was not allowed to speak to anyone else. Now when she started to cry, she fled to the bathroom to gain control, not wanting to awaken her roommate. Hot tears on her face and cold feet on the terrazzo floor remain an all-too-clear picture of her first years at Visitation.

"I remember seeing you during those years," I told her. "You were in the novitiate during my junior and senior years at Visitation. I never dreamed that you were having such a hard time. I don't think we ever spoke."

"No, we wouldn't have because novices then remained very much in the background and didn't interact unnecessarily with others. I remember seeing you too, though, in the gym and in the dining room. You were one of the new students and I worried about how you were getting along. So many of the girls in your class had been together for many years, and I was concerned that they wouldn't accept you."

"How ironic," I answered. "You were worried about me and I was getting along just fine—I was much happier than I had been at my former school. And it never once occurred to me to think you were unhappy. I remember how you smiled all the time. Every time we left the dining room, you were standing in the doorway, nodding and smiling at all of us."

She shook her head. "That was the front I put on each day. I cried all night and smiled all day—what a miserable way to be!"

After two years, when the time came for her first profession, she had to see the bishop, who awaited her in the convent parlor. It was one of his duties to meet alone with each young woman seeking profession to ensure that she was doing this of her own free will, not being coerced by family or other pressures.

She entered her side of the wooden grille that at that time separated the cloister from all visitors. Archbishop Byrne was tall and austere, his sober face topped with a crown of beautiful white hair and his eyes like blue flint. An efficient and competent bishop, he was not noted for personal warmth. Now he regarded the young novice before him.

"Do you want to profess vows?" he asked her.

"No, Your Excellency," she answered in a small voice.

The bishop's face revealed a flicker of emotion. "No? Then why are you here?

"Because I will to profess vows."

"What is this you say? You don't *want* to, but you *will* to?"

"Yes. I'm being called to this and I know it is right and I will it. But I really don't want to."

After a pause he said, "Well, that seems authentic. You are certain you are not being coerced?"

"Yes, Your Excellency."

Three years later the scene was repeated in the same parlor. Still unhappy but still convinced, the woman now called Sister Mary Paul accepted for life the black habit and veil designed nearly four hundred years earlier by Saint Jane de Chantal.

After the trying years of apprenticeship, joy finally found Sister Mary Paula. The custom for all nuns aspiring to final profession was to make a ten-day retreat to reflect on the meaning of a consecrated relationship with God. During this time, Sister finally experienced peace, that profound sensibility known as the peace of Christ, the peace that surpasses all understanding. Finally, it felt *good*, not just *right*.

The gift of her vocation was now fully apparent. She spent a good part of her ten days in retreat on the rooftop of the Convent, being bathed by the sunlight while she prayed, inundated by her new happiness and peace. More than fifty years later, each time she recalls this period, she is overcome with the same sense of serene joy and she feels again the golden warmth of the sun.

Teaching in the school, Sister Mary Paula filled many roles over the years. She had the eighth grade for twelve years and made a pact with her students to read any book they recommended to her as particularly good. She set her herself to the task of reading at least a book a week, two in the summer, of children's and teen literature. There were usually some girls who were interested in some special area not shared by their classmates.

One might be absorbed in ballet, another in horses—interests they needed to talk about. The other girls thought they were showing off, but Sister Mary Paula could perceive their need to share their experiences. She read all the books she could get on ballet, or horses, or whatever the driving passion was, and made herself available to talk with the girls about it.

Later she taught in the high school, covering English, Latin, Spanish or French as the need arose. The school at that time was divided into two strands, curriculum and activities, rather than in the present configuration of lower, middle and upper schools. She was made director of curriculum, with Sister Jane de Chantal as director of activities. Sister Mary Paula saw that she needed an administrative degree to meet the North Central Accreditation Association's requirements, so she took classes at Saint Thomas toward that end. She also completed all the course work needed for a master's degree in Guidance and Counseling. In the late 1950s the faculty of both local Catholic colleges had found it too cumbersome to come to the convent to teach. The decision was made to send the sisters out to continue their education even though the relaxing of rules permitted by Vatican II was still a few years away.

Sister Mary Paula also took a course in Linguistics at Saint Thomas and was fascinated by it. She felt it was the coming thing in education and the school would benefit by having a staff member schooled in that area. This spurred her to attend Georgetown University in Washington DC for a master's degree in Linguistics.

There she completed all the course work but returned home to write her thesis. Back in Saint Paul she experienced a psycho-logical block that prevented her from writing. She procrastinated and made excuses until the sisters' governing council became exasperated and ordered her to complete the thesis. Instead of boosting her up, the command deflated her ego and took all the starch out of her resolve. She became too demoralized and depressed to even begin. This directive was issued before the redemptive discovery of Bamie's bedspread that later brought so much healing to Sister Mary Paula. Her self-confidence was too fragile to sustain the blow of condemnation she felt she had received. She never did complete the degree, although she regained enough psychological strength to move on to other areas of work and study.

A job opened up at the College of Saint Thomas and, although it was highly unusual for a Visitation sister to work outside of her community, the sisters agreed with her that it might be good for her to experience another environment. She applied for and received the position of associate director of religious education at Saint Thomas. It was a welcome change. She traveled around the state giving presentations and workshops to parish personnel and helped design a master's program that is still in place at the College, now the University, of Saint Thomas. While working at Saint Thomas she also completed a master's degree in theology, including the thesis, and that helped restore her diminished sense of self-worth. The mind that had been so frustrated in the kitchen and the garden was happiest when engaged in productive, intellectual activity.

After leaving Saint Thomas in 1983, Sister Mary Paula was invited to join a committee to help organize the annual meetings that became known as the Salesian Conferences. These are gatherings of Visitation sisters, Oblate sisters of Saint Francis de Sales, laypeople and Oblate priests, the religious order of men who follow the teachings of Saint Francis de Sales. With cloister rules more relaxed, the sisters were now free to meet and exchange ideas, both spiritual and intellectual.

One of the outgrowths of these meetings was the establishment of a Scholar's Seminar. Interested members meet every year or two and engage in scholarly research pertaining to Salesian history and issues. Sister Mary Paula has contributed many scholarly essays to this seminar. The dynamic charism of Saint Francis continues to flourish in this environment through the papers that are printed and distributed among the Oblate and Visitation communities.

Sister Mary Paula also continues to use her intellectual talents in editing many of the written documents of the school, where she has been a board member for many years. She nourishes her spiritual life and that of others by participating in a group formerly known as the Daughters of Saint Francis. The members study Salesian virtues and their application to their lives. They also commit to saying certain prayers and following religious practices. (Recently this group changed its name to the Association of Saint Francis to accommodate the men who have joined the "daughters.")

In 1998 Sister Mary Paula helped organize a joint celebration of the history of the Visitation sisters in the United States. Georgetown was heading for its two hundredth anniversary, the Wheeling community was going on one hundred and fifty years and Saint Paul was nearing one hundred and twenty-five years. The idea came up in committee that in addition to celebrating, rejoicing and being grateful, they should give back by creating service projects that would include their schools.

A group called VISTORY was the result. The name is an acronym for Visitation in Service to Others through Responsive Youth. Every year up to fifteen students from each of the four operating Visitation high schools meet and engage in service to the poor of the city they are visiting. They come from Saint Paul, Georgetown, Wheeling and Saint Louis to help in day care centers, homeless shelters, eldercare and other non-profit places that welcome volunteer help. It is an opportunity to increase the social consciences of the girls while acquainting them with their sister schools. The model is a balance of service, education, spirituality and fun. Each day begins and ends in prayer so the students see spirituality as part of their Christian commitment, not just "doing good." Sister Mary Paula plays an important role in hosting the students when they come to Saint Paul and accompanying the groups to other Visitation schools.

At seventy-five she looks back on her long life with the satisfaction of feeling she has answered God's call and served His purpose for her. I asked her to articulate her thoughts about the future of Visitation. She answered with confidence.

"If Visitation had to dissolve, it would not invalidate for a minute what my life has been pledged to. Our numbers are diminished, but we must remember that a charism is carried by an institution, never by just an individual. I will continue to work to maintain and enhance the order, but the back-up is the laity, carrying the Visitation spirit into the future. Groups like the Association of Saint Francis give laypeople the opportunity to participate in the Salesian charism.

"The attendance at the annual Salesian Conferences is now composed of seventy percent laypeople. It started with religious, but now it is filled with laity who not only attend and participate, but who also present and teach."

Sister Mary Paula's love for and devotion to Salesian ideals are apparent in the pattern of her life. From her early creation of textbooks that included black children in the culture of learning to her establishing VISTORY, which brings the students of the Visitation schools together, she has used her gifts to express her vocation.

Through her research and scholarly writing she has extended knowledge of the history of the Visitation Order far beyond her original cloister walls, and her active participation in the Association of Saint Francis ensures that her storehouse of knowledge has instructed and influenced the other members. By personally showing interest in her students beyond the classroom, she has broadened their idea of schoolwork to include the messages of the heart that Saints Francis and Jane intended.

While still a high school student, Sister Mary Paula had hoped to win the scholarship that would help her realize her intellectual potential. Then her spiritual intuition intervened and led her to pray, not that she herself would win, but that the girl who would best use the prize to glorify God would be the winner. Having won, she accepted the accompanying responsibility. God had chosen her and her duty has been to give back whatever God desires. Her life is a witness to the fulfillment of her promise.

SISTER MARGARET AGNES

I will always think of Sister Margaret as the "runaway nun." After sixty-five years in the convent, her eyes still gleam with excitement when she speaks of the times she has escaped its confines and rules, self-embraced though they were. Her smile is mischievous and her wispy white hair, standing out from her head like a halo, still bears traces of the golden blonde it once was.

"I'll bet you were a pretty girl," I tell her, as we sit together in the parlor. When I started this project, the parlor had felt strange and stiff; the saints in their frames looked down from the walls at me with somber eyes, and the little chairs seemed spindly and formal. Now it feels as comfortable to me as my own living room.

"I never worried overmuch about being pretty," she laughs, her New York accent softened by the lilt of her parents' native country, Ireland. "I wasn't one for looking in the mirror or thinking about the boys. Do you know now, I had my whole life planned by the time I was six years old?"

"*Six* years old?" I echoed. "That's quite a feat!"

She leaned back and looked at me with satisfaction. "When I was six years old, I told my mother that first I would have a candy store. I was thinking there could be no grander future than to have a shop filled with candy and be able to have as much as I wanted, being the owner and all. And then I said I would be an artist. I was forever messing around with chalk and pencils and such, and I thought my artwork would make me famous some day. And then I said the last thing was I would go into a convent to die. So I guess I was a prophet because I've done all those things. Well, almost all; I'm not dead yet. But I'm ninety-eight years old, so that can't be too far off now, can it?"

"By the looks of you I would guess you could still be around here quite a good long while," I said. "I'd like to hear about your candy store. Did you really own one after all?" Sister Margaret leaned forward on her chair as she began, her eyes shining with the memories she summoned.

She was born in 1908 in the Hell's Kitchen neighborhood of New York City, the child of Irish immigrants. In this tough area she and her little brother were tenderly cared for and never got hurt on the often dangerous streets. Her father, Daniel Doyle, was a private chauffeur for a prominent businessman and, while his salary wasn't large, the job afforded a rare privilege. Each summer the boss moved with his family and servants to a beautiful estate in Massachusetts. The Doyles had their own private cottage on the estate, and it was here, at the end of the tree-lined driveway that swept down to the public road, that little Margaret set up her candy shop.

"It wasn't a proper shop," she explained, laughing. "Just a little stand my father put together for me, but I thought it quite lovely, and I sat there many days selling candy to all the grand families that drove by. They all knew me, you see, for they all knew each other's chauffeurs, and they didn't mind being fleeced a bit by Daniel Doyle's daughter. I'd buy the candy bars for five cents and sell them for a dime, so I made a good profit every summer in spite of eating much of my own trade. It was enough to finance my art supplies when we'd return to New York in the fall."

"Was your name Margaret then as well as now?" I asked her, picturing the audacious child who so cheerfully robbed the rich to help not the poor, but herself.

"Yes," she answered. "And that's unusual, I know. But I wasn't given a new name in religion except that they added Agnes to the Margaret. My mother had not given me a middle name, but I got one when I became Sister Margaret Agnes."

Like most Irish immigrants, the Doyles were devout Catholics, and Margaret was introduced early to a sense of the sacred. Weekly Mass and Confessions were a part of her routine, as well as frequent visits to the church for private prayer. The atmosphere of the building brought a strange a comfort to her; even on the dark days of winter when she and her mother would slip into a pew in the dim and nearly vacant building. Prayer came easily to her. From an early age she was aware of God's presence. It was as though a bright flame glowed around and within her small section of the pew, filling her with wonder and peace. She was seldom ready to leave the church as soon as her mother was, reluctant to leave the circle of light behind.

"You must have attended Catholic schools," I said.

"Oh my, yes. That was very important to my parents, and both my brother and I went to the sisters. The tuition wasn't so terribly much in those days, but even if it had been more expensive I think they would have managed it somehow; it meant that much to them. I went to Catholic high school as well, to Saint Margaret's Academy, run by the Sisters of Charity." She chuckled. "I couldn't get away from that name, Margaret. I was as much at home with the nuns as I was with my parents. I always knew I'd be one some day, but I kept saying to myself, 'Not yet. Not yet.'"

"Why do you think that was," I asked, "when you seemed so convinced it would be the right life for you?"

She thought for a bit. "I think it was the obedience part that held me back. I liked doing things my own way, and I didn't want to give that up. My mother had a friend who was a nun, and every time we visited her in her convent, I'd come away thinking I was glad I wasn't in yet."

"Why?" I asked again. "Was she a gloomy person?"

"No, not at all," she laughed. "She was pleasant—very nice. I just didn't want to give up my freedom. I used to talk to God about it quite a bit, and I could hear Him saying, 'Don't you think it's time now, Margaret?' I suppose I should have been scared but instead I'd just tell Him, 'Not yet, Lord. I know you want me, and I'm coming, but not yet.' And He always let me off the hook."

"It sounds as if you had a pretty comfortable relationship with the Almighty, not so permeated with a sense of guilt and sin as some Catholics of your era."

"Well, I learned early that some sins aren't as terrible as you think," she smiled. "I think I was in about seventh or eighth grade when this happened. It was the night before Holy Thursday, and for some reason I decided to go to Confession. Now the school children were supposed to go on Saturday with the school group. The nuns would be in the church and would line us all up and see to it that we stayed long enough to say our penance, don't you know. But this particular night I wanted to go when the grown-ups did. When it was my turn, I entered the confessional and started to speak. This parish pastor was kind of a grump, and right away he could tell I was a child, not one of the adults."

"'What are you doing here?' he asked me impatiently. 'You should be going with the school group. Get along now. Go home and come back Saturday with the sisters.'

"I was so mad I marched home, stomping all the way, and I slammed the door when I came in. I told my mother what had happened and said that I wished that priest were dead. She was horrified.

"'You could be struck dead for saying such a thing!' she said. 'You'll have to tell that in Confession now. That's a terrible sin!'

"Well, there was no help for it," Sister Margaret said now. "I'd have to go back on Saturday, and I kept wondering how I was going to say I'd wished a holy priest dead. I rehearsed my speech over and over, and when I joined the group on Saturday, I made sure I got into the line where the assistant priest was hearing Confessions, as I didn't want the pastor, not then or ever again."

"Weren't you about scared to death?"

"Yes, I surely was, thinking about being struck dead and all. And wouldn't you know, the sister was trying to get the confessional lines even and keep us children moving along, and she pushed me right into the pastor's line. I was so scared I forgot the speech I'd rehearsed so carefully. I went in and knelt down; when he slid the panel back, I blurted right out at him, 'I've done a terrible sin, Father. When you wouldn't hear my confession on Wednesday night, I was so mad I said I wished you were dead.' I could hear something that sounded like a rumble, or a chuckle, on the other side of the box, and then he pushed the screen back so we could see each other.

"He said, 'Well, now you can see I'm still with us so a lot of good that did you!' He was still laughing when he closed the screen, and somehow I stumbled out the rest of my confession. But I wasn't scared anymore. And that was my first insight into knowing that a lot of our so-called sins are all in our own heads and not in the mind of God at all."

"So, do you credit this cranky priest with freeing you from a fear of God?"

"Partly, but not entirely. From the time I was very small I felt like I knew God pretty well, and that He knew me. It was especially strong when I was in church or receiving Communion, but I was aware of Him often during ordinary times too. He filled me with a kind of lightness, a feeling that is different from happiness, but still quite like it. That feeling made the most mundane things kind of glorious in a way."

Margaret hadn't read Saint Francis De Sales yet, but she was practicing Salesian Spirituality. By allowing her awareness of God to guide her daily actions as well as her times of deliberate prayer, she was following Francis' assertion that the ordinary life is made extraordinary when lived to its fullest for the love of God.

After graduating from high school, she got a job working as a secretary in a publishing house, following that inner voice that kept saying, "Not yet" to the convent. During the evenings she was able to pursue her artistic interests, as she had been accepted at a prestigious New York art academy that offered free tuition for night classes to talented young people who qualified. She studied drawing and calligraphy as well as furniture design and art history. This was at the time of the Great Depression, and her salary was very small, so she was especially appreciative that it cost nothing to attend.

"Did you have any social life?" I was curious as to how she interacted with others.

"Not really," she answered, "and the interesting thing to me is that it didn't bother me. I didn't realize it at the time, but I thought about it after I entered the convent. I had a few girl friends, but never one of those intense relationships that other girls had. I'd hear them talking about who was their 'best friend,' and I hardly knew what they meant. I never had a date, never went to a dance or a party. I lived at home with my parents and was perfectly happy going to a movie with my father. It never occurred to me I might be missing something."

"Did you regret it, after you were in the convent, and looked back on the life you had missed by not participating?"

"No, I can't say that I did. It was more of a curiosity than a regret. I could see that I was different from most people. My parents were married and were happy together, and my brother married too, so I didn't have anything against the married state as such. I had just never thought of it for myself. I honestly never missed the parties and such that other girls thought were so important."

Margaret passed her days enjoying her job and pursuing her artwork. She had been promoted to private secretary of the head of the publishing house, and her salary grew larger. This was good, as she was carefully stashing it into a savings account. She could feel the call to enter the convent drawing near, and she wanted to go to Europe first. All her life she had dreamed of seeing the sacred art of Italy, and she hoped to immerse herself in it before withdrawing from the world. By now she had also learned something of Saints Francis de Sales and Jane de Chantal, and she wanted to visit Annecy, France, where they had established the first Visitation monastery. She went to Europe by herself, not wanting to be part of a tour that would make shopping and sight-seeing its focus, and traveled in Italy and France for a month. The rumblings of World War II were poised above Europe like a dark specter, but she was oblivious to either political or social turmoil. Her business was spiritual.

She spoke to no one of her plans for the religious life. "I had always kept my thoughts to myself, and I didn't tell my parents until I came home from Europe."

"How did they react to your news?"

"They were surprised, my father more than my mother, I think. She was probably more aware of my inner life than Dad was. When I actually left, he kept saying, 'You'll be back, you'll be back.' But I never did go back. Once I knew it was time to go, I told God I was finally coming in, and I never changed my mind about that."

"How did you know it was finally time?" I asked. "And how old were you by then?"

"I was twenty-nine when I entered in 1937, and I made my final profession in 1943 when I was thirty-one. I can't tell you exactly how I knew it was time. I could feel my 'not yet' weakening each time God spoke to me, and one day I just thought, 'It's time.' That's when I quit my job and went to Europe."

Margaret came home from Italy and France still uncertain of which convent to join. She had been consulting with a Passionist priest who often met with her and others who had spiritual interests. He believed that her quiet nature would prefer a contemplative order to an active one, and she agreed. He didn't think the Carmelites would be right; their rule was very strict and demanded fasting and other physical hardships. He thought her independent spirit might rebel at the demands of such total obedience.

He suggested that she visit the Visitation Monastery in Brooklyn; he knew their chaplain and introduced her to him. On his advice she went to be interviewed there, but it was not a happy visit. The Novice Mistress who met with her seemed very cold and haughty, not at all gentle as the French sisters in Annecy had been. She seemed surprised that Margaret had not been to a proper college, only the art academy and a business school for secretaries. Then she asked her to sing and Margaret was mortified.

"I was never a singer. I felt so embarrassed and stupid when I croaked out a few bars, and of course Sister Snooty looked appalled. I figured if they took me at all they'd want me to be a lay sister, so I could do the shopping and other tasks that require leaving the monastery, but I didn't want that. I wanted to be a fully professed nun, and the life I sought did not include being an errand runner!"

Margaret could hardly find the handle of the door when she left, she was crying so hard. She cried all the way home, convinced that the last thing she wanted to be was a Visitation nun. "If that's the Visitation, then phooey on them!" she hissed to herself through her tears.

While checking the phone book to verify their address so she could write the Brooklyn sisters a note of thanks, but no thanks, she noticed an entry she had not seen earlier. There was a Visitation monastery in Riverdale on the Hudson. Something flashed an alert to her that *this* might be the Visitation she was looking for. On impulse she called and made an appointment with the Mother Superior.

"What a wonderful difference that was!" she exclaimed. "This sister was very warm and cordial to me, and we talked for a long time. She invited me to come back the next week to meet the council. Now that sounded frightening—*The Council*—I pictured them all lined up like the Sanhedrin, waiting to judge me.

"But it was nothing like that. They saw me one at a time and were not in the least intimidating. The first one was a very elderly nun who entered in a wheelchair, and she was gentle and respectful. The second was equally kind, and the third and final was very sprightly." Sister Margaret laughed. "She sat sideways to me like a confessor, and I found it very easy to talk intimately with her in that position. I don't know if she did that deliberately, knowing that Catholics were used to pouring their hearts out to a listening ear, or if it was just an accident. Her name was Sister Agnes, and I felt very comfortable with her. While we were talking, I had a strange experience. I heard a voice in my head say very clearly, 'That one will help you when all the others turn against you.'"

"Goodness," I said. "Did a day come when they turned against you?"

"No, they never did, and I sometimes wondered why I had heard the message so clearly. Much later it occurred to me that maybe Sister Agnes had worked behind the scenes in getting the others to accept me. I was a difficult nun—a hard postulant and a hard novice, but they put up with me."

"Why were you difficult? Were you rebellious over the rules?" I wondered.

"No, quite the opposite. I was really quite obedient and docile. But I had always been different from others. I heard a different drummer, and my head was often in places where the others' were not. For instance, one night when I was supposed to be in bed sleeping, the Novice Mistress came in and found me sitting in the windowsill, looking at the stars. I was completely wrapped up in the experience of the night sky, and when she told me to get back to bed, I said I *wanted* to look at the stars. I think I said it in a way she found strange. They thought me a kind of mystical type, and they found me odd, foreign. God was very present to me at all times; I was very aware of His nearness, although I didn't tell them that was why I sometimes seemed to be somewhere else."

"Did you have these mystical experiences often?" I asked.

"Yes," she answered slowly. "I had some I still do not speak of; they seem too personal, just between me and the Holy Spirit. But I'll tell you one I remember so you can see why the others thought me so strange. I was up on a ladder putting a scriptural passage on the wall. Most monasteries have a set of pious statements from scripture to use as inspirations for meditation, and we had a place in our refectory for writing out a thought for the day or week. I don't remember which one I was writing, but it was something about love or charity. Suddenly it was like God was right in that sentence; it was so real to me, and I knew I had to worship immediately. The emotion was so intense I realized I would fall off the ladder if I started to pray there, so I climbed down quickly and knelt right there on the floor. I felt His presence so keenly I wasn't aware of my surroundings. I went back later and finished the sentence, but I could see the sisters looking at me, thinking how odd I was."

"Maybe you're right," I ventured, "in thinking Sister Agnes worked behind the scenes to help the others accept you. It doesn't sound as if your 'strange' ways prevented you from being fully professed."

"Yes, I made my final profession in 1943, and Riverdale was my home until 1980 when I came to Saint Paul. But," she added, her eyes sparkling, 'I didn't stay in Riverdale the entire time. I'd been there about twenty years when I got a restless feeling that I should be somewhere else. I didn't want to quit Riverdale, but I did want to get away from it for a while. I felt like I was getting stale and needed a change, so I asked for a leave of absence."

It was a very unusual request for a cloistered nun to make, but Sister Margaret was an unusual nun. The Mother Superior granted her wish, and a local priest found her a job as secretary to a religious education director in Cincinnati. She lived in a convent with a group of Notre Dame Sisters and wore lay clothes, except for a small veil. When the director left to return to college, that position ended, and Sister Margaret got a job in a nursing home. There her eyes were opened to how much times had changed. She had entered the convent during the depression, leaving a job that paid her $14.50 per week. Now the nursing home was giving her $100.00 a week, more money than she had ever imagined having at her disposal. She saw this windfall as a chance to realize her dream of going to Jerusalem. She intended to return to Riverdale, but when Jerusalem beckoned, she thought once again, "Not yet."

"I worked for a year and saved my money until I had enough to go. I didn't want to go as just a sightseer," she explained. "A group that would include scripture study with the visits to the sacred places in the Holy Land was what I wanted. And I found just such a tour from Saint John's University in Minnesota, made up entirely of priests and nuns. We had Mass every morning, exploration each afternoon and scripture study in the evenings. It was perfect—one of the most meaningful times of my life and I will never forget it. The air was alive with the presence of God. What they say about Jerusalem is true; there is a story in every stone."

After the trip ended, Sister Margaret stopped briefly in Cincinnati to see the Notre Dame Sisters once more, but her allotted time was up and she returned to Riverdale. She was barely back when she happened to pick up a magazine published by the Association of Contemplative Sisters. There was an ad in it for a summer scripture study conducted by the Jesuits for contemplatives. It was past the application deadline, but she figured she had nothing to lose by applying. To her delight, she was immediately accepted, but now she had the task of telling Mother Superior that it was time to hit the road again.

This caused some consternation. "What's this I hear?" cried Mother Superior. "You want to leave us again? What's the matter with you that you can't stay put?"

Sister Margaret threw herself on the Mother Superior's mercy, arguing her case that the course would increase her knowledge of scripture, and she could bring back the fruits of the class to share with the other sisters. And as an added benefit, it offered room, board and tuition—free!

Now her eyes twinkled at me. "How could she refuse a deal like that?" Sister Margaret chuckled. "She let me go, and of course I did as promised and brought back some wonderful scripture interpretations. I had three great summers with that group. The first was in upstate New York, the second in Milwaukee and the third somewhere in Wisconsin at one of the Jesuit universities."

"Did the Jesuits fund this venture?" I asked.

"That's the best part," she laughed. "The whole shebang was sponsored by a Minneapolis brewery. We all got a laugh out of knowing that beer money was paying our way and said it was too bad that free beer wasn't included."

"How in the world did the Jesuits get tied up with a brewery?"

"We learned that a Carmelite nun had gone begging to different businesses in Minneapolis, explaining that the sisters needed instruction to grow in faith and knowledge, but they didn't have any money for tuition. The brewery president thought that was a worthy cause, so he provided the money and the Jesuits provided the teaching. It wasn't just Jesuits either, although they ran it. We had Zen priests as well; they understand meditation so well. It was Thomas Merton, you know, who helped open the door to that kind of studying."

I wondered how the other nuns had received their sometimes strange sister in the role of scripture instructor. They considered her odd and eccentric; did they take kindly to her teaching?

"The teaching, yes," Sister Margaret said. "But the rest, no. I told you I was a difficult nun. I know I caused unrest and made it difficult for Mother Superior to deal with the others. My wanderings made them restless and, perhaps, a bit envious. They began to ask for permission to go on family trips and such. One might say, 'My brother has offered to take me to Ireland this summer. Why can't I go?' When permission was refused, they didn't understand that it was okay for me because my travels were always tied to study and learning. They were asking for social opportunities."

Monastic rules were beginning to be relaxed by this time, as the reforms of Vatican II were underway, and the Catholic world was starting to feel its effects. But they weren't loose enough yet to permit cloistered monks and sisters to go on secular travel jaunts. However, when word came from Rome that it was now permissible for nuns to leave their monasteries to attend regular college classes, Sister Margaret was ready to grab the gold ring as it came around. There was a Catholic college just two blocks from her convent, within walking distance, and she quickly enrolled there. Once again her sisters were annoyed. They either had college degrees already or were not inclined to higher studies, so she was the only one who went.

"Did you get a college degree then?" I asked.

"No, I didn't want to bother with that. Too many required classes in things I wasn't interested in. I only wanted to take theology and philosophy and so that's all I did."

Although not feeling particularly close to her community, Sister Margaret was content with her studies, her prayer life and her occasional artwork. She drew pictures with biblical themes and lettered documents for the convent to use. She acquired a small printing press and made greeting cards and bookmarks for the other sisters. But her meditations and scriptural studies occupied her most intensely, and the years went by quickly.

By 1978 it was apparent that not only was their community no longer growing, it was shrinking. The emergence of an active laity in the Catholic Church meant that fewer and fewer young women were seeking to enter religious life. The sisters decided they would have to close their monastery and separate, each sister praying for discernment as to where she should go.

"I really didn't know where to go," said Sister Margaret. "Preoccupied as I was with my interior life, I didn't know all that much about the other communities and how they functioned. But I knew I was ready for another adventure and didn't just want to go off somewhere that wasn't exciting. It was then that Sister Mary Regina arrived on one of her visits. She came regularly to all of us to see how we were getting on. I told her I didn't know where to go, and she instantly said, 'Why don't you come to Saint Paul and see how we operate?'

"Those were her exact words," Sister Margaret laughed. "I can still hear her; I liked the way she said 'See how we operate.' And I decided to take her up on it. When Riverdale closed, I came straight to Saint Paul, and it was all on account of Sister Mary Regina."

"So, how did they operate?" I asked her. "Did you find it so very different from Riverdale after all?"

"I certainly did. The first thing one of the sisters said to me when I came in was, 'Welcome to Vis!' Let me tell you, I was horrified. I remember thinking, 'Oh dear, I hope they don't use slang here. I knew I wouldn't fit in a place that didn't speak properly."

"Did you not like slang at all, or was it just when it was applied to religious things?"

"I didn't like it was when it was used for words that are supposed to be sacred. Remember, I was born in Hell's Kitchen, and I can handle a little street language, but not when it comes to matters of religious vocabulary."

I could sympathize with her there. I told her that I had been less than edified upon meeting an associate pastor from Blessed Sacrament Parish who told me he worked at "Blessed Sack." Some of the kids in my Catholic grade school, Incarnation, called it "Inky," and the lovely name "Our Lady of Grace" had a basketball cheer ending in "O-L-G, O-L-G Rah, Rah, Rah!"

"Oh my, that is bad. But for the most part Visitation was not like that. That first greeting was unfortunate, but the sisters were gracious and kind to me. Sister Mary Regina was a perfect lady; they all were, really, but she set the tone, and everyone was very respectful. They were less formal than we'd been in Riverdale, but that was to be expected as we had been completely enclosed. Well, most of us were; I did have my escapades but even I was certainly in more than I was out. Here the sisters had a school to run, and they had a lot more contact with the outside."

Sister Margaret settled into her new life in Saint Paul, pleased that she had selected an active community. She had wanted an adventure, and the liveliness of the community was a change from the more sedate Riverdale. With her little printing press set up, she was soon making cards to be sold in the school store, The Peddler. She wasn't a teacher, but she could contribute to the educational endeavor this way.

I asked her if she continued to have mystical experiences in her new home. She looked at me as though perhaps I didn't have good sense and said, "But of course. That has never stopped. My relationship with God has just kept strengthening over the years. We don't talk as often as we used to, but there is less need to, as we understand each other better."

Feeling somewhat chastened for having missed the obvious, I asked her if the Saint Paul sisters had found her as odd as had the Riverdale group. She cocked her head at me and answered, "I am a difficult person and will always be perceived by others as such. Even though the community here welcomed me as much as possible, after several years I felt the need to get away from them, too. Not for good, mind you. Just for a while until I could once again figure out where I might really belong. I had my artwork, of course, but I couldn't teach, and I did odd jobs like working in the students' dining room and as portress. But once again, I was not really fitting in."

"Did you ask for another leave of absence?"

"I did, although this time it wasn't as easy. By this time Mary Denise was Mother Superior, and she wasn't as easy to get around as the superiors in Riverdale had been. There was something about the First Federation sisters—the cloistered bunch—that was more innocent, maybe gullible, than the active sisters. We were less for governance, for process. These Second Federation women were more canny, more sophisticated in how to handle people. Mother Mary Denise gave me a year and said that by the end of it I would have to decide if I were committed to Saint Paul. If not, I would have to choose another community."

"Did that seem harsh to you?"

"Not at first. I always liked to start out on a new venture, and this time I picked Toledo, where I lived in a high-rise apartment instead of in another community of nuns. But you can't escape it if that's how you're bent. I still connected with a religious community and received spiritual guidance from a priest who served them. He helped me to discern where I truly belonged. I was gradually led to see that the Saint Paul Visitation might really be the making of me as a nun, and I was pretty sure I would return there. It was almost Christmas, and I was lonesome for the sisters and wanted to go home for a visit. But when I wrote Mary Denise and asked if I might come, she was quick to reply, 'No way.' I had asked for a year to decide, and I wasn't to come back until my decision was clear. Was I back for good, or just until I got restless again? she wanted to know."

"So you had to celebrate Christmas alone in Toledo?"

"Yes, and that was hard. But later I could see that she was right in drawing the line. I had been allowed to shilly-shally too much, and it was time to get down to brass tacks. I would definitely return to Saint Paul, but I found I still I had one more 'not yet' in me. I can see why I drove people kind of crazy."

"What was the 'not yet' this time?" I asked.

"I had been studying the life of Mother Mary de Sales de Chappuis, an eighteenth century Visitation nun who was instrumental in starting the order of the Oblate Priests of Saint Francis de Sales. She was a remarkably holy woman who has been neglected in the religious literature of that period, and I wanted to go to Switzerland and research her life so I could write about it. I believed she should be brought to prominence, to help her advancement to beatification and, possibly, canonization.

"I had just written to Mary Denise asking her to let me return to Saint Paul when I spoke to my spiritual director about going to Switzerland. I thought the poor man was going to have a stroke. He said, 'You didn't go and say anything to Mother Superior about Switzerland when you asked to return to Saint Paul, did you?'

"I told him, no, I was asking *him* for *that* permission, not Mary Denise.

"He said to me, 'Now honestly, don't you see you're sending mixed messages all over the place? You can't stay away for a year and then humbly ask to be welcomed home while putting in a slick request for a little trip to Switzerland before you show up! Do you want them to think you've really gone around the bend this time?'"

I was disappointed in the priest's answer and asked her, "Didn't you get to go to Switzerland?" I was sorry to hear her say no. I had a hunch she would have done a splendid job of getting Mother Mary de Sales de Chappuis some good press, and that she regretted it hadn't happened.

She read my mind. "Maybe you'll have to do it now, Elsa, since I didn't get to."

"Have mercy, Sister Margaret," I begged. "I'm going to have all I can do to bring the lives of you sisters living *here* to the page without going off to Europe to learn about some nun I never heard of until today."

She smiled philosophically at me. "We never know what the Lord will ask of us, do we?"

Sister Margaret returned to Saint Paul when her year was up and has remained ever since. "Not every single minute," she amended. "I took advantage of every class I could, and also made many retreats while I could still get around, but no more leaves of absence, no more trips to Europe."

She continued her studies in art as well as religion, concentrating in her later years on icon art and calligraphy. Taking a class in manuscript at Saint John's University, she became familiar with the artists working on the new *Saint John's Bible* and keeps in touch with them regularly. They send her a copy of each page as it is completed. Only in the last year has she had to quit drawing and painting, as arthritis has made her fingers too stiff to continue.

"So I spend my time with my flowers now," she smiled. "I raise African violets, and I have a whole indoor bed of them, as well as an outdoor garden when the weather is warm. I grow herbs too, even lavender although we have no use for it here. It's fun to watch it grow and it smells wonderful. The nuns in France love their perfumes, so they put it between their sheets and scent their habits, but the American sisters have grown away from that."

She is the refectorian too, getting the prepared food to the table and putting it away when meals are finished. She'd like to get out more, but now she must use a walker and that makes it difficult.

She is grateful that her community has not succumbed to the informality of guitar masses. "They're a travesty," she says. "I know many people think they're wonderful because the young folks like them, but I'm glad we still have an organ. It seems that every now and then someone will pull out a guitar and a piece of music and say, 'You'll like this; it was written by a nun.' Now, I want to know what difference it makes if the pope himself wrote it if it's just a bit of drivel? Having a nun write it doesn't automatically make it music."

The future of Visitation remains unclear to her. She has no doubt that the school will continue; the laity will take it over and many arrangements are in place to ensure that happens. The Visitation Order will be represented through the living spirit of the school, but she has a hard time believing that young women will continue to enter the convent.

"Girls today don't seem to be attracted to the spiritual life. They want to do good deeds and be social activists, but the contemplative life—what's that? And yet among the laity, the more mature laity, there seems to be a greater consciousness, a greater awareness of prayer life. Who knows where that will lead?"

She recognizes that she is old now, and her time is drawing close. She still prays the Office five times a day, but not always in the chapel. She is tired by the end of the day and retires immediately after supper, praying in her room.

"Has it been a good life for you, Sister?" I ask softly.

"Oh yes, it has. I have many wonderful memories, and I am closer than ever to God. His grace surrounds me, and I can feel His presence. But I can't tell exactly when I'll go to join Him."

Death seems to hold no terror for Sister Margaret. Like Huck Finn, she harbors a desire to "strike out fer the territory" and perhaps regards it as her last, great adventure. I can't help thinking that maybe the reason she has lived so long is because each time God has said to her, "Margaret, are you coming home now?" she has answered, "Not yet, Lord. I'm coming, of course, but not yet. Trust me, as I have trusted you. It's soon, but not yet."

SISTER JANE DE CHANTAL

Marie Smisek was born in Saint Paul in 1925. Like many families struggling in the era of the Great Depression, the Smiseks didn't have much money, but Marie was barely aware of it. Her dad's occupation helped account for much of that; he was an ice cream maker at the Crescent Creamery in Saint Paul and nearly every day brought home frozen treasures from his workplace. The Smisek children watched for his car, and when it turned the corner of their street, they and the neighbor kids rushed to meet it, jumping on the running boards for the ride home. Reaching through the open window, they begged him to tell what he had brought. Sometimes it was ice cream sandwiches or bars, sometimes popsicles; whatever he had, he handed out to the eager children like Santa Claus distributing toys.

"Those were the days before freezers," I said to her. "How did you keep it from melting?"

"We didn't keep it," she grinned. "We ate it."

Mrs. Smisek was a frugal housekeeper, and while the family lived simply and economically, they never went hungry or ill-clothed. They didn't have much in the way of extras, but between the ice cream and a dime for the movies every Saturday, they were as rich as they wanted to be.

There were three children: Lorraine, a year and a half older than Marie, and Robert, three years younger. Sister Jane de Chantal smiled when she told me how Lorraine got her name.

"My dad was stationed in the Alsace/Lorraine region of France during World War I, and he became very attached to the country and its people. He met a small orphan girl whom he loved very much. He wanted to adopt her, but army regulations would not permit it, so he had to come home without her. For a while he tried to keep up a correspondence with the orphanage that housed her, but then they lost contact. He grieved over that loss for a long time; he never forgot the little girl.

"Later he met and married my mother, and when their first child, a daughter, was born, he named her Lorraine. Then I came along a year and a half later, and this time he thought Alsace would be a perfect name for the second daughter. Mother had gone along with the Lorraine bit, but she drew the line at calling me Alsace." Sister Jane raised her eyes to heaven and said, "Thank you, Mother." Then she looked at me indignantly. "Can you imagine going through school with a name like Alsace? The other kids would have eaten me up!"

The Smisek family was devoutly Catholic, faithfully attending Mass every Sunday. "We never even thought of skipping it; it was just something one did without any question. When we were little, we children came downstairs every night and said our prayers, kneeling around our mother. We would come in our little sleepers or nightgowns and pray aloud. Even if we had company in the house we did this. It was just part of our normal routine."

From an early age Marie was especially devout. Her dad often made visits to Saint Luke's and would take her with him because he knew how much she loved to kneel with him in front of the altar. She sensed a special peace in the presence of the Blessed Sacrament.

"We were brought up to love God," she said. "He was a very real presence in our lives whether we were at home or in school or anywhere. But He was especially real to me in church, even when it was dark and empty of other people. When I was in fifth grade at Saint Luke's, our teacher gave everyone a holy card, and mine depicted the famous painting of Jesus knocking at the door with a lantern in His hand. I was only ten years old, but I knew what it was, what it meant. Jesus was knocking at my door for me. I kept it to myself—kind of pushed it to the back of my mind—but it was always there and I knew it."

Marie attended John Marshall High School after she graduated from eighth grade. Many of her friends went to Saint Joseph's Academy or Visitation Convent, but her family couldn't afford the tuition, so the Smisek children went to public high school. John Marshall was in a lower-middle-income area, and the students came from different ethnic backgrounds.

"Our school had about a third each of Jewish, white and black students and it was a wonderful mixture. When I hear now what a big deal everyone makes of diversity, I wonder what all the fuss is about. We were all friends at Marshall; there wasn't any difficulty about which group you were in. I had great high school years—lots of dances and other activities."

Art was her favorite subject and she had a talent for it. She sometimes wished she had more skillful teachers; she realized she could go further with better instruction, but otherwise she was content.

Her other important class was religion, taught in the evenings by seminarians for students who attended public school. The young men talked to the kids about religious vocations, asking them to examine their hearts and see if they thought God might be calling them.

Sister Jane shook her head now at her own stubbornness. "I don't know what kept me from telling those nice men I had already received my call. I *knew* I was going to enter the convent, but I didn't talk about it. They would have been so pleased to hear that I was committed, but I wasn't thinking about them. One, especially, seemed to sense that I was interested, and he gave me some written materials on religious vocations, but I still wouldn't discuss it with him or with anyone else. I just kept living it up in high school and having fun."

Money was too tight to send Marie to college, but that was all right with her. She got a job with the U.S. Navy as a civilian secretary and took some art and English classes at night at the university. Those were the only classes that interested her, and she was taking them for her own pleasure, not to get a degree. The convent was a persistent image, but it was in the back of her mind, and that was where she preferred to leave it for the time being.

Then one day she was invited by the sister of one of her friends to attend a weekend retreat at Saint Catherine's. It was a chance occurrence, as another girl had been invited first but at the last minute was unable to go. The idea appealed to Marie.

"Did you see it as a chance to pray about your vocation?" I asked. "Maybe get some guidance about it finally?"

She laughed and shook her head. "No. I should be ashamed to say that what was attracting me was that it was a beautiful October weekend, and I knew the lovely campus would be a great place to sunbathe. They had apple trees, and I pictured myself lying on the warm grass and soaking up the sun and eating stolen apples. And that's exactly what I did. I didn't attend a single conference or service.

"And I didn't have any guilt about it—I just felt like a lazy cat in the warm sun all weekend. But when Sunday afternoon arrived, it did occur to me that I'd better get into the chapel and hear a little bit, as my dad would be picking me up and was sure to ask me about it. So I hurried in and got in on just a few minutes of the last talk, and then Benediction started. It was during Benediction that I heard a strange, rumbling sound coming from the roof of the chapel. It was built of stone, and I thought that the roof was disintegrating, preparing to come down. I was scared to death; it was a horrible sound. It kept on and then something inside me said, "Yes or No?" And no one else heard the rumbling; that was apparent. I didn't answer immediately; I thought, 'I know what you mean, Lord, but I really only came here for apples and sun-bathing.' It was a tremendous shock to realize that while I hadn't been thinking of Him at all, He came anyway with that knock. So then I said, 'Yes,' and all the noise subsided. I was weak as could be."

"So you did have an epiphany after all, Sister Jane. It sounds like the kind of mystical experience I've only read about."

"I don't know what it was, Elsa, but it was very powerful. And I've never regretted my answer. Not for an instant. When Dad came, I was very subdued, and I think he sensed that because he didn't press me for an account of my weekend. I didn't tell him what had happened to me in the chapel; it was too new and unsettling. But the subject of my vocation had definitely moved from the back of my mind to the front."

"Now the question was where to go. I didn't know anything about religious orders, but we had a family friend, a Father Gabriel Dieffenbach, and as it turned out, he helped me. He dropped in at our house from time to time, and one evening when he came over I happened to be the one who let him in. Before my parents joined us, we sat together on the davenport talking when he suddenly said, 'Marie, do you have something on your heart?'

"It was quite a thing for me to hear him say that because I had not yet, never, told anyone about my calling, not even my parents. But I answered him, 'Yes, I do.' And so I told him. We stopped talking when my parents joined us, but he must have thought about it a while because a few days later he came over again.

"He actually asked my parents to leave the room, saying that he and I had something we must discuss alone. They went out into the yard; I think they were so used to obeying anything a priest told them to do that it didn't seem that odd to them. He said to me, 'We've got to do some talking here.'"

Ever since that day in the chapel at Saint Catherine's, Marie had been praying the rosary to the Blessed Mother, asking her where she should go. The Carmelite Order appealed to her, but she feared the life would be too hard, as they were very strict. She also didn't want to become a Saint Joseph sister; they were a teaching order and she had no desire to teach. She trusted that Mary, the Mother of God, would eventually tell her where she belonged. Now she shared these thoughts with Father Dieffenbach.

"Father," she said, "I've been praying for guidance. I've told Mary that if her Son wants me, she's going to have to help me, because I have no idea where to go."

"'It seems clear enough to me,' he answered. 'I think you should go to the Visitation Convent.'"

She turned to me and said, "You see, his mother and sisters had gone to Visitation, and he knew all the Visitation sisters. He thought very highly of them and believed it would be the ideal place for me. My first reaction was to protest that I didn't speak French, but he assured me that the language of their community was English, even if they were a French order." She added, "You can see how little I knew about them!"

Marie did not immediately reveal the subject of her conversation with Father Dieffenbach to her parents. But a few days later, she decided the time had come. Her mother was ironing in the kitchen and looked up when Marie said, "Mom?"

She answered, "Yes?"

Marie said simply, "I'm going to enter the convent."

Her mother said, "Ohhh?" and then called to her husband, who was in the basement. He came upstairs and she said, "Marie has something to tell you."

When Marie told him, he made no response at all, just looked at her and went back down the stairs to the basement.

"How did you feel when neither of them said anything to you?" I asked. I couldn't imagine making a tremendous announcement like that and being met with silence.

She answered, "I was relieved. I felt good because I didn't want them to cry or make a scene. I knew they wouldn't oppose it. They didn't have to talk it over with me; we were not an effusive family, but we understood each other deeply; we often didn't need words. My brother and sister didn't say anything either. My sister was gone—she was married and living in Texas—and my brother had graduated from high school by the time I actually went in."

She was eighteen when she told them, but didn't enter until she was twenty. There was no doubt in her mind that she would go, but she needed time to disengage from her old life. Her friends and relatives urged her to change her mind; aunts and uncles said she would never be able to hug her mother again. Her friends worried that she wouldn't have any fun, ever again, and that she would have to cut off her pretty hair. Her male friends were especially upset; she received three proposals of marriage during that time. Their pleading didn't faze her. When the time came, she knew she was ready.

Father Dieffenbach had made an appointment for her to see the Mother Superior at Visitation, after which she went back and met the sisters' council. With its dark entry and grilles separating the cloister from the extern areas, the convent was very different from anything she had seen before, but it felt right to her. She wanted an order that was very thorough, one with a way of life that would be new in every way. They set her entry date for September 8, traditionally considered the birthday of the Blessed Virgin.

"My mother sewed my postulant outfit herself, and she and my father drove me to the convent when the day came. My brother showed his emotion by making sure he wasn't home when I left; that was his way of letting me know how much he cared. It was my dad who broke down when we got to the convent door; he just sobbed." She sighed. "My poor papa."

"Did you cry, too?" I asked.

"I cried a little bit, but not like he did. I had done all my sobbing, maybe for a year or two. My mom held up but—and I didn't know this until years later—she almost had a nervous breakdown that night, because she felt she would never see me again. My brother told me about it, but not until I had been in the convent for years."

"When they left, the sisters brought me up to my little cell. It was a nice room with a bed and a white bedspread—nothing extraordinary—I didn't have my little dressing table with the big mirrors, but it was plain and clean and good. The next morning before my parents came back to visit me, one of the sisters brought me up to the tower to show me the view. She thought it would be fun for me, but I could almost see my house from there. That set me off and I cried and cried. Poor Sister; she had meant to treat me to something nice, and instead I nearly had hysterics.

"Thank goodness, I finished before Mom and Dad came; they brought me some roses a friend had sent me. They were meant to be delivered the day I went in, but they had arrived the next day. Mom said, 'Honey, I thought you would want your flowers,' and then handed them to me. We hugged and they could see that I was all right, that I was going to be okay here."

"What happened to the flowers?" I asked. Postulants were not allowed to have personal possessions.

"You know, I can't remember," she answered. "They may have been put on the altar but I don't know. I just handed them over right away to the Mother Superior."

"Roses sound like a gift from a boyfriend," I teased. "Had you left a special boy behind when you entered?"

She smiled. "Yes I had, but it wasn't he who sent the roses. He sent me a box of candy that I wasn't allowed to keep either, but I opened it and read his note before I turned it in."

"What did it say?"

"It said something like, 'I think I'm already missing you too much.' I never saw it again so I'm not sure of the exact words, but I knew he was thinking about me."

Life in the novitiate was hard, but not as bad as Marie had worried that it might be. Shortly before entering, she had seen the movie *The Song of Bernadette*, the story of the nineteenth century French saint who had endured much harsh treatment from her Mistress of Novices.

"Sister Mary Patricia was my novice mistress, and she was very strict with me, but it was nothing like what poor Bernadette went through. I accepted it because I believed it was what the Lord wanted. Sisters Mary Gertrude and Mary Christine were novices with me and we had a good time being together. Their presence helped me adjust to convent routines, and we learned together the importance of being obedient. It was very different from home, but I had known it would be."

"Were you ever tempted to leave when the rules seemed especially hard?"

"No, I never once thought of leaving. I came with the expectation that I was here to stay. It was so definite when I had to say *yes* or *no* in the chapel at Saint Catherine's, that it was a bond between the Lord and me. Not to be broken. I didn't want to break it and I knew He wouldn't."

After the first year, Marie was accepted into the community, given her new name and clothed in the familiar black habit of a Visitation nun. Sister Jane de Chantal laughed as she showed me the snapshot taken of her that day, wearing a girlfriend's wedding gown and veil. The gown was way too big, but Sister Mary Patricia tucked it in and tied it tighter in the back somehow. She said no one would see it anyway; only the front would show through the opening in the chapel enclosure.

"The ceremony is supposed to be very solemn, and it really is," she assured me. "But so often some little glitch will occur that everyone behind the monastery grille sees while the group in the outer chapel has no idea what's going on. In my case it was my bridal veil. When the bishop leaned through the grille window to bless me with his lighted candle, he set my veil on fire. He was oblivious to it and so was the congregation, but the sisters behind me were frantically slapping out the flames before my hair and dress were ignited too. I could feel them patting at my head and shoulders, making sure the fire was out, while I had to kneel there and look attentive."

The newly clothed sister received her guests in the garden after the ceremony, and none of them knew that anything had gone amiss. Later, though, she returned the dress and had to apologize for the ruined veil.

After her formal acceptance into the community, a new novice mistress was appointed, and life became easier. Sister Mary Helen was not as strict as Sister Mary Patricia had been, focusing less on rules and more on prayer. She taught her charges how to meditate, which enriched their spiritual lives considerably.

Sister Jane de Chantal made her first profession on June 25, 1946, and her final vows in 1948. The community soon discovered they had a talented artist in their midst and revised their opinion that the newly professed nun need not teach. While still in the novitiate, she had been sent to Sister Francis de Sales to learn calligraphy, and the older woman had reported her beautiful work to the others. They felt the gift that had been given by God to Sister Jane should be put to use for the good of the school; they had no one to staff an art studio for the students. Knowing that she had taken a vow of obedience, she set about becoming a teacher, even though that wasn't what she had planned.

She started out by taking correspondence courses in English. Because she had never cared about getting a college degree, she hadn't bothered to get her records from the university, so she lost those credits. Now she had to start from the beginning. Sister Mary Helen helped her with her classes; it was she who taught her to write with clarity, and Sister Jane will always be grateful to her for her help. She was among the generation of sisters who did not leave the convent to study; she completed her coursework under the guidance of the visiting teachers from Saint Thomas. To her surprise and delight, Sister Jane found that she enjoyed teaching art. She set up a studio and worked with her pupils in various media: charcoal, pencil, oil and watercolor.

"The Lord always supplies us with what is needed, you know," she told me. "He gave me enthusiasm for teaching, something I hadn't expected, and I loved being with the girls. They produced some fine work and I was proud of them. On visiting days it was fun to show my parents and friends my little studio, and they were pleased that I had found work I loved to do."

She went along happily with her studio art classes. Sister Irena, a Benedictine nun, came to Visitation daily to teach History of Art to the students, as that was a field in which Sister

Jane had no preparation. Then, one day early in the summer of 1960, the Mother Superior called her to her study. She told her that Sister Irena was no longer available, nor was the layperson who had also taught there at one time. Sister Jane was told that she would begin to teach History of Art in the fall.

She was stunned. "Elsa, I couldn't believe what I had just heard. I had no background in it, none!"

"What did you say to her?" I asked.

"I said, 'Yes, Mother,' and then I went out into the hall and fainted."

"How awful! Did anyone see you? Did Mother Superior know that you had fainted?"

"No, I just came to, picked myself up and dusted off, and decided I'd better start to study. I read and read all that summer to prepare for class. I *never* went to a class unprepared—even if I was just that one step ahead of the students—I was prepared. I was good at anticipating their questions; I remembered all the things I hadn't known right up until that summer, so I had a good idea of what the students might ask. And, wouldn't you know, once again the Lord provided: I learned to love teaching History of Art."

The class became the stepping stone to one of the greatest pleasures of Sister Jane de Chantal's teaching career. She teamed up with two lay teachers, one from the History Department, the other an English instructor, and together they designed a humanities course.

"It was such fun!" she beamed. "We had a ball. The girls loved that class; it was very popular. I taught the art portion, and it was wonderful working with those two brilliant men, showing the students how the pieces intertwined and fit together as civilization advanced. We taught it until about 1988."

By then Sister Jane had been a successful and happy teacher for thirty years; she who had been sure that teaching was the one career she would never choose. She sensed when it was time to quit, though; some inner direction told her that it would be wise to begin to wind it down.

"I quit the studio art first and then, a couple of years later, the humanities course. That was a disappointment because it brought an end to the class. My services were free, but if the school were to continue it, they would have had to hire an outside teacher, and that was too expensive for an elective class. And yet, that inner voice guided me to end it, and I talked about it with the Mother Superior. By then many of our rules had been relaxed, and we were no longer simply told what we must do. We had help in discerning what we were best suited for."

Though she no longer teaches, Sister Jane's influence is still evident in the work of her former students. One of them, a Saint Paul artist, recently had an exhibit of her work in which she featured a portrait she had painted of her beloved art teacher. Modest Sister Jane did not mention this to me, but the student's mother, a former classmate of mine, told me about it.

"It was a wonderful afternoon for both of us," she said. "I drove Sister Jane de Chantal to the exhibit, which was titled 'Faith, Hope and Love.' We were admiring the various paintings when Sister spotted one of a woman in a black habit.

"'Oh look,' she said. 'I see a Visitandine habit—did she do a portrait of Saint Margaret Mary?' I told her to look at it carefully and as we drew closer she realized it was of herself. She was really astonished and pleased; I think she was especially happy that she was represented in the original habit of the order. The portrait was titled 'Inspiration and Guidance.' Sister Jane nurtured her students' talents; they owe much to her."

Another student painted a beautiful set of the Stations of the Cross for the sisters. They are in the monastery so the public does not see them, but Sister Jane brought one of them to the parlor to show me. It depicted Jesus being stripped of his garments, exquisitely designed and painted in oil on wood.

"I remember so well when she did them," said Sister Jane. "She started the set when she was a junior and worked on them all that year and the next. Many evenings and Saturdays she would come with a classmate who was her model. After they finished, I was so delighted and grateful for her work that I asked her if she would finish the mural started by the class of 1940.

"Sister Jane Margaret was the art teacher then, and she had wanted her seniors to paint murals representing the four Cardinal Virtues: Prudence, Justice, Fortitude and Temperance. They only completed three, so I asked my student to do Prudence, the one they had missed. Happily, the murals were actually painted on canvas, not the wall, so they could be removed and reinstalled when we moved to Mendota Heights, but all those years they had hung there incomplete."

We walked together down to the hall outside of the students' dining room to admire the set, now complete, thanks to Sister Jane's tutelage and her student's willingness.

Sister Jane continues to stay involved with the school in other ways. For many years she had a homeroom, which helped her get to know the girls. Every Wednesday, before classes start, she prays a decade of the rosary with those students who come to the chapel. She works with the Fine Arts Society, deciding which visiting artists should be invited to school and which plays and cultural events they should attend. She watches auditions for the talent show to make sure the acts are in good taste. She explained that students sometimes haven't developed the best judgment about what is appropriate and what is not; she helps them see that there are boundaries that should not be crossed.

"And in the monastery there is always work to be done. I do portressing, gardening, cleaning dishes; isn't that the same in every home? That the dishes are *always* there, waiting to be washed?" she laughed.

Her words pin-pointed the charism of the order: even ordinary tasks like washing the dishes are transformed into the extraordinary when done willingly and for the love of God. Prayer remains central to Sister Jane's life. She knows that trusting in the Holy Spirit has sustained her through difficult times and kept her steadfast to the vows of her vocation.

"It's ironic, is it not?" she asked. "My hardest times have been in the monastery and the easiest in the school. When I entered, I believed that teaching would be the last thing I wanted and monastic life would be my greatest joy. But teaching turned out to be wonderful, and it's been living in community that has been my biggest challenge."

"How has it been difficult?" I asked.

"We have made changes that I believe have diminished the original spirit of our community."

"Do you mean the changes initiated by Vatican II?"

"No," she answered quickly. "Not at all. Vatican II was a great thing, something the Catholic Church badly needed. I think that it was in our *interpretation* of the changes that we sometimes erred, and we are living now with the consequences of what we did. We went too far in dropping customs that were part of the glue that held us together. We are no longer attracting young women to join our community, and I believe it is because they don't see that we are that different from the secular world."

"But you still have a special spirit here," I protested. "I feel it when I come here. There is a very real sense of peace that pervades Visitation, a kind of spiritual energy that I don't experience in most other places. And you, as well as your sisters, convey a kind of serene presence to me when I am with you."

"I think I know what you mean, and I believe that is the work of the Holy Spirit, not just of us individually," she mused. "I'll give you an example. Some time ago I spent a week visiting my sister, Lorraine, in a setting where she was hospitalized. In the latter half of her life she has struggled with alcohol and has been tormented in many ways.

"The day I was leaving to return home, a woman who was in the place with her told me she hated to see me go. She said it was because it was so much more peaceful when I was there; everything felt more calm. It never had occurred to me that I might have that effect on others, but that's what the woman said. Now, that's not because I'm some especially saintly person—I know I'm no Mother Teresa—but I think that those of us who are consecrated to God may bring an awareness of Him to others."

She sighed. "That's one of the reasons I regret that so many of us are no longer wearing habits. When people see us in the clothing of a religious, it signals to them that we are representing something besides just ourselves."

Sister Jane still wears her habit at all times, although it has been modified from the original style. With her black jumper and short black veil, she is identifiable as a nun everywhere. She still keeps the old one in her closet, though, and intends to be buried in it.

She looked thoughtful. "Our holy founders had to make changes they didn't feel good about, so I pray to them when I'm discouraged about where we are today. You know, when the order started, Saint Francis wanted each sister to go out once a month and work with a poor family. They were to return, of course, but they were meant to go out and visit, as Mary had visited Elizabeth when she was pregnant and needed her. But the archbishop at the time thought it was not proper for sisters to go into seedy neighborhoods, and he said they must remain in the cloister. Saint Francis felt bad about it, but he was always obedient to his superiors. He said it must be the will of God if the bishop told him to do it.

"And it turned out to be a very good thing after all. After his initial reluctance Saint Francis came to accept it willingly and so did Saint Jane de Chantal. I'll show you what she wrote about it." She handed me a page from the community's *Mission and Spirit* document. I read:

> *...and after much consideration and difficulty, for it grieved our Blessed Father to change the original simplicity of his little Congregation as he thought this less spectacular way of life would, for this very reason, lead to more lowliness and leave us humble and small, he nevertheless gave in, being mindful of Divine Providence. And soon afterwards he told me that when all was carefully considered and weighed in the balance, it was best for us to be religious with solemn vows, and that God had had His way in the face of his own personal aversion; and he blessed God for this, remaining extremely happy about this solution.*

"So you see," Sister resumed, "God will always find a way for his work to be done. If one door closes another opens."

"That happened literally when some of your convents closed, and the sisters needed to find new homes, didn't it?" I remarked. "They turned to your house and you welcomed them in."

"Oh yes, and they've been so good for us. Each one who came brought her own special gifts. It was hard for them to leave their monasteries but they never complain. I only wish they would be more willing to speak up. Sometimes I worry that because they weren't here at the beginning, they may feel they aren't really part of our community. But they are, and I hope they know how much their presence here means to us. My goodness, if they weren't here we'd be down to five people."

"There would be seven if Sisters Mary Frances and Katherine hadn't left for the Minneapolis monastery. Was it hard for you to lose them?"

"We miss them very much, but it wasn't hard in the sense that they obviously felt called. It was a really strong and sincere conviction that they were to be among the poor, and it was the right place for them to be. I think they are very happy in this new expression of their vocations, and we're glad that they're happy. We couldn't wish them back among us, knowing that they are following God's will as they feel it to be."

I took my leave of Sister Jane de Chantal at the front door of the convent. Always gracious, the sisters walk with their guests and open the door for them. We embraced and then she gave a radiant smile.

"I'm not saying that the Visitation spirit has disappeared here," she said. "I just want it to continue. I know that often when things appear to have died, they become reborn. So I pray—we all pray—for ways to ignite the flame again. I do trust that the Holy Spirit will continue to guide us, even when I doubt the wisdom of some of the things that have occurred. I know we don't always get our way in how things work out. Acceptance and obedience are the way of religious life."

SISTER MARY IMMACULATA

I worried from the start that Sister Immaculata would be a tough nut to crack. Ninety-three years old and nearly blind, she still wears the full seventeenth-century habit and veil. It contrasts oddly with her Ray Charles–style wrap-around sunglasses and the little red motor-scooter she uses to maneuver around the monastery. The day I presented my writing plan to the community she had no questions, crouched over her handlebars in the back row, her expression impenetrable behind the dark shades.

Sister Marie Thérèse had warned me. The other nuns were enthusiastic about the project and most of them signed themselves up for interview times with me. Sister Immaculata had to *be* signed up.

"What does Elsa want to talk to me about?" she had asked Sister Marie Thérèse plaintively.

"She's talking to all of us, Immaculata," Sister Marie Thérèse answered. "She wants you to tell her about your vocation."

"Boring subject," said Sister Immaculata as she swiveled her motorized seat around and scooted away.

But now her turn had come, and I awaited her in the convent parlor, tape recorder and microphone set up.

"I don't know what I'm doing here," she said crossly as she wheeled her scooter toward me through the door. "I can't see, I can't hear and I can't remember anything. I'm no good to you."

I made a quick decision to meet fire with fire. "Well, you can talk," I snapped back. "That's obvious."

Her black glasses glinted as she tilted her head back, but I saw a hint of a smile on her lips. I breathed easier; I had guessed right.

"I'll try to make this easy for you," I said in a softer tone. "Sister Marie Thérèse told me you weren't eager to be interviewed."

"Well, I thank you for that," she answered. "It is certainly not my idea of a delightful thing to do."

Sitting down and pulling my chair close to her, I asked her to tell me a little bit about her childhood and family. She started slowly but warmed up as her memories, like a third person, began to join our tête-à-tête in the parlor, a few at a time and not always in the most chronological order, but vivid nonetheless.

She was born and baptized Mary Helen Binzel in 1913 in Beaver Dam, Wisconsin. When she was ten, the family moved from Beaver Dam to Marshfield, where her father owned and operated a cannery. There were two children, Mary Helen and her brother, Rudolph, who was three years older. Rudy was a joy to Mr. and Mrs. Binzel, as he was bright and well-behaved, a good student, always eager to please. Mary Helen was their problem child. She was willful and fun-loving, always more ready to go out and play than help in the house or do her homework. She found school difficult and boring, and was a poor student.

Her parents bemoaned her lack of seriousness and compared her, unfavorably, to her brother.

As she spoke, I could see that her crusty exterior was a thin front for a warm heart and active sense of humor. The frisky girl she had once been darted and winked behind her forbidding glasses. She chuckled affectionately at herself as she recalled her naughtiness as a child.

"Besides the fact that I was a poor student, it really bothered my mother and father that I didn't particularly like going to Mass, and I thought the missions and retreats at church were even more boring than school. They seriously worried that I would come to no good end. And," she laughed again, "I have to admit I didn't improve much when I went to high school."

Her friends were carefree kids like herself, uninterested in school and intent on having fun. Their activities were harmless, consisting mostly of playing baseball and basketball together, but they neglected schoolwork, and none of them graduated with any distinction. If only she could behave more like Rudy, and less like Mary Helen, her parents often said sadly.

College sounded abhorrent to her, but her father insisted she go. And, he added, at least the first two years must be at a Catholic college. In the fall of 1932, Mary Helen reluctantly packed her suitcases and left home to attend the College of Saint Catherine in Saint Paul.

Predictably, she did not do well there. The Saint Joseph sisters who ran the all-women's school did not approve of her unladylike behavior. She was frequently in trouble for skipping classes and sneaking down to the riverbank to smoke cigarettes. She would have been sent home for good but for the intercessions of a Sister Jeanne Marie, a dean and counselor. She saw a good heart hiding inside the rebellious tomboy and asked the others to be more patient and understanding with Mary Helen. With Sister's help and encouragement, she was able to last out the two years prescribed by her father.

"She was my savior," Sister Immaculata says now. "She was like a guardian angel, and I really loved her. If all the sisters at Saint Catherine's had been like her, I might have stayed there for more than two years, but they just let me know in a lot of ways that they didn't approve of me. Of course I couldn't really blame them; I was a bit of a rascal."

She went to the University of Wisconsin at Madison for her third year, but that didn't prove to be the right place either. No one scolded her for smoking and skipping classes; they simply gave her poor and failing grades. Instead of finishing college, she went to a business school during what would have been her senior year. That was the only course of study she ever remembers liking. The subject matter made sense to her in ways that Latin and literature never did.

"I'm no scholar," she laughed. "You're probably wondering why I'm in a convent when I'm no good for anything. I'm not fit to teach, and I can't even sing. I've never been an asset in the chapel."

"You do make me curious," I answered, "although I can't help wondering if you're as hopeless at everything as you say you are."

"The sisters here are a good bunch. They've been awfully patient with me, and I guess I did a good enough job back when I was younger. I liked the work I had; I mowed the lawns, worked in the garden and washed an awful lot of dishes, but now I can't do much of anything but pray." She laughed again. "But that's what I'm supposed to be doing, so I guess that's okay too."

"What did you do when you finished business school?" I asked. "If you entered the convent, you must have learned to like church a little bit."

"No, I hadn't discovered church at that time. I went back to Marshfield and worked in the bank there for about ten years. I still had friends there, and my family, of course. I knew I was a disappointment to them, but it's not as if we didn't get along at all."

She described her years in the bank along with her active social life, going out with her friends and having a good time. She never had a serious boyfriend, saying that early on she had known that marriage wasn't right for her. She liked boys well enough but couldn't see herself living with one of them. She enjoyed the freedom to come and go as she pleased.

Her father was running the cannery and now had Rudy to help him, but Rudy wasn't well. He had developed kidney problems, and effective treatment for his condition didn't exist at that time. Dad and Rudy approached Mary Helen about joining them in the cannery, thinking that it would be prudent to have another family member learn the business. At first she wasn't very eager, but decided she owed it to the family to be cooperative for once. She was glad she had done the right thing, because shortly after she settled into the business, her father died of a stroke. Now she and Rudy ran the plant together, and they developed a friendship, at last. As children they had not been close; there was too much distance between their intellects and interests. But, in the cannery, they felt the bonds of blood relationship erasing the old indifference, and they worked well together.

They managed the business and cared for their mother, who was becoming frail with heart disease. When her weak heart stopped beating, Mary Helen and Rudy buried her next to their father. Mary Helen felt the loss deeply and regretted not having been a more dutiful daughter while both parents were alive. Through her tears, she took comfort in knowing that she had been of some help to them in the end.

Looking back, she says that those life-changing events caused her to reflect more soberly on what our existence is about. "After my father died, I began to get a little respect for religion.

Going to church wasn't the chore it had once been, and I began to pay more attention to the Mass and the sermons. I even began to pray."

After her mother's death, her prayers intensified, and attending church became a source of strength to her. She felt the stirrings of something deeply spiritual within her and found going out with her friends less and less attractive. There was now an emptiness where there had once been loud laughter and careless fun. She started driving to Minneapolis several times a year to make religious retreats at The Cenacle, a Catholic establishment offering retreats and seminars to women seeking spiritual direction. I noticed the mischievous smile appearing again on her strong-boned, angular face.

"I think my mother and father were working on me from heaven. I spent a fair amount of time realizing there were lots of things I could have done to make their lives easier while they were here. I realized how much time I had wasted, running around to bars and clubs, joining in the empty nightlife that you see in those places."

She continued helping Rudy with the cannery for another five years, but her interest in it was flagging. Her trips to The Cenacle increased in frequency, and she also looked up her old mentor, Sister Jeanne Marie, at Saint Catherine's. The two women had many discussions about prayer and its purpose. One hot August day, they talked so intensely they didn't realize how late it had become, and Sister Jeanne Marie invited her to have dinner with the sisters and stay overnight.

The next morning they resumed their discussion and Sister Jeanne Marie said to her, "You know, you may be surprised to hear this, but I don't think what we're talking about is just ordinary devotion. I think we're seeing a religious vocation."

Mary Helen's heart seemed to skip a beat. The same thought had been on her mind but she had pushed it down, believing it was too late for her to realize such a dream. "But I'm too old, Sister," she remembers protesting. "I'm forty years old; no one would want me now. All the religious orders accept only young women."

Sister Jeanne Marie regarded her thoughtfully. "Have you heard of the Visitation Sisters in Saint Paul?"

Mary Helen had not, but her interest was piqued.

"They accept many different kinds of women, women in various stages of life," Sister Jeanne Marie said. "I think you might want to get to know them. See if your desires and theirs aren't more alike than you believe."

Sister Jeanne Marie made arrangements with Sister Jane Margaret, who was Mother Superior at the time, and Mary Helen went to see her. Jane Margaret is still remembered as one of Visitation's most beloved sisters, admired for her energetic compassion, great piety and sharp Irish humor.

"She must have hit just the right spot in me," Sister Immaculata told me. "I was fond of her right away, and I guess she didn't think I was that bad after all. We talked quite a while, and then she invited some of the other sisters in to meet me. They asked me to stay overnight and spend a few hours with them, see the grounds and everything. I was pretty happy with the welcome they gave me, I have to tell you. They were really wonderful."

"Did you find the environment depressing?" I asked her. "Some of the sisters have told me they were quite put off at first by the spooky entrance with its heavy door and peephole."

"It didn't seem strange to me," she laughed. "I was a product of Prohibition—it was just like a speakeasy, and I was no stranger to them."

Mary Helen drove home to Marshfield the next day, her heart filled with warm wishes and her head with good advice. The sisters had suggested that she pray about her experience in their monastery, talk it over with her priest and with other nuns she knew, and then let the Mother Superior know what she was thinking. Obediently, she did just that.

But she knew it wasn't time that she needed to realize she was ready to embrace a new life. She could have asked to be admitted on the day of her initial meeting, she was so certain. Visitation was what she been seeking since losing her parents and finding God. It was another concern that held her back, one she knew she would have to confess to Mother Jane Margaret.

Returning to the monastery a few weeks later, she revealed her weakness to the Mother Superior. She told her that it had been easy to give up running around to bars and hanging around with friends who had nothing on their minds but the next good time. She had already done that to a large extent and didn't miss the excitement that such encounters had once provided. But her addiction to cigarettes was another matter.

Mary Helen had smoked cigarettes, heavily and daily, for more than twenty years. She could not imagine a life without cigarettes. People who have never experienced substance addiction have trouble understanding how compelling the need to satisfy it is. To lifelong smokers, a day without the "lift" nicotine provides is joyless. These addicts wonder how they can manage to be happy with all their sensations dulled and deprived.

Mother Jane Margaret received Mary Helen's admission with the equanimity that so beautifully defines the Visitation spirit of flexibility. Instead of lecturing her about self-discipline and advising her to come back only after she had conquered her bad habit, she took her hand and smiled encouragingly at her.

"Perhaps, my dear," she said, "Perhaps you wouldn't have to give it up all at once. Surely we should be able to find a room in the monastery where you can go and smoke if you feel desperate. That way, you can taper off until you feel comfortable without cigarettes. We should not let a thing like that stand in the way of you realizing your vocation."

Mary Helen's eyes filled with tears of gratitude. The last thing she had expected was to have her vocational call so completely acknowledged that any impediments to it could be easily handled. Mother Jane Margaret didn't look down on her for her weakness; she saw it as a temporary little hurdle that would be overcome in time.

The word "empowerment" was not used in the 1950s the way it is today. But as I heard the story, I realized that Mother Jane Margaret had empowered Mary Helen. Her non-judgmental acceptance had given Mary Helen the confidence and strength she needed to overcome her craving. Sister Immaculata never used whatever special smoking room might have been found for her. On the way home to Marshfield that day, she threw out the last of her cigarettes and never smoked again.

She and Rudy made arrangements to leave the cannery. It wasn't hard, as Rudy had hired a good manager who wanted to buy it from them. Saying good-by to her old friends wasn't hard either. She still liked them, but spending time with them no longer had much meaning for her. The cloister beckoned, and with her new-found certainty that it truly was the right place for her, all her thoughts and desires were turned towards its peaceful sanctuary.

She entered the convent in Saint Paul on November 25, 1953. She was forty years old and felt like an old lady compared to the other postulant, Margaret Ann Burke, who was only seventeen. But in humility she knew she had as much to learn as anyone, no matter what age. She needed to learn how to become a nun.

At the end of the first year she was given her habit and veil, a way of dressing that she has never abandoned. It proclaimed her new identity and, though she could have modified it when many of the other sisters did, it was important to her to keep it. Along with the habit, she was also given her new name, Mary Immaculata.

"That is an unusual and beautiful name," I said to her. "Did you like it when you received it?"

"No," she answered quickly. "I was terribly embarrassed. You see, it was the Marian Year, 1954, and Sister Jane Margaret thought it would be fitting. She had asked me if I had a preference for any particular name, and I said I didn't care as long as it had 'Mary' in it. I knew I wanted a 'Mary,' but I hadn't figured on so much Mary—that's a lot of Mary to carry around all your life. I have lived with that embarrassment for fifty years. You might know Jane Margaret would go and overdo it."

"But it's a beautiful name," I protested. "Why don't you like it?"

"Because there was nothing immaculate about me and there still isn't. I didn't think I should have the name."

"Did you think you should have been called Mary Magdalene," I teased her, "because you thought you had been so wicked?"

She laughed again. "Well, it might have suited me better, but here I am, still trying to live up to it after all these years."

"What types of work did you do in the convent?" I asked, curious to know what talents of hers had materialized.

She had filled a variety of roles, most of them removed from the educational mission of the school. That continued to hold little interest for her, but she enjoyed the domestic tasks that helped keep the place running. She washed a lot of dishes and spent many hours as the convent's *portress*, the charming name for receptionist that has followed the sisters from their original home in France. She enjoyed answering the phones and greeting visitors. In the summer she worked in the garden and mowed the lawns, and in the winter shoveled the walks. She loved being outdoors and during recreation was usually to be found on the ice rink, ball diamond or tennis courts. She hitched up her skirts and pinned back her veil to lob shots over the net or crack her bat against the ball, running to first base in her laced-up black shoes.

And she prayed. The call to which she had responded with such relief still spoke to her from the center of her being, encouraging her to live the virtues Saint Francis de Sales had patiently described so many years ago. The ordinary life becomes extraordinary when lived in the light of God's undying love. The most humble task is heroic when performed willingly and cheerfully to honor God. *"Vive Jésus,"* she whispered in the French language that Saint Francis had spoken. "Live Jesus." Try in all things to be like Him and turn your thoughts to Him a hundred times a day as you go about your work and play.

"It sounds as though your life here has been happy," I offered, "with its balance of work and prayer and fun."

"Yes, I have been happy. I've lived with some wonderful women and they've been very good to me. Of course, it wasn't always easy, being the odd-ball nun, you might say."

"How do you mean that?" I asked.

"Well, most of the others are what you might call a lot more ladylike than I am. My tomboy ways used to irritate Sister Mary Patricia and some of the others something fierce. And of course, I couldn't teach and I couldn't sing—just didn't act much like a nun, I guess. But they never turned me out so I must have been of some help here."

She smiled as she remembered another job she had especially enjoyed. Around the time of her final profession, the sisters had begun going to Saint Catherine's to attend college, and Sister Immaculata frequently drove them to and from school. She loved hanging around her old campus without having to attend class. Free from any regulations, she wandered around the lovely grounds, stopping in to chat with various sisters, especially her beloved Jeanne Marie. The chapel was a favorite place too, and she spent happy hours there, waiting for the sisters to finish their work and ride home with her. That came to an end when the sisters drove themselves, but it had been a nice hiatus from routine.

"I'm surprised that in all this time you never worked in the business office, with the experience you had at the bank and then actually running a business with your brother."

"That was fine with me," Sister Immaculata said. "If I'd been asked I'd have done it, of course, but I was always happier working outside than in a stuffy office. Sister Mary de Sales was in the business office when I came, and she was very particular. To tell you the truth, I don't think she thought I had a lot of sense, and that was okay as far as I was concerned. It's easier to turn your thoughts to Jesus from the back of a mower than from a column of figures."

The changes of Vatican II had relatively little effect on Sister Immaculata. She found it easy to accept the new liturgies and rituals as she had only been in the convent a few years and did not have a lifetime of habits to change. The deeper theological implications were not important to her, never having been intellectual or reflective. The simple life she had embraced remained largely unchanged, the guiding spirit of Visitation intact.

She sometimes grows sad when she considers how few sisters remain in her order. She believes that women are not becoming nuns much anymore because they have discovered they can do the Lord's work outside of the convent. In this age of the laity, much of the work that religious used to do is being done by laypeople—the unique entity known as sisterhood may not survive the current trend.

However, she acknowledges, this may not be all bad. As long as God's will is being accomplished, it shouldn't matter who is performing the tasks. If the spirit of Visitation is kept alive, the charism of Saints Francis and Jane de Chantal will continue to flourish. She believes the school is a vital force for carrying on the mission.

"And," she adds, "what we think now may not be at all what will happen in the end. We feel like we're in the twilight of our order now, but we've been through big changes before."

I thought of their expulsion from France after the Revolution; the small band of Visitation Sisters struggling through the snows of the Alps into Italy. They hid the sacred relic of their beloved founder in one of their meager bundles, knowing they could never return to the land of their birth. It was the end of the world as they knew it, and yet they lived to flourish throughout Europe and, eventually, in the new world of America. The monastery at Annecy in France, founded by Saint Jane de Chantal, has been restored and remains the spiritual heart of the Visitation order today.

"Have you ever visited Annecy?" I asked her, as our time together came to a close.

"No," she answered, "and I have no desire to. My travels led me here, to Saint Paul, and that is close enough to our holy founders for me." She took her dark glasses off and looked dimly but directly at me with her beautiful, ancient eyes. "God will find this old body here when He comes looking for me. He won't have to go all the way to France."

SISTER MARY DOROTHY

If it's true that the meek shall inherit the earth, then Sister Dorothy stands to gain a portion about the size of Australia. Limping along with her walker, her nearly useless left arm and hand resting on one of its handles, she radiates a joyful innocence that belies her physical and mental limitations. Her unlined face and wide eyes make her appear twenty years younger than the sixty-nine she is.

She came slowly into the parlor, settled herself carefully into a chair and propped her walker against it. She was already speaking. "I just couldn't sleep last night, Elsa. I was so excited about talking to you today and thinking of all the things I want to say. I hope I haven't forgotten too many of them." She fumbled for some bits of paper in the pocket of her dark blue sweater.

"It looks as if you've been writing down those thoughts," I said, as she began to shuffle the scraps into order.

"I certainly have and there are more things in these books and folders I brought too." She gestured toward a big fabric bag hanging from the hook of her walker. "I have pictures from Rock Island of all the sisters there and of our beautiful monastery and bell tower. I was hoping you might want to see them."

Sister Dorothy has not been a lifelong resident of the Saint Paul/Mendota Heights Monastery. She had arrived in 1992 when her community had reluctantly closed the convent in Rock Island, Illinois, merging their shrinking numbers with other, larger houses. Five of them had joined the Visitation community in Saint Louis, and six came to Saint Paul.

"There's so much to say I don't know where I'm supposed to begin." She looked worried.

"You're going to do just fine," I assured her. "I'll ask you some questions, and you can just answer them naturally. Why don't you start by telling me when you were born and what your name was before you became Sister Dorothy."

"I can do that," she said, sounding relieved that the questions were easy. "I was born in 1937, and we lived in a little town: Kent City, Michigan. My parents had me baptized Elizabeth Anne, but they called me Betty." She smiled. "My dad always called me his little Betty. He was a doctor and he was the hardest-working man you ever saw. He almost never got any sleep; he was so busy taking care of sick people, getting up in the middle of the night to go to their houses and still going to the office every morning. But he always made time for his little Betty."

She thought about this for a bit and then added, "I don't want to give the impression that I was more important to him than the other kids. Daddy never played favorites. He loved us all equally. But because of what happened to me when I still very little, he knew that the family needed to give me extra time to learn things."

She was the second child of five born to Paul and Emma Sue Yegge. A brother, John, preceded her by eighteen months, and a sister, Mary Lou, arrived when Betty was nearly three. Then there were no more children for ten years when, to everyone's surprise, little Pauline showed up. Betty's father had a sister, a Visitation nun in Rock Island, Illinois, named Sister Mary Pauline Yegge, and the new daughter was named in her honor. Five years later another girl, Kathleen, was born, so Betty was a young woman by the time her family was complete.

The Yegges suffered a serious blow when Betty was two years old. She contracted encephalitis and hovered between life and death for days. When at last her skin cooled and the convulsions ceased, her parents rejoiced and thanked God for sparing her life. But it was soon evident that the miraculously recovered little girl was not the same one who had endured that blast-furnace fever. They could see that her alertness had changed, and much of her precocious vocabulary had disappeared.

Sister Dorothy smiled, only a little wistfully. "They told me that before I got sick, I was really smart. My dad had examined all the children in town, and he said I was the smartest little girl he had ever seen." She offered a mischievous grin. "They said I was even smarter than my brother John, and believe me, John is really smart."

"Did the encephalitis hurt your arm and leg as well," I asked?

"No, only my mind was affected by that, they told me. But just as I was getting stronger from my illness, I began to have bad stomach pains. I cried so much they thought it must be my appendix and so they took it out. Somehow, a mistake was made, and I bled inside from the operation, and that caused me to have a stroke. So that's what crippled my arm and leg."

I thought of how hard it must have been for a doctor to see his own child so wounded in brain and body while he labored to heal other people's children. And Mrs. Yegge was pregnant with Mary Lou. She soon became exhausted from taking Betty daily for physical therapy to a town several miles away while still looking after little John. To the family's dismay, Betty was not cooperative in therapy.

Sister Dorothy shook her head sadly. "I wish I could have understood then how important it was for me to do the exercises they tried to make me do. My mother says I just wouldn't work my arm and hand no matter what they did. I guess I must have wanted to run around because I was willing to work my leg, but I was just stubborn about my arm." She waved the nearly useless appendage at me. "I might be able to do more with this now if I hadn't been so stubborn then."

I could see that it still troubled her to reflect on her obstinacy. "You were just a tiny child," I reminded her. "You didn't refuse because you were naughty. You didn't know any better, and they didn't have any way to explain it to you."

"Well, that's true, I know. I've been told that. I guess I still blame myself sometimes, although I know I shouldn't. God must have had a reason for needing me to be this way."

The word, *needing*, caught my attention. Sister Dorothy hadn't said God *wanted* her to be impaired, as though He were some capricious being who thought it might be interesting to see how she handled it. There was a deeper implication that she was a useful part of God's work; there was a *need* that her condition was fulfilling even though the reason was not easily apparent.

"Sometimes people blame God for the way things are," I said. "They say it's unfair to send afflictions to little children, and that a loving God wouldn't do that. Did you ever feel that way?"

"Oh no," she answered solemnly. "Even when I was little, I don't think I ever blamed God. I loved God, and I trusted Him." Her face brightened. "Do you know the one subject I was good at in school was religion? I don't know why I liked it so much or

how I could do so well in it, because I got D's and F's in everything else." She sighed. "I still remember seeing my mom sign
my report cards with all those D's and F's."

"I don't think that would happen today," I told her. "Now
they have classes for children with special needs, and the teachers
don't give them marks that make then feel like failures."

"Well, we didn't have any of those, but Dad went to the
school and told them I was doing the best I could, so they always
passed me on to the next grade anyway. I never had to stay behind.
But religion was the only thing I really understood." She brightened again. "When it came time for my First Holy Communion,
the priest gave me private instructions to make sure I knew what
it was all about, and he told my parents he was very happy with
how well I understood it. I didn't make my First Communion in
a group with other kids. I made it on Christmas Eve at Midnight
Mass with my family, and I know it meant more to me than if I
had been a normal child."

"It sounds as if your home was a happy place."

"It was very happy. I had a wonderful childhood because
God blessed me with such good parents. My mother was so
kind and loving. She was always interested in seeing how much
I could do, and she taught me how to dust and make beds. I did
lots of cleaning while she did the canning in the summer, and we
had a good time working together."

She smiled as a memory of her mother came to her. "One
of the best things she did was to teach me how to embroider.
She gave me a piece of unbleached muslin. Do you know what
that is?" I nodded. "It had a little kitten with a red nose marked
on it, and she showed me how to cross-stitch it. I still love to
embroider and do needlework."

"I've seen your beautifully embroidered dish towels at
the Merrie Market," I said, mentally kicking myself for never
having bid high enough to win one. The Merrie Market is Visi-

tation School's yearly fundraiser, and the students, parents and sisters contribute items to its silent auction. I made a mental promise to obtain a dishtowel at the next one, no matter how high the bid. It suddenly seemed important to own a piece of her needlework, elaborately and painstakingly stitched in spite of the crippled hand.

We Catholics place a lot of store in our relics, objects that of themselves have little significance, but are valued because they were once owned or touched by a holy person. I was beginning to realize that Sister Dorothy, this humble nun, was such a person. Sitting in her presence, I became aware of a feeling of awe. Words from the book of Exodus, whispered in my head, "Take the shoes from thy feet, thou art standing on holy ground."

I brought myself back to the parlor. "I think it's a real tribute to your mother that she taught you to make the most of yourself by being able to do so many things. And your father made sure you weren't held back at school. He must have been a caring person too."

"Oh, he was. I'm surprised he lived as long as he did because he spent his whole life taking such good care of his patients that he didn't take care of himself. He died of a heart attack when he was only fifty-five."

She described the life of a small town's only doctor, a man so exhausted that when the phone rang in the middle of the night, as it often did, he would pick it up, say, "This is Dr. Yegge speaking," and then fall right back to sleep.

"Paul," his wife would whisper, nudging him. "You're on the phone with a patient."

That roused him to alertness again, and soon he could be heard starting his car to see to whatever need had awakened him. In spite of his demanding schedule he saw to it that he paid attention to his children, especially little Betty. Nearly every Saturday morning she accompanied him on his rounds of home visits, waiting patiently in the car while he visited patients in their houses. As they headed for home, they would stop for her special treat, doughnuts.

"I think I have my dad to thank for my vocation," Sister Dorothy offered. "We talked a lot when we went out on Saturdays, and he often asked me what I wanted to be when I grew up. I told him I wanted to be in a convent, and he never said I couldn't because of my disabilities. He told me to say my prayers and listen to God. He said that God would let me know if that's what I was to do."

At age eleven Betty went for a month-long visit to her aunt, Sister Pauline, at the Visitation monastery in Rock Island. She considers it to be one of the happiest times of her life and remembers how she wanted to return there. "It's surprising to think how much I loved it when I was so happy at home. It wasn't as if I wanted to get away. But I just felt so right there, even more at home than at home, if you know what I mean."

Though only in fourth grade, she begged her parents to send her to Rock Island to school. She insisted that she wanted to be with nuns instead of in the public school the town offered. Her mother said she couldn't bear to have her little girl go so far away from home; they would only see her at Christmas and in the summers. They compromised and sent her to Mount Mercy in Grand Rapids, which was only thirty-five miles away. Her mother drove her there every Sunday evening and picked her up on Friday afternoons.

"I loved Mount Mercy; the nuns were so kind there. But I still kept thinking about Visitation and was sure that I would be allowed to enter there some day. The Visitation sisters are such wonderful women. They take people with handicaps, people like me, if they know they have a religious vocation. And I really knew I did."

Betty Yegge was received by the Rock Island community

immediately following her high school graduation from Mount Mercy. She would have liked to go to college first, as she felt that she would then have had more to offer the sisters. "It's like my brain is hungry to know things, but I can't read fast enough to understand a lot of what I want to know. It's frustrating to be such a slow reader."

Although she couldn't teach in the school, the Visitation nuns valued her myriad other qualities. Her humility, the patience with which she bore her infirmities, her gentleness towards all and, especially, her great love of God endeared her to the community. She was happy in their novitiate. With her was a woman who had entered later in life, and she mothered Sister Dorothy in a way a younger woman might not have. She helped her get dressed and reminded her where to go and what to do.

"Her name was Sister Christina and she was my angel. I don't think I would have caught on to all the things a sister has to do if she hadn't been there to help me. Of course, there were a lot of things I never did learn. When I entered, the Liturgy of the Hours was in Latin, and I couldn't say it. I never did learn how. You can imagine how happy I was when it changed to English, and I could finally say it with my sisters. I couldn't keep up at first, but having it in English made it so much easier."

"Was that after Vatican II?" I asked.

"It was really during it, not just after it. The sisters talked about the changes a lot and I wanted to understand them, but I have to admit I couldn't read the documents the way they could."

"Many of us found them pretty hard," I assured her. "Church language has never been exactly easy reading."

"I liked the changes, especially because of the switch from Latin to English. And I liked not having to get dressed in my habit anymore. It was really hard to get all those layers on just right and then pin my veil with only one arm working right. I always had to have help. But now I can dress myself and I even tie my own shoes.

"I was happy, but some of the sisters weren't. Five of them left us. Not all at once, but still, they left, and it felt like a big, empty hole in our community. They were all teachers and very bright women, and we missed them terribly. And, of course, not many women entered convents anywhere after Vatican II. It wasn't just us at Rock Island."

The remaining Rock Island sisters struggled to keep the school running with their reduced numbers. Sister Dorothy couldn't teach, but she took pride in accepting more responsibility in the school. Given six rooms to clean, she was pleased that she did it well without supervision. She also walked the students from their piano practice rooms back to their classrooms. Sometimes she could tell they weren't practicing when they should have been. Her brother and sisters had taken piano lessons, and Mrs. Yegge got after them when they didn't practice, so Sister Dorothy knew what to say to the errant students. She liked taking on her mother's role and helped ensure the children did what they were supposed to.

In spite of their efforts, the sisters were unable to continue the school. Lay teachers required salaries, and the building and grounds needed more attention than the little community could afford. In 1978 they made the difficult decision to close the school.

"That was hard," Sister Dorothy remembered sadly. "We knew that whatever happened was God's will and we needed to accept it, but we had to do a lot of praying." She brightened, "But, of course we had more time for prayer, as we didn't have so much work to do."

In 1992, their numbers down to eleven, the sisters closed the convent, each one praying to the Holy Spirit to guide her to her next destination. Some went to Saint Paul, others to Saint Louis. Sister Dorothy had hoped at the time that the separation would be temporary; that the two communities would eventually merge. But that was not to be, and the sisters remained apart.

"Six of us came to Saint Paul/Mendota Heights," said Sister Dorothy. "Sisters Carmelita, Cecilia, Ambrose, Christina and Anna Mary. I thought it would be wonderful to go to the Minneapolis monastery that was being established and work with the poor, but I couldn't."

"Why not?" I wanted to know.

"Instead of being a help, I would have created more work for them. Their house doesn't have any of the things a handicapped person needs, and they would have had to spend too much time helping me. It was hard to decide who would go where, but we did it." She laughed. "When Ambrose settled on Saint Paul, she was really worried that there wouldn't be decent dirt here for her garden. She wanted to haul twenty pounds of Rock Island dirt to Saint Paul."

I would love to have seen Sister Ambrose in her garden, the way Sister Dorothy described her. She was from Luxembourg, having come to the United States with her father during World War II. When in the classroom, teaching French to her students, she was all elegance and propriety. But her true passion was revealed in her garden, and all pretences were dropped. She put a big, floppy hat on over her veil and trudged out to the garden with her trowel and other tools. Working under the hot sun, she planted and trimmed, weeded and harvested for hours at a time, coming in only when thoroughly soaked with sweat. Her face would be as red as the radishes she loved to grow.

"The only thing Sister Ambrose ever complained about was the artificial leg she had to wear," Sister Dorothy said. "She had to have her leg amputated up to the knee and she called the leg 'Saddam' because it inflicted so much pain." She shook her head. "She really hated that thing.

"Only Sister Carmelita and I are here now from our original

six. When Christina and Anna Mary died, it wasn't unexpected because they were pretty elderly, but when Sister Cecilia died, it was a terrible shock. She had gone to Saint Louis for a retreat, and when she was there, she had a heart attack and never came home." Sister Dorothy's large eyes became moist with tears. "I miss her so very much," she sighed. "You can't believe what a wonderful person she was. She and my aunt, Pauline, were my two favorite nuns in the world. I know they're in heaven and I'll be with them again some day, but right now I miss them."

She smiled then, with a little twinkle in her eyes. "At least I *think* I'll be with them. A priest once gave us a kind of test here to see how we're doing spiritually, to assess ourselves. I did come out pretty good on it. It said I'm humble and obedient and things like that, so I guess my character isn't too bad. And my aunt, Pauline, gave me a card once and she had written something like, 'I don't know what this place would be like without you. You are so helpful and dear; it would be awful to be without you.' I tried to find it to bring to you but I couldn't. But I know it said something like that. So I'm pretty sure God will let me into heaven."

"That sounds like a safe assumption," I answered, wondering how I'd score on a test that assessed humility and obedience. They are two virtues not much prized by women today, perhaps because we miss their intended meaning and equate them with unassertiveness and acquiescence. To be *humble* is to be modest, rather than arrogant, and has nothing to do with humiliation or degradation. To be humble is to live in joyful simplicity and be willing to serve others. Saint Francis de Sales is quoted saying, "Humility is true knowledge."

The word "obedience" is also anathema to most women, as it connotes subservience, especially with regard to husbands and other dominating males. The "obey" has been excised from the old wedding vow, "To love, honor and obey." Modern women refuse to consider themselves subject to their husbands, the words of Saint Paul notwithstanding. We do not submit to being dominated by anyone. But to a nun, the virtue of obedience is not viewed as being coerced to do the will of another. Her obedience to her superior, signifying obedience to the will of God, is embraced willingly to further her spiritual growth. It is a discipline she knowingly seeks, not something forced upon her. One of the Visitation mottoes, "All through love and nothing through constraint," emphasizes this belief.

Sister Dorothy went on to tell me about the only other Rock Island nun now remaining in the Saint Paul/Mendota Heights convent. Sister Mary Carmelita has developed a condition that causes water to collect in her brain, robbing her of much of her personality and intelligence. Sister Mary Denise told me it was unlikely that I would meet her, as she is unable to hold a conversation anymore. But it is her *spirit* on which Sister Dorothy concentrates.

"She's so peaceful and happy," she told me. "Most of the time she sits in her chair at the end of the hallway, and I go and sit with her. We listen to music and smile at each other. She's kind of like my mother is now, because Mother has Alzheimer's and isn't the way she used to be either."

"Your mother is still alive?" I asked in surprise.

"Oh yes. She's ninety-four years old and lives with my sister in Dayton, Ohio. I go to visit her every summer for a month. We stay in the beach house on Lake Michigan that our family still owns, and different family members come and stay, too. Mother doesn't talk much anymore, but she's always so glad to see me and I love being with her. It makes her happy to just have us near her."

Again, I noticed the difference between Sister Dorothy's values and those of our secular world. It was clear that to her a human's essence doesn't lie in the body or the mind. The mother she always loved is still there, her soul intact beneath the diminished intellect and aging body. I thought of how I had wept and railed and struggled when my mother lost her bright mind to the same condition. All I could see was loss, both hers and mine. I failed to realize that her spirit was behind the vacant eyes; I thought only of what was not. A stronger belief that we are eternal beings having a temporary journey in our bodies and not the other way around might have allowed me to let my spirit connect with my mother's, bringing more peace to both of us.

Sister Dorothy continued talking about her mother. "It was my mom who gave me a special book, a commentary that has really helped me to understand the bible. That was in 1970, way before she got Alzheimer's. It was hard for me to read at first, but I kept at it. I never would have understood the bible as well as I do now if it weren't for that book. All my life I've wanted to be a better reader and I'm still learning."

She said the sisters don't let her get up for morning prayer anymore, as they think she needs her rest, but she sits up and listens to it through a speaker in her room and reads along with it. "So in a way, I'm there. I attend all the other Offices, and every other week I read aloud at midday prayer. I have to practice it quite a bit to get it right, so I work hard at that. I'm making headway; I do better now than when I started."

She still hasn't learned to read music and admits that it's one thing she hasn't tried. All those black notes on the page look pretty daunting. But she sings and knows the melodies by heart.

"You're never too old to learn," she said earnestly. "I hate to admit it, but I never read our holy founders until lately. Their works were read *to* us when we were in the novitiate. People kept telling me I didn't have to read it because they say I live it, but I wanted to find out for myself." She smiled conspiratorially. "And you know what? I found out there are a lot of things I don't do, or don't do well enough, so now I'm really working to be a better person."

"God help me," I thought. "If she thinks *she* has to work at being more humble and holy, where does that leave me?" I felt my inherited patch of earth shrink again.

Sister Dorothy will celebrate her Golden Jubilee in 2008. The time has gone so fast it's hard for her to believe it's been nearly fifty years since she made her first profession. "I'm sixty-nine years old, but I don't feel any older than when I entered. I feel like I'll live another fifty years so I'm not going to give up on learning."

That sense of awe that visited me earlier came back again. I felt reverence for the courage and determination this woman has been quietly exhibiting for more than a half century. With many odds against her, she has refused to feel victimized, choosing to see life's gifts, not its difficulties. She has labored to understand complex ideas and to express them in careful, accurate speech, and she has succeeded.

I asked her what she wanted for Visitation's future. She said she hoped that more women will turn again to monastic life; that they will see the beauty in being more spiritual.

"We must keep the spirit of Saint Francis de Sales alive; his spirit is priceless."

"How can we do that?" I asked.

"Through prayer," she answered firmly. "A return to prayer is badly needed, and faith and courage are needed too. I think sometimes we give up too easily when our prayers aren't answered right away, or not answered the way we want them to be. Laypeople need to learn to meditate too, not just nuns."

Sister Dorothy's faith and courage were tested recently. On July 15, 2005, the beautiful building that had been home to the Rock Island nuns was destroyed by fire. The newspaper pictures were so devastating to her she could hardly bear to show them to me. The obliteration of one's history is painful, and all the former Rock Island sisters grieved the disaster.

They no longer owned the building or grounds; those have passed through several transformations, but the building stood in silent testimony to the lives the sisters once shared there. It was a physical reminder of the thousands of prayers that had flown to God from their hearts, the vocations that had flowered behind the lovely stained-glass windows.

"It felt like my heart had been torn out of my body when I heard about it," Sister Dorothy said. "It's as though there was a big hole there, and I could feel it like an ache. It made me feel sick."

"How did you deal with such feelings?" I asked. "You speak of it calmly now, but I know that last summer you had tears in your eyes each time it was mentioned."

"It didn't happen quickly. I was very sad for at least three or four months, but I prayed a lot, and I began to think, 'Why be so down?' I began to see that I had no real reason to mourn. You can't deny grief when it is there, but you don't have to hang on to it. In the end everything in this world will be gone, and we will all be one with God. That old saying, 'You can't take it with you' is really true when you think about it."

This woman who has been called brain-damaged looked directly at me with her large, clear eyes as she continued.

"A lot of people think that life is supposed to be fair, and they get angry when things happen that hurt them. But life isn't fair; it doesn't work like that. Life is going to offer many hurts, and you just have to go on and not give up. Some people fare well and others fare poorly; I feel I've fared very well and have been given many blessings, and I thank God for them."

As I left the convent after our meeting, I wondered how many of us would agree that Sister Dorothy has "fared well" in her life. Early illnesses robbed her of a major share of her functions, both mental and physical. She learns slowly and with difficulty; simple acts like walking, buttoning a coat or tying a scarf take her five times longer than most of us, and she knows there are many things she will never understand.

Yet she chooses to focus on the things she has, not the things she lacks. Grasping the essentials of faith, she trusts utterly in the goodness of God, knowing that He watches over all of us with love. No matter how she fares in the eyes of the world, she knows she will always fare well in the hands of God.

SISTER CAROL ANN

Some are called to religious life with a summons so immediate and insistent it cannot be denied. God's invitation to Sister Carol Ann DePresca came gradually and quietly; for many years she did not understand what she was hearing.

She was the youngest of three children, born in 1944 to Michael and Helen DePresca on a farm in Long Island, New York. Her parents had thought their family to be complete with a fourteen-year-old girl, June, and a nine-year-old boy, John. Carol Ann's birth was not unwelcome to her parents, but it was a surprise. In some ways the little girl often felt like an only child, as June and John were too old to play with her and her closest companions were the farm animals: dogs, rabbits and kittens from the barn. She paused often from her play to listen to the haunting calls of the whippoorwills. Farm life gave her a love of nature and a feeling of being free.

When she was six, her mother enrolled her in a school named Saint Francis de Sales, a choice that Carol Ann now regards as prophetic. Her older brother and sister had attended a different Catholic school, but Helen DePresca felt strongly that little Carol Ann belonged at Saint Francis.

"I never asked why my mother sent me to a different school from the one June and John had attended," she told me when I wondered about the reason for the change. "I wish I had asked her before she died, but I didn't think anything of it then. I do know that my mother was very attracted to the church that was just across the street from the school because it was warm and homey, but that was nothing new. She had also loved it when she sent the older kids to a different school. Yet, for some reason, she believed I belonged there and look where I am now: in a monastery founded by Francis de Sales."

The most significant event in her early school years occurred on the day of her First Holy Communion. Like almost all little girls, she was thrilled with her pretty white dress and veil, the gifts and excitement surrounding the party-like atmosphere. But on that day the Blessed Mother seemed to enter her life and has continued to be a major influence on her.

"You would think it would be Jesus I was drawn to on such an occasion," she said. "After all, it was He I knew I was receiving, but it was His mother who occupied my attention. I clearly remember that the first thing I wanted my mother to do was to take a picture of me with the beautiful statue of Mary that stood in front of the church. Her face had for me a haunting, contemplative gaze, and I was drawn to it."

It was the custom then for devout Catholics to pray a rosary on Fridays, so every Friday when Mrs. DePresca came to drive her daughter home from school she stopped in at the church to pray. Carol Ann would hurry to cross the street to join her there as soon as classes were dismissed. Her goal was to visit that special statue and feel the peace and happiness that surrounded her when she was there.

Elementary school days passed happily until Carol Ann was in the fifth grade and her family decided to sell the farm. They moved to the suburbs, more than twenty miles from their former home. That was considered quite a distance in those pre-freeway days, and she had to change schools, enrolling at Saint Aloysius. It was a bad experience for the young girl.

"This is not easy to say," she admitted to me, "but the nuns there were… not nice women. There's just no other way for me to put it. After being with the loving sisters who had been my first teachers, I was frightened and miserable. The sisters at my new school weren't nasty to me because I was too timid to defy them, but I observed how harsh and mean they were to my more outspoken classmates.

"The worst thing for me was that through them I developed a fear of God, where I had previously had only love and trust. They taught me that God was a big judge in the sky, watching my every move so He could trip me up and send me to hell. I couldn't understand it. I read the religion books that told of God's love for all people, and I remembered the good God my former teachers had talked about with such confidence.

"My classmates and I didn't discuss it at the time, but years later, I learned that they had been crippled spiritually in the same way as I. As adults we recognized the harm those nuns had done us; they violated our innocence and trust, and that is a terrible thing to do to children."

More than fifty years later, Sister Carol Ann still looks sad while speaking of Saint Aloysius. She remembers how she missed visiting the beloved statue of Mary that had represented the peace of her old life.

It was a great relief to her and her fellow students when they graduated from Saint Aloysius and entered Saint Mary's

High School, run by the Sisters of the Immaculate Heart of Mary. These teachers were very strict with the girls, but were not mean. Their God might be a dictator and a rule-maker, but was not vengeful and angry, waiting to catch you in a mistake so you could be punished. Under the less negative guidance of these sisters Carol Ann lost some of her fear, but did not really begin to regain her early confidence until her senior year of high school when her class made a religious retreat at The Cenacle.

The Cenacle Sisters are a group of nuns who manage retreat centers for women throughout the country. Their mission is to provide opportunities for quiet reflection and prayer, offering respite from the daily cares of the world. Listening to their encouraging talks on the goodness of God, Carol Ann felt some of the spiritual peace of her childhood restored. It was a reassuring experience, and she knew she would return to The Cenacle.

High school had been a maturing and emancipating experience for her, and Carol Ann felt herself growing up during those four years as she discovered the world beyond home and family. She had many friends of both sexes and enjoyed participating in school activities as well as the parties and dances with their promise of romantic possibilities. Earning her own money by babysitting brought her a good feeling of independence, and she looked forward to graduation and a "real" job.

Despite her few unhappy years at Saint Aloysius, Carol Ann feels that her Catholic education was invaluable. It taught her that her religion had significant meaning to her and sowed the seeds of what she now realizes was always the deepest desire of her heart—to know God. She considers her Catholic education to be the most important gift her parents gave her.

After finishing high school she found work in a brokerage office and immediately began taking night-school classes to enhance her skills. She found the brokerage business was complex and fascinating and quickly recognized that education was the tool to professional advancement. The office personnel were both friendly and competent, and this new milieu was satisfactory to her in nearly every way.

But once settled into her new job, she realized that the desire to return to The Cenacle had not left her. She went back for a weekend retreat and connected almost instantly with one of the nuns, Sister Margaret Garvey. The two women established a warm relationship.

"There was something about her, some special quality that I couldn't put a name to, but in a way she personified for me what I thought a nun should be. I would just look at her and think, 'there's something extraordinary about her—I don't know what it is, but I know I want to see more of her.'"

She went frequently to visit Sister Margaret, though to her surprise and dismay, her parents did not approve of this involvement with the retreat center. She wondered why such devout Catholics would be opposed to her desire to associate with the sisters. They could only answer that there was something odd about her going there so often, and they urged her to focus on other interests. Not knowing how to handle controversy, Carol Ann did not argue, but she continued her visits without telling them.

She and Sister Margaret talked of spiritual matters, but also laughed a lot and chatted about ordinary things. Carol Ann would ask silly questions about how nuns went to sleep with those big veils on; about what it was like to wear a habit and live in community. She was curious, and the older woman answered her questions with good humor.

"I wondered about those things, too, when I was a girl," I said to Sister Carol Ann. "I think we all did. There was something so *hidden* about the sisters who taught us in school. They always looked so calm and clean with never a wrinkle in their clothes. We couldn't imagine one of them dashing out of her room in just her slip like our mothers did when they were in a hurry. My friends and I liked walking past the back yard of the convent on Saturdays when we knew the sisters would be doing their laundry and hanging their clothes outside. We kept hoping for a glimpse of underwear or nightgowns, but those clever nuns always hung the sheets on the outside lines, and no one got a hint of what was behind them."

Sister Carol Ann smiled. "That was the kind of nonsense Sister Margaret could talk with me about. But we also talked more seriously about religious life, and I especially remember a particular time when I went to visit her. She greeted me at the entrance where a strange feeling of comfort came over me. As she closed the door behind me, I remember thinking that I wouldn't care if I never left again."

Carol Ann began to realize she was getting quite interested in religious life and thought perhaps she should really pursue the idea, maybe even consider entering the convent. She was profoundly affected by her relationship with Sister Margaret, describing her as "one of those people who seem so perfect that you just kind of sit and marvel at them."

Then one day she went for her scheduled visit and was greeted by a sister she didn't know. She was told that Sister Margaret wasn't there. She was surprised, explaining that her visit was scheduled, but was told, "You don't understand. She isn't *here* anymore."

Carol Ann was so dumbstruck she couldn't say anything. She felt like the ground was falling out from under her. The nun at the door took pity on her confusion, invited her to come in and sit down and said she would send one of the administrator sisters to her. When that sister joined her, she told Carol Ann that Margaret Garvey had left the convent and would not be back. When asked where she had gone, the sister said only that

Sister Margaret had left to live in the world.

Carol Ann remained with the administrator for an hour or more, trying to sort out her feelings. When asked why she had been seeing Sister Margaret, she replied that she had been seeking spiritual advice and direction. Possibly a vocation.

This was in the early 1960s and she was unaware of what was going on in many religious houses. As the reforms from Vatican II swept over the Catholic world, priests and sisters were reevaluating their vocations and deciding, sometimes hastily, that they wanted to be part of the new laity. Some felt that a consecrated life would prevent them from participating in the great upheaval brewing in the Church; they wanted to be part of the wave of the forward movement. The monasteries that had seemed so nurturing to spiritual life now felt like confining fortresses from which they could only watch the parade going on in the streets below. They wanted to join the march, and many did.

The sister said she would assign another nun to guide her in her spiritual search, but Carol Ann hardly heard her. She was hurt that Margaret had left without a word of farewell to her, and that this sister was providing no explanation for what had happened.

She said, "I was terribly confused, to think that she had left no message for me. When I started to see my new advisor, Sister Rita, I held her at bay for a long time. I'm sure I feared emotionally and psychologically that the same thing could happen to me again.

"But I continued to see her, and in time I loosened up a bit and relaxed my fears. She was a beautiful woman; her personality was even lovelier than her looks, and I began to believe that maybe I could trust the vocational call that still seemed to be whispering inside of me.

"So I persisted until I had to leave the area for a month. It's funny: I don't remember now what the occasion was—something to do with work, or a scheduled vacation—I only know I was away for some weeks. When I returned, I went to see Sister Rita right away. I didn't have an appointment, but thought that since I was in the area I'd just drop in to say hello. If she were busy, we could choose another time to get together.

"At the door when I said I had come to see Rita, I was told that she had left. It didn't dawn on me that they literally meant *left*; talk about being slow to get it! I was ushered into the parlor where I was informed that there was a letter for me. I must admit it was a beautiful letter. In it Rita said that she had left religious life, but hoped that I would continue to pursue it. She urged me to talk to the Mother Superior.

"I was so disheartened that I took the letter and just went away. I remember going out to the car and reading it over and over. And I thought, 'never again.' I drove away from The Cenacle, vowing that I would not return, ever."

These episodes were devastating to Carol Ann, but she convinced herself that she had been mistaken in believing she had a calling. She made excuses to herself, thinking that had it been a *real* vocation she wouldn't have let a couple of disappointments stop her. God would have interceded and called her back to The Cenacle, but that did not happen.

Taking stock of her situation, she realized that she was not quite twenty years old, had a good job and friends in New York City—an exciting place to work. She would continue her night classes, focus on her career and personal life and forget this vocation illusion. Her resolve worked for her, and she advanced steadily within her firm, achieving higher positions with supervisory powers and working with high-level corporate executives.

She felt fortunate to be working with large groups of people, not only from New York but from other parts of the country as well. Her outlook on life broadened and she became more knowledgeable, flexible and, most of all, accepting of others.

Those years were worthwhile and rewarding, and she would not trade them for anything.

Her decision to avoid The Cenacle lasted a long time, but she was still a devout person whose prayer life was important to her. Being disillusioned about religious life did not mean that she did not wish to continue growing spiritually. She began thinking about how much she had loved The Cenacle, apart from any desire to enter it permanently, and, in her late twenties, assembled the courage to go back and attend another retreat.

This time Carol Ann was emphatic in stating that she did not wish to have *any* one-on-one sessions with a sister, an opportunity that is offered to every participant. She listened to the lectures, participated in the prayer services and enjoyed having the time to quietly reflect and contemplate. It was a good experience, and she decided to make a yearly retreat, or at least attend special days of prayer there, from then on.

Manhattan was a great place, full of opportunities. Her work paid well and she loved the professionalism of her office. She was respected and, in turn, respected those with whom she worked. She had many friends, especially an older woman with whom she developed a close relationship. This woman treated Carol Ann with the affection of a mother toward a grown-up daughter, and they dined in fine restaurants and shopped together in the beautiful New York stores.

Romantic love presented itself to her; there were two young men to whom she was especially attracted, but neither offered a marriage proposal. They didn't ask her, and she was too shy to give a hint of her feelings to either of them. Then, in her thirties, she went through a period of feeling she neither wanted nor needed to be married. This view was strengthened by her noting that several friends and family members had less-than-perfect marriages. Seeing their unhappiness, she assured herself she was better off single.

After she lost interest in being married, she did receive some proposals, two especially serious ones. She feels she was mistaken in continuing to see these men long after she should have realized that it was their persistence, not her fulfillment, that caused her to continue. In doing so, she was not being true to herself and was, consequently, learning there is no real happiness in doing something in which one doesn't believe. Since then, she feels she has been much more attentive to the quality of any relationship.

A dozen or more years passed this way and, in her late thirties, she cautiously made friends with a Sister Alice at The Cenacle. Alice was newly arrived there and was outgoing and effervescent. Carol Ann told her what had happened to her with Sisters Margaret and Rita, and received assurance that Alice wasn't going anywhere. She had just returned from a posting in New Zealand, which she hadn't liked at all, and said she wasn't leaving the Cenacle again until the Lord called her home to heaven.

Sister Alice became Carol Ann's spiritual advisor, with the understanding that it was not a religious vocation they were exploring. She was true to her promise not to leave. She remains there today, and the two women correspond and are good friends.

By the time Carol Ann was in her early fifties, her sister and both of her parents had died. June went first, after a short, brutal episode of pancreatic cancer. Her death was very hard on their parents, Michael and Helen, both of whom were ill and frail themselves by then with heart disease, and the doctors advised against their attending June's funeral. Michael died just four months after June, and Carol Ann quit her job to care for her ailing mother.

Helen lasted several more years, but suffered a series of devastating strokes and heart attacks. Eventually she had to be placed in a total-care facility, and although she no longer recognized her daughter, Carol Ann visited her every day to ensure she was receiving proper care.

"It made me almost physically sick to see her like that, but in spite of the pain I learned the valuable lesson of compassion. Many of the residents of her nursing home had families who hardly ever came to see them, and I felt very sorry for them. I hurt for them as well as for my mother. Because my relationship with her had been somewhat distant, especially after she had so strongly voiced her opinion about my spiritual quest, I finally recognized how God intervenes as the Ultimate Healer. My heart went out to her beyond belief. I realized I had never really understood my mother clearly. I could forgive all and recognize she had done the best she could, according to her beliefs."

Sister Carol Ann paused in her narrative, her eyes misting at the memory of her losses. She said her forties and early fifties comprised the worst, hardest time of her life. She and her brother, John, supported each other as well as they could, but they were both aching with grief.

"One morning, not long after my mother's death, I began to wonder what I was going to do with the rest of my life. It's curious, but even with all my praying and introspection, especially with my earlier consideration of religious life, I had never asked myself that important question. What was it God wanted me to do? What was the purpose of my life?"

She looked directly at me, saying, "Doesn't it strike you as unusual that I had never overtly asked myself the most important question of one's life?"

I could only reply, "I don't know that it is unusual; we are each unique and God speaks to us at unexpected times in unexpected ways."

Sister Carol Ann said that as she was pondering this weighty question, she went out to get her mail and there in the box was a brochure from The Cenacle. She had received their brochures for many years, advertising retreats and days of prayer, but this one contained an invitation she had never seen before. It said, "Come and see." She read further, "For those who might think they wish to look into religious life." She felt an immediate click, as if her brain had just turned on. She had just, for the first time in her life, asked God what her purpose was, and this invitation arrived.

She phoned Sister Alice and asked what she thought it meant. Why had she never seen this invitation before? Sister said that perhaps she wasn't meant to see it until now; that the Holy Spirit often speaks to us when we least expect it. Carol Ann signed up for the program, which was a few weeks away.

She had never thought about a community other than The Cenacle during the time she had considered a vocation. But this conference presented views of many different orders, and the women were told they should learn about them while they were exploring the idea of religious life.

Carol Ann thought first of the Carmelites as they had always had a kind of mystical aura for her, but she learned they had an age limitation and she was too old for them to consider her.

The work carried out by The Little Sisters of the Poor was also attractive to her. From an early age she had felt drawn to elderly people and wondered if helping to care for them were her purpose, but on visiting, she found the sisters to be less contemplative than she wanted. She felt their lives were so busy fulfilling their mission they had not enough time for prayer.

Sister Alice thought Carol Ann should look into a Dominican contemplative order that had a monastery in the South Bronx, but she wasn't interested. She didn't generally like nuns' habits and was concerned about the neighborhood. The South Bronx had a reputation as a tough place. When she said she was worried that she'd need a knife and gun if she were she to live there, Sister Alice laughed and insisted they should visit anyway. They made an appointment and went together to the beautiful Dominican Monastery.

Carol Ann felt her resistance melt almost immediately. The sisters were very gracious and looked lovely in their white habits. Why had she thought them so unattractive and been worried that they lived in a dangerous place? After an afternoon with them, she decided to give them a trial. She would spend six weeks with them, immersing herself in their lives and seeing if theirs was the order she should join. Surely, God would give her guidance, now that she had finally asked to have her purpose in life revealed.

"I spent an enjoyable six weeks with the Dominicans," Sister Carol Ann said. "I began to feel as though maybe I belonged there and so did they. After two weeks they asked me to take psychological tests; it was a requirement of the diocese. After Vatican II, when so many left their religious orders, some dioceses became quite careful in discerning those who were not stable enough to keep a serious commitment.

"My tests must have shown that I was okay—the sisters were happy with the results—but I kept thinking to myself that it was weird. Something didn't feel quite right after that; I can't put my finger on it. They expected me to stay and enter their order, but I knew I needed more time to think it over. I was not at peace with the thought of belonging to their community, even though I was very fond of the sisters, and I stay in touch with them to this day. They understood and did not pressure me; we knew if it were right for me, I would eventually come in. If not, then the Dominican life was not God's will for me."

After telling Sister Alice that she was still searching for the right place, Carol Ann was encouraged by a friend to look into a Visitation Community in Brooklyn. She wasn't very interested, as she had never heard of them, but decided she had nothing to lose by visiting. The day she drove to their convent, she passed a bay whose beauty caught her attention in an unusual way. The water was sparkling in the sunlight; the sun seemed to dance on the waves in a manner she had never seen before. It almost took her breath away. It was at that moment of delight in the water's beauty that she recalled the name of the first school she had attended as a child: Saint Francis de Sales. Though not staffed by Visitation sisters, she knew he had been the founder of their order. The dancing sunlight, combined with that sudden recollection, felt like a sign to her, and she approached the monastery with a light heart and an awakened interest.

The Visitation Sisters there gave her a booklet containing many sayings of Saint Francis, and she realized she had been reading them all her life on holy cards, but had not known they were his words. His advice to be gentle with yourself, to cease worrying about the morrow, to be who you are and accept yourself as you are, seemed especially appropriate to her at this stage of her life. She felt she was being called to the Visitation Order by Saint Francis himself. His words spoke to her inner core, her very nature.

The sisters in Brooklyn were gracious, serving as a significant introduction to the teachings of Saint Francis de Sales. She wanted to visit more than one of their monasteries to see how they differed in following Salesian life.

Her next step was to attend a Salesian Conference at Georgetown Visitation, where she found the sisters to be very warm, but extremely academic. Carol Ann knew that she had neither preparation for, nor interest in, teaching in any capacity. To her, it seemed as though the Georgetown Sisters lived in and for their school, and she felt she would not fit in well there.

Sister Alice was worried that Carol Ann would keep on seeking, never finding, and would finally abandon the search. She was sometimes tempted to do just that, as she had enjoyed a full life in New York that she could easily resume. But she felt sure she had received a genuine call from Saint Francis de Sales, a call that could not be ignored. She just needed to make certain that the community she chose would be the right one for her.

Upon visiting Saint Paul/Mendota Heights, she found the community to be welcoming and friendly. Although they, like Georgetown, had a school, not all of the sisters were directly involved in its operation. Carol Ann believed that there she could grow spiritually in religious life without having to work in a school. Although still not completely sure, she eventually decided that maybe it didn't matter so much where one goes; it's that one's conviction must be strong enough to believe in God's will and follow where He leads. She discerned that God had led her to Mendota Heights. The year was 2001, she was fifty-seven years old, and it was time to put her trust in His call.

She said, "I would be remiss not to mention my brother's reaction during this period of time. When I confided to him my desire for a religious life, he told me it was the best news he had heard in years. I always knew John to be deeply but quietly spiritual. I also believe that, if he hadn't married at twenty-one, he would have become a priest or a brother."

Carol Ann was received as a postulant in the Visitation Monastery in Mendota Heights. She began to study basic theology and, for the first two years, attended classes at the Jesuit Novitiate House with aspirants from different orders. Specific Salesian Spirituality was taught back at the monastery in Mendota Heights. After two years, she made her first profession and was no longer considered a novice, but a "First Professed."

Her doubts continued to surface from time to time, and, four years after entering, she asked to visit a First Federation Monastery to see if a more completely cloistered community was what she needed to lay those doubts to rest. A week there convinced her that she would have trouble adapting to the old rituals they still practiced. The sisters seemed to be very normal, happy women, and she concluded that the lifestyle must work for them, but could see it wasn't right for her.

She returned, resuming the familiar cycle of prayer and continuing her duties. These included going out to shop for the monastery's food, a task some dislike but she enjoyed. She was also the assistant sacristan, performing the detailed tasks of caring for the altar linens and sacred vessels. Her most fulfilling work was in managing the Retreat Center and attending to the needs of the retreatants.

"I feel richly rewarded in this work," she said. "I believe in the importance of maintaining the integrity of a place of retreat by adhering to a monastic atmosphere of quiet. Our property is extensive and lovely, and the attendees often take long, contemplative walks. They also are welcome to join the sisters for the Liturgy of the Hours and our Eucharistic celebrations. I receive positive feedback from them, as they say they are refreshed and renewed. They tell me that being here, experiencing silence in the presence of God, is just what they need."

Because she has taken her first, or temporary, vows, Carol Ann bears the title of Sister, but still has not professed final vows. Recently, she asked for, and was given, a year's extension to deliberate further.

"Six years may seem like a long time to decide," she smiled. "But if you take it in the context of my whole life span, it's really not so very long. Discernment is a broad picture. It is much, much more than knowing where you want to be or should be. I used to be of the opinion that I was seeking God, but the reverse is true. God has been seeking me. That is true of all religious.

"You might say I'm at a standstill, or stuck, if you will. I remain uncertain of where I'm called to live out my religious life. You might say I believe I'm following my spiritual calling, but I'm not sure I'm at the right address."

I asked, "Are you saying you are sure of your vocation to the Salesian life, but you still may want to live in another community to once more test it against this one?"

"Yes, perhaps I feel it would be irresponsible of me to do less. I think if I were on my deathbed and God asked me if I couldn't at least have tried and given it my all, I'd know I wouldn't have kept my promise to Him. What would that say about my purpose in life? My father used to tell me that I wouldn't respect others if I didn't respect myself. You can only be true to another if you are true to yourself. I think that what I am doing will bring me peace. And even if I were to leave religious life, I would know that I had explored every possibility. Even if I do not stay in religious life, I will always value it because I have learned to go deeply into myself, and that is a valuable thing.

"Perhaps the reason I remain unsure is due to some of my experiences here. I know that a vocation comes from God, not a community. But you are placed in a community that you expect will care for your vocation and encourage its growth. Within five years of my time here, three sisters have left: one during her novitiate years, one before final profession and still another after many years as a fully professed sister.

"I'm still a new religious and find it only natural to assess the impact this has had on me. Each parting has been difficult and left me with many questions. While I did not specifically enter for any of these women, I enjoyed a good relationship with each one. I do have many misgivings, concerns and doubts about community life. I know that faith doesn't necessarily eliminate doubts.

"A priest I consulted told me that the call to follow God doesn't mean we can predict or legislate, but to be ready to go where we are led. And I have learned that God does not violate who we are, but actually works with and through us as we are, not as we think we should be. That is why I think it is so important for me to monitor my feelings and not neglect what goes on inside. I feel strongly that collaboration and collegiality are very important; perhaps they are practiced more diligently in other communities than here. Maybe I should consider this in order to be better prepared and informed for a lifelong commitment to Visitation. I wish I didn't have to say these things, but that's how I feel. I have done the best I could but, looking back, I think I made the mistake of keeping my vocation in a beautiful little box and didn't want anything to interfere with it. I feel like I was wearing blinders, but now they are off."

Sister Carol Ann was quiet for a bit, reflecting on her words. Then she shrugged and gave a little smile. "But who knows? Things may turn around. Once I would have fallen down laughing if anyone had told me I would be a nun, and yet here I am. I've been thrown so many curves in my religious life, who's to say I won't remain here?"

When she entered religious life as a postulant, the Mother Superior posed the question according to the entrance formula, "What do you ask?"

She gave the proper response gladly, "For the gifts of perseverance and conversion."

Sister Carol Ann continues to pray for perseverance and conversion. To that end, she struggles on, bravely trying to discern her place in the kingdom of her belief.

SISTER MARIE THÉRÈSE

Sister Marie Thérèse Conaty was born in Richmond, Virginia, in 1929, into one of those fairy-tale families that our angry world often claims never really existed. "Too good to be true," we scoff. Her father, Walter Conaty, was known as a self-made man, a son of Irish immigrants. Not born into wealth, he acquired it through education and hard work. And, he would have added, with the help of his Catholic faith.

He started as a young lawyer taking cases for railroad companies, including the Chesapeake and Ohio. The executives there quickly noticed his bright mind and strong character, and soon had him working exclusively for them. He rose in importance in the company, becoming a highly paid executive himself. Being a serious young man, he was devoted to God and his work, more interested in going to Mass than to parties.

But in large businesses, some socializing was expected, and at a company event Walter met the pretty daughter of an older colleague and fell deeply in love. Mary Gilmore was a graduate of the Visitation School in Cardome, Kentucky. Her mother had died when Mary was very young, and her father had sent the little girl to the sisters "to become a lady." It seems he got his money's worth. According to Sister Marie Thérèse, her mother was gentle and gracious, a soft-spoken and cheerful woman—bright, curious and an accomplished musician. She was impressed by Walter's strong Catholic faith and his considerable bank account; she wanted a family and she wanted a husband who would be a good father and a willing provider.

The young couple married and settled happily into fertility and prosperity. Over the years they had eight children, although to their sorrow, one daughter died in infancy. The other seven children got along well together and filled their home with music and laughter. Edna Rose, nicknamed Eddie, the second-to-last child born to the Conatys, was one day to become Sister Marie Thérèse. She smiled now, as she described her family life to me.

"Elsa, you just can't imagine what a wonder my mother was. Dad was so serious and stiff, but we watched her gentle him; we could see before our eyes how she softened him and helped him relax. Poor Dad," she laughed, "he was so smart, but we kids did think he was a little boring. We loved him; he just wasn't very exciting. Mother was the light-hearted one; the fun revolved around her, and Dad kind of watched us. He didn't really take part, but you could feel him loving her and loving the way we interacted with her."

"You make it sound like every child's dream of a perfect home," I told her, "with seven happy children dancing around the piano and your dad looking benevolently on like Abraham over the tribes. You kids must have been good friends with each other."

"We had our differences, of course, and argued and wrangled sometimes as children will. But I honestly think our mother helped us keep it to a minimum. She influenced us so strongly, and we could just constantly see that there were better ways to behave than being horrid to each other. There was a lot of affection among us.

"You see, Mother calmed us, just as she calmed Dad. She taught us, not with words, but by modeling, how to be gentle with ourselves and others. It was her greatest gift to us, and our father's greatest gift to us was his regard for Mother."

"Did you pray together?" I asked, thinking that a family whose faith seemed so important might have been into many devotional practices.

Sister Marie Thérèse said that they did to some extent, but they lived their faith more than praying about it a lot. They went to Mass every Sunday and were loyal about confessions and the Stations of the Cross, but it was her father who was the biggest one for prayer. He went to Mass every morning before work, carrying a special little book in his pocket. His wife, the former Visitation student, had taught him to love Saint Francis de Sales, so he frequently used a booklet Saint Francis had written called *How to Assist at Mass.*

Sister said, "When I was seven, we moved to Huntington, Virginia, to a really big house that had a wide landing on the staircase with stained-glass windows. I think Dad loved the house because the landing looked like a chapel. He gave Mother a statue of the Blessed Virgin and placed it on the landing on a pedestal. My brothers made a *prie dieu*, a kneeler, for him, and he would stop to pray there every night while coming up the stairs.

"I can still hear Mother calling to him from the bedroom," she said, tilting her head back and imitating her mother's high voice, 'You can come to bed now, Saint Joseph. You've prayed enough for one night.'"

"It sounds like your background was blessed in every way. You not only had all the material things you wanted, but every spiritual and emotional need was tended to as well."

"You know, it's true that we did have wonderful times in our family. We wanted for nothing, of course, and had privileges that we could see the other kids in town didn't have. For instance, if our family wanted to travel by train from Huntington to Richmond, we rode in a private car. Every summer my sisters and I attended a beautiful camp at Fort Scott in Cincinnati, where we met girls from well-to-do families from that area. The other girls in our town didn't go there. We had railroad passes and could ride on the train for free anywhere we wanted to go. While we enjoyed our gorgeous home and beautiful clothes, I think we knew that our happiness didn't come from just being comfortable. There was so much love and laughter among all of us and then, of course, there was the music. Just imagine all that joy and then, on top of it, the beauty of Mother's music. The house was filled with the sounds of her piano and of the different instruments we kids were learning."

"You sound like the Trapp Family Singers," I teased. "Maybe you should have called yourselves The Conaty Conservatory."

"Maybe we would have, except for Dad. He couldn't carry a tune. You'd think with all their differences that my parents weren't well-suited to each other, but they were. They complemented each other in so many ways, and they each had the greatest esteem for the other's qualities. That carried over to the way they treated their children.

"Dad wasn't as emotionally warm with us as Mother; getting close and intimate wasn't easy for him. But he cherished the closeness we had with her and with each other. We could all see the special friendship that Mother enjoyed with my oldest sister, Mary. I think I learned to value friendships among women by observing Mother and Mary; maybe part of the reason I've been so happy as a nun is that I treasure my friendships within this community of women.

"When Mary got married, Dad bought the house next door so she and her husband could live there, and Mary and Mother could still see each other every day."

"Did her husband mind?" I asked, thinking how unusual that would be in today's world of fiercely independent young married people. "Most beginning couples I know want to distance themselves from their families; they're so eager to prove that they're totally self-sufficient."

"To tell you the truth I'm not sure anybody asked him," she laughed. "I suppose he must have agreed to it, but I don't remember any talk about it. He loved our mother too. I think everybody did."

One of the ways Mrs. Conaty entertained the family was by telling stories of her days in boarding school at Visitation. Eddie was especially fascinated—entranced, really. It seemed to her that it had to have been the most perfect place in the world to go to school and she begged to be sent there. Her brothers and sisters thought she was crazy. They all went to Saint Joe's, just two blocks from the house, and they had a great social life there. Eddie's sister Liz was a cheerleader, and the brothers played basketball, so they had loads of friends, both boys and girls, always at the house after school. But it was something Eddie couldn't give up on wanting to do, and when she was twelve they let her go.

"Did it meet your expectations?" I asked.

"It was everything I had pictured and more. I loved the sisters, and I made good friends with the boarders and the other students. And, you see, I had that pass for the railroad so I could go home whenever I felt the least bit homesick. I had a ready-made social life when I got home because of my brothers and sisters, so I had the best of both worlds."

"Did going to school at Visitation get you thinking about wanting to be a nun?"

"You know, it was never far from my mind. Even before I went there the idea must have been somewhere in my head or I may not have insisted so strongly on going. But my religious vocation was a gradually growing thing; it didn't ever hit me suddenly that I was being called to this life."

"Nothing dramatic like Saint Paul on the road to Damascus?" I asked.

"Oh my no—just a slowly dawning realization." She paused and then looked tenderly reflective. "But... there were significant moments, too. I remember a time when I was a junior, and we older girls were giving a picnic for the younger students. We were all outside enjoying it when suddenly the bell in the tower rang, and I remember looking up and thinking, oh my God, there really *is* a God! This stuff is for real—there's *meaning* here. It took my breath away; I almost had to sit down on the grass. Elsa, it was as if He had smiled at me from the sky and said, 'Hello, I'm here.' The sense that He had spoken was very real to me."

"Did you tell anyone about it?"

"No. Although I came close to telling my mother once. It was her custom to give each of us children a diamond ring when we reached our sixteenth birthday, which she fashioned from stickpins that her father had worn. He had been an executive with the Chesapeake and Ohio, too, and had beautiful clothes and jewelry. When she came to the convent at Cardome to visit me for my sixteenth birthday and give me my ring, I really wanted to tell her then, but I didn't."

"What kept you from telling her?" I asked.

"I think... I believe I knew it was news she would not want to hear."

"Did you think she wouldn't approve of your becoming a nun?"

"That might not be the best way to put it. It wouldn't exactly have been disapproval. Mother was a devout Catholic, and she certainly loved the nuns who had taught her at Visitation. She knew their lives were good. But the idea of having your own daughter leave home forever—well, I think that might have felt like a terrible loss to her. Mother loved all of us so much—I didn't want to propose anything that might make her sad until I had to."

"And so you let the moment pass?"

"I let the moment pass."

Two years later Eddie graduated from Cardome, and this time she resolved that the moment would not pass. At the reception, still wearing her white gown and holding her bouquet of roses, she told her mother that she wanted to be a nun and to stay at Visitation. Her mother quietly whispered to her, "We'll talk."

When she returned home, both her parents sat down with her. There was never any question of their not respecting her wishes; they did not try to talk her out of it or ask her how she could be sure. Instead, they told her she could follow her heart, but that she must do some more growing up. She must go to college first. They added, she could go to any college in the country, with one exception. Georgetown Visitation was out. Because living with the Visitation nuns had been her only experience, they felt she needed to test her attachment to them to be sure it was more than just emotional.

"I could see their advice was wise," Sister Marie Thérèse said. "I really believed my heart was in the convent and that I would be there some day, but I could see their point that eighteen was too young an age to make a permanent commitment to anything."

"Had you had any boyfriends up until then?" I asked, my layperson's curiosity showing. Most of us wonder about how romance has played out in the lives of nuns.

"Oh my yes," she answered, laughing. "I had dated many darling boys so I was no stranger to that excitement. But none of them had ever said, 'Hello, I'm here,' in quite as compelling a way as God did that day at the bell tower in Cardome. You know, I had the example of my mother's married life and also my sister Mary's, so I wasn't a bit opposed to marriage. I could see the attractions it held, but it didn't call to me the way the convent did."

"So what happened next?"

Sister started thinking about college choices; her parents had given her *carte blanche*, so her options were almost unlimited. Having been a bright student, she wasn't worried about being admitted to whichever institution she chose. In the end, she decided on Mount Saint Joseph in Cincinnati, for several reasons. They awarded her a scholarship and, while her family didn't need the money, it was a good feeling to receive such a welcoming affirmation. Also, one of her older sisters, Liz, was there, and that sounded cozy. The two young women were good friends so they knew they'd like sharing college life and would also enjoy going home together as often as they pleased, thanks to those ubiquitous railroad passes. Finally, Cincinnati was attractive because it was so familiar to her. All those summers at Fort Scott Camp made it feel like another home, and Eddie had many friends in the area.

"I've often wondered what shape my life might have taken if I had picked another school," Sister Marie Thérèse said thoughtfully now. "Nothing happens by accident, I know, but I had the possibility of so many other places! The whole country was open to me, and yet I was led to Cincinnati. There was a reason I needed to be there, not somewhere else."

I was curious. "You make it sound portentous," I said. "How did that particular city come to signify such importance in your life?"

"We can never predict what will happen to us," she said softly. "We think we have everything so programmed out; I was just swimming along with the plan I had made. I loved Mount Saint Joe's; I was majoring in music there and having a wonderful time. I had had an excellent violin teacher at Visitation, and the music teachers at Saint Joe's were thrilled with my preparation. I was just awash in music, having the time of my life playing everything I loved and dreaming of the day when I would graduate and then enter Visitation Convent. My religion classes kept deepening and increasing my faith; there just wasn't anything that could go wrong.

"And then, during my sophomore year I went with friends to obtain a Red Cross swimming instructor's license so I could be a summer counselor at Camp Fort Scott. I had spent so many happy summers there I thought it would be a good service to help young girls as I had been helped. I passed my tests and was accepted as a swimming instructor. My heart was filled with joy, and I hadn't a worry in the world as I packed my bags and headed to Fort Scott for a wonderful summer. And there I fell in love with the camp doctor."

"Not you!" I said. "Not the girl who had known without a doubt since she was sixteen that she was headed for the convent!"

"I'm afraid so," she smiled, shaking her head. "And the worst of it was, it was the same for him. The minute we saw each other we knew that we were meant to be together. Everyone hears of love at first sight, but we actually experienced it. It was a great gift and we have both always known it."

"What in the world did you do?" I asked.

"Well, one of the first things we learned about each other was that he was planning to enter the Jesuits as soon as he completed his medical training and I, of course, was going to become a sister. We had a great deal to talk about, as you may imagine. We realized very quickly that we were both service-oriented people. Robert—his name was Robert Bamberger—had never been interested in establishing a practice and becoming a rich doctor. He thought that by combining the priesthood with his medical degree he could become a medical missionary and serve the poor. We began to dream of going to Africa together, or South America or India—wherever we would be most needed."

"Did you begin to discuss marriage that soon, even though you both felt you had religious vocations?" I asked.

"There wasn't any way we couldn't; the love between us was so strong. We each felt that God had brought us to a certain point in our lives where we would be sure of our love for Him, and then He brought us together so we could express that love as a married couple. Our feelings were so deep, and the way before us so clear, we couldn't help but feel we were being guided by the Holy Spirit. Every word, every gesture between us was like a prayer.

"That summer of love was so gorgeous; I remember every moment of it clearly. I used to look into his eyes and think, 'How beautiful the eyes of God must be, when Bob's are so unbelievably lovely. How can even God's eyes surpass this beauty?' The weather was perfect that summer, and we took long walks together, holding hands and planning our future."

Eddie was to be a junior at Saint Joe's the next year and Bob would be in his senior year of medical school in Cincinnati. "Did you call each other Eddie and Bob?" I asked, wanting to form as clear a picture of the young couple as possible.

"I called him Bob, but he would have none of this 'Eddie' nonsense. I was his Edna Rose, and he refused to use my nickname. He said my name made him think of Saint Rose of Lima, and he compared me to her. I knew I was no saint, but that's just how romantic he was. He was a real idealist, one of those who just sees the best and most beautiful in everyone."

She had many opportunities to see Bob's particular form of idealism in action. When they returned to Cincinnati in the fall, he often took her with him on his hospital rounds and she was touched by the caring tenderness he extended to every patient. He was unfailingly gentle with each one, listening to their stories and calming their fears.

"I learned so much about him by watching him. I could see the way people were drawn to place their trust in him; even the very sickest smiled and spoke of hope when they were with him. He was a born healer."

Bob and Edna Rose saw as much of each other as possible during that year in Cincinnati. Their love for each other grew with each encounter, and their only question was when to marry and under what circumstances. They decided to become formally engaged at the end of the academic year, and Bob presented her with a ring on the day of his graduation from medical school. Both of their families were delighted; everyone felt that a happy destiny had brought them together.

At first they planned on marrying immediately, but Bob would be interning in Washington DC and Eddie still had a year of college to finish. She remained at Mount Saint Joe's while he started his hospital work in DC, but they were still able to see each other frequently. Those handy railroad passes were at her disposal, and her youngest sister, Kate, was by now a student at Georgetown. Eddie could stay with her when she came to town. Her sister Liz was working in Washington and dating a local district attorney, and one of her brothers was also there working in law. It seemed that half her family was in town to share the joy that she and Bob were feeling. It was an incredible year. Eddie could hop a train after her last class on Friday, spend the weekend in DC, board a Pullman on Sunday evening and tuck into bed. She would arrive in Cincinnati on Monday morning in time to go to her first class. When the school year ended in June, she was set to graduate at the same time Bob completed his internship, and then they would marry.

One of those idyllic weekends in DC, everything changed. Bob and Edna Rose started on one of their many long walks— their favorite type of date, as it left them free to pour out their hearts to each other. Bob began to tell her that he had been seeing a new confessor, and that many of his old feelings about the priesthood were surfacing. Edna Rose felt her heart go still; her brain retreated to a silent spot miles above. She could only listen, as she began to understand all too well what he was trying to say. He told her he had been troubled for several weeks, but that a few nights before an incident had occurred that gave focus to what he was feeling. He felt that the Holy Spirit was again speaking to him, this time more clearly than ever before. There had been a fire in a nearby Trappist Monastery and the medical interns had been called out to help.

"I saw the monks, Edna Rose," Bob told her solemnly. "I saw their house and the way they live, and it seemed that I was being called to join them. Not just called, but something stronger. It wasn't exactly a command, but it was more than an invitation. It was a call for each of us to return to the vocations we believed we were to follow before we met each other."

"So you see," Sister Marie Thérèse said to me, "we needed to start talking about religious vocations again. It was a very long walk. Both my heart and my brain needed to come to the reality of what Bob was saying. We thought we had this behind us, but we hadn't. We could see that we needed to deal with it again."

My eyes filled with tears as I listened to her. "Oh Sister," I barely breathed. "Weren't you just dying inside?"

"Not just inside; outside, too," she answered. "I would have followed him anywhere. Into Africa, or the worst slums of our country or any country. I loved him totally with a love I knew had been blessed by God. And I knew that he loved me in the same way. There was never a moment's doubt between us. Our devotion to each other was completely valid; it was a sacramental love."

"And so there was no sense of betrayal? Were you not hurt beyond belief by what he was telling you?"

"'Hurt' would never be the word to describe it. I understood that it was impossible for Bob to betray me. Elsa, I knew as clearly as I know that you and I are sitting here together, that all I would have had to do was remind him of his promise to marry me, and that would be the end of it. He was not asking to be released from that promise. He was just telling me what he believed the Holy Spirit had told him."

"And so you let him go."

"He was not mine to keep or to let go. He belonged to God, as did I, and we knew we needed to listen to this new message He was giving to us. We had both found God before we found each other, and He had given us this miraculous gift of love that we knew we would always have."

"Except that you would not have it as husband and wife. You could agree to live apart and be content to share it spiritually?" She heard the incredulity in my question.

"The contented part didn't happen immediately," she smiled. "He took me to my train that evening and I climbed into my familiar Pullman berth, but I didn't sleep on that trip, not even for a moment. I lay awake all night, staring out at the stars, hearing the iron wheels of the train carrying me far away from the world I had thought was mine. It was a long time before I slept well again. Although there would be more discussions, I knew that Bob and I would never marry, that it was not to be. God had given us a great gift, and now He was telling us we would have to live it in another light from the one we had pictured.

"After we were engaged," she said, "each time I visited home, I prayed before the statue of Mary that was on our staircase. Each time I knelt down I took off my engagement ring and placed it in her hand, asking for her help in living up to its meaning. Now I was being given her answer."

"Did you continue to see each other up until your graduation time?" I asked.

"Oh yes. We needed to be together to comfort each other and also to figure out how to handle this. Our friends and families had such happy expectations for us, and we didn't want to break the news suddenly to them. And the first thing for Bob was to talk to the Trappists. Before he and I fell in love, he had planned to enter the Jesuits, but now that had changed.

"He said to me, 'If we're going to do this, it has to be all the way for me. I cannot live in the world without you, so I will have to go into cloistered life.'

"Poor Bob," she sighed. "He suffered so. I didn't realize it at the time, but he suffered more than I did."

"How do you mean?" I asked. "He was the one who changed everything. If he hadn't experienced that intense new calling, you would have been getting married."

"Yes, but once I had accepted it, and I really did accept it as the voice of God, I was able to return to my original intention of entering Visitation. I was more innocent in some ways than Bob." She laughed. "Or maybe just more ignorant—kind of dumb. He was smarter than I was, deeper. I think he saw more clearly than I just how much we were giving up. Maybe it was a kind of protection for me to have not realized it all at once, the way he did."

"And yet when you did finally realize the entirety, there were no regrets?"

"You may find this hard to understand, but there were not. You see, by the time I came to fully understand, I had been in the convent for many years. I have been a happy nun. I didn't pine for him—didn't wish that we were married and feel sorry for myself. Most days I was like Maria, singing the sound of music and running over the hills under the sun. Except I didn't have to leave and marry Captain von Trapp to keep on singing. My love for Bob stayed firmly in my heart, and I knew that I lived in his."

"So how did you finally tell your parents?"

"That was hard. My mother was especially disappointed, and I knew that Bob's parents were, too. Imagine: they had this gifted son who had the whole world before him. It wasn't just my girlish love that made me think he was something special. He was brilliant, a leader in every way and yet completely human. He had been quarterback on his high school football team, a top student, handsome but not conceited. He was devout and yet he had a rich sense of humor. To be around him was to be constantly entertained, charmed and enlightened at the same time. His parents' background was humble; his dad was a grocer, and they had an old rattletrap of a car and a very modest home. And now, here was this magnificent son, a scholar and a doctor to boot. And he was going to become a monk and retire from the world. It didn't take a lot of imagination to understand how they must have felt!"

"How did you wind up managing it?" I asked.

"Bob finished medical school in June and immediately entered Gethsemane, the Trappist monastery in Kentucky. I graduated from Mount Saint Joe's, but he did not attend as we had already said our final goodbye. You don't want to do that any more times than you have to."

"Was it terribly hard?"

"It was hard, and yet there was a certain peace to it because we both believed so firmly that we were doing the right thing. We knew we would always be together in spirit and that God was leading us where we needed to go."

"Did you go directly to Visitation then?"

"No, my parents thought it would be well if I took a trip to Europe first, and it seemed like a good idea. I had come to terms with our decision, but I had the summer before me as I wasn't to enter Cardome until the fall. My sister Kate had just graduated from Georgetown Visitation—it was a two-year college at that time—and it was kind of her graduation gift too. Dad didn't want us girls to go alone, so my brother Tom agreed to take us, but once again, our plans were changed in a way we could not have foreseen. Kate became very ill and couldn't go, so just Liz and I went with Tom and his fiancée. As it turned out, Kate had Hodgkin's disease, so it was very serious indeed.

"I came home from Europe and entered Visitation in Cardome, Kentucky, on September 8, 1950, the feast of the birth of Our Lady. Shortly before I went in, I was a bridesmaid in the wedding of the couple who had been Bob's and my closest friends. The fact that I could do that with a peaceful heart told me I was ready to become a nun. I gave my engagement ring to my father and asked him not to tell me what he did with it. I didn't want to know."

"So you and Bob were both in Kentucky, living your separate but similar lives. Could you communicate with each other at all?"

"Oh my no, not in those days. Everything was very strict then; this was pre–Vatican II, remember. But I learned years later how well Bob had done in the monastery.

"At Gethsemane they recognized his unusual gifts, as did nearly everyone, and he was assigned to study under Thomas Merton. Merton was actually his novice master. In fact, later when Merton died in Thailand, it was Bob who identified the body. They were very close; Bob understood Merton's struggles and the validity of his quest more then anyone, I think."

Once again, I became aware of the remarkable spiritual leaders whose lives have brushed against this small convent of sisters in Saint Paul. Earlier I had learned that Mother Teresa lived with them each time she came to Minnesota, had sat with them in the very parlor where I was sitting now, and spent evenings talking and praying with them. I felt the reality of the links that connect those who are entirely dedicated to God. They share a spiritual attraction that draws them together.

Now Sister Marie Thérèse was telling me that as soon as Bob was professed, the Trappists sent him off to learn to be a psychiatrist. It became his job to screen the young men seeking entrance to the monastery. "People choose monastic life for a lot of reasons, you know, not all of them healthy. Bob had that combination of holiness and psychological expertise to weed out the unstable men from the inspired." She smiled. "There are religious nuts everywhere, you know. Monasteries and convents don't have immunity to them, and not everyone who thinks he's been called to the life has a genuine vocation."

"How do you define a religious nut?" I asked.

"Well, if an aspirant to the convent entertains a picture of herself constantly flopping around the tabernacle having ecstasies, that would qualify," she said, laughing. "Religious life is hard work, and prayer doesn't automatically flow from your heart just because you have a vocation. A relationship with God is something we all have to work at constantly; it has to be tended like a garden. The life can be romanticized; you, of course, know that yourself from being married so long. How many marriages aren't based on a real calling or commitment to the life, but on infatuation or sexual desire or even a need for security? It's the same with religious—we really have to examine our motives and reach an understanding of why we're here."

I thought about this for a bit and said, "You seem to have done all the requisite self-examining. You and Bob really did it together when you decided to part from each other."

"That's true," she said thoughtfully. "I was a willing novice. It felt right and good to be in the convent, and I was happy most of the time in spite of the many losses I experienced during the first few years."

"Losses besides Bob?"

"Yes. My sister Kate, as I told you, was very ill, and she died a few months after I entered. It was my dad, not Mother, who came to tell me how bad it was getting. Dear Dad, not an emotionally demonstrative man, but he was crushed by this, and he felt he had to spare Mother from being the one to break the news. He said to me, 'You're going to have a baby sister in heaven, very soon, I fear.' And he was right. She died not long after that. Leaving Bob was a kind of dying, and now I had lost my little sister."

Kate's death was not the last one for the family that had once been so happy, solid and secure. Less than two years later, Mary, the oldest girl, developed breast cancer and died, leaving her husband and four young children. She was just thirty-eight. Mrs. Conaty, devastated by the death of another daughter, did her best to bear up, but suffered a massive stroke just four months after burying Mary. Within days, she too was gone. With the joy of his life taken from him, Mr. Conaty began to fail. He tried to hold together but the heart was gone from him, and he was never really himself again.

"My brothers looked after him and took good care of him, but he couldn't recover his spirits. He lived eight years after Mother died, but they were sad years, for him and for all of us. And here I was in the convent, wondering what I was to make of all these losses. It was clear that we each enter this life alone and leave alone; we sustain each other as best we can on the way, but each of us has to work out how to live with ourselves and figure out our relationship with God."

Sister Marie Thérèse confessed that she had missed Bob terribly during that period. She wanted him to share her grief and help her understand the mysteries of death and loss. But these were the 1950s, pre–Vatican II, and cloister rules were strictly followed. Contact between them was unthinkable.

"Did you have regrets then about not having married?" I asked.

"Not about the marriage, no. I truly had accepted that both Bob and I were to honor our religious vocations. But I wanted to be with him in person, not just in spirit. I wanted to talk to him, and I needed to hear his words of comfort. With prayer you can accomplish anything, you know, and I eventually found peace of mind. But I think it would have been easier and better all around if I could have seen him then. As it was, I didn't get to see him for many years."

I was astonished. Somehow, as this story unfolded, I had pictured them parting during the summer of 1950 and never seeing each other again. "You mean you've seen him, actually talked to him? How did that happen? When did you get in touch?"

My questions spilled out. "Of course," she smiled. "In fact, I saw him just this summer. I made my annual retreat at Genesee—saw him every day for two weeks."

I sat back in my chair, letting her words register. "Let's back up a bit," I requested. "Tell me when you reconnected and how that came about."

I learned that after Vatican II, sometime in the 1960s or early '70s—she couldn't remember exactly when—Bob had come to Saint Paul to attend a conference. He was no longer in Gethsemane in Kentucky, having been sent to the monastery of Genesee in New York. By then he had been ordained and was a priest as well as a monk. He had been elected Abbott in Genesee, eventually serving as the Superior General of his entire order. He called her convent from Saint Paul and received permission to come and see her and say Mass for the nuns.

"What was it like, seeing him after all those years?"

"It was as though no time had passed," she answered instantly. "It was like a repetition of our first meeting; it was so obvious that we were both still deeply in love. We knew that anyway, but it was wonderful to be together and be able to say it again."

After that meeting they started a correspondence that has remained steady over the years. They have seen each other many times, always for reasons having to do with spiritual growth. This summer's retreat was the second she has made at his monastery.

Sister Marie Thérèse considers Bob's decision to contact her one of the greatest gifts of her religious life. He became the bellwether against which she weighed many of her decisions, especially as the fallout from Vatican II began to inspire more changes in the way the sisters lived. She would ask herself what Bob would think of each proposal. Would he see it as sensible?

"Many of the changes were hard to accept. They resulted in more freedom, including the wonderful freedom of being able to write to Bob, but they disrupted the orderliness of our lives and we lost much graciousness and beauty, many of the things that held us together. I sometimes wish we still had them."

"Like what?" I asked.

"Oh, there are so many," she answered. "Where to start? We used to have an antechoir, for one thing. When the bell rang for prayer, we would assemble in the antechoir and ask for grace to perform the Office and to praise God, and then we processed in with ceremony. Now the bell rings and we fly in from all over, arriving raggedly, rustling pages to find the place. We want to make the same intent, but it's very different from doing it in a uniform way. The dining room is another example. We talk now at every meal—we talked once a year in the old days. We had a lector who read to us, and each meal was a time to listen to God, not talk to each other. Saint Francis taught us to take every hour and live it fully, offer it and accept whatever comes in that hour. It is living in the moment, as we are meant to do, and that was easier under the old structure. There was a time when I knew what I would be doing in twenty-five years on any given day, and that is a very solid life, very secure."

She has no doubt that Bob's letters helped her remain stable inwardly as the outward structure of her life altered. He helped her see that it is the bedrock of our love for God that matters, not the way it is expressed. One letter was particularly affirming to her in that it helped her with her sense of self-confidence. She believes that her most pervasive personal sin is her feeling of inadequacy.

"How is that a sin?" I asked. "Many people lack self-confidence in some area, but I've never thought of it as a sin."

"By sin, I mean a lack of trust in the Holy Spirit. If we really believe that He guides us in whatever we do, then we have no need to keep doubting ourselves. We are who we are meant to be. All my life I've looked for the approval of others to assure me that I'm doing a good job. If I give a speech I have to hurry to someone who I know was in the audience to ask if I made sense, if I did okay.

"What this letter did was to assure me that I am adequate. In it he told me that he knew I would have been a wonderful wife and mother, and that we must look at all we've both accomplished by following the call of our vocations instead. And you know it's true." She smiled at me. "Sometimes I think I've had everybody's children but my own. Interacting with my students over the years and being able to influence them to live in the light of God has been one of the great joys of my life."

"And Bob's love has fueled the fire that helped you do that?" I asked.

"Absolutely. He has informed my vocation in every way, bringing me closer to God. The love I feel has touched every child I ever worked with and touched my sisters in the community. I am grateful that I have been so loved all through my religious life right up to today. The validity of our love has lasted through all these years, and that is extraordinary. It's something close to a mystery because I would not keep him from following his vocation, and he would not keep me from following mine.

"He says he owes so much to me, and I think that's because I didn't hold him to his promise; he would never have parted from me without my encouragement. He can see what his life has meant as a monk and a priest. We recount the things we've accomplished living apart that we could not have done had we married. Just this summer he said again how grateful he is to me; I winked at him and said, 'You'd better be.'" Then she smiled at me and added, "We plan to spend eternity together, you know."

She said that after she returned from Genesee in August, she had a letter from him in which he said they might never see each other again in this life. She hopes he is not feeling premonitions of death, as she continues to count on his guidance. "Only in these last several years have I felt my vocation to be a burden, and it was a relief to talk to Bob about that and have him help me."

"How have you felt burdened, Sister?" I knew she had just stepped down after six years as Mother Superior and wondered if her responsibilities then had been heavy.

"It's hard being in charge of an aging community," she answered. "I like to do things I do well, not the things I'm not suited to. That's one of the reasons I came to Saint Paul/Mendota Heights even before Cardome closed. We had shut down our high school there and that was hard for me. I loved teaching English, and I loved the contributions I could make with my music to both the school and the monastery.

"Now in Cardome we were going to start two new programs, a Montessori school and a home for the elderly. We came here to learn how to teach Montessori from Sister Mary Denise, and I could see that I didn't like it. I had been a high school English teacher all my life, and I had no talent for working with little ones. And I was certain I had no desire to take care of old people.

Sister Mary Regina offered me the opportunity to come here on loan and teach English, so I did. It wasn't easy having a foot in each community, as I flew back and forth between Cardome and here for eight or ten years. I could talk that over with Bob then, and he always helped me.

"And this summer I could tell him about my discouragement at feeling I was running a nursing home after all. This time there wasn't any Sister Mary Regina to bail me out and give me a job I liked. I poured this out to Bob, and he was wonderful. He told me I am experiencing the cross; so much of my religious life I've been delighted, and now I need to become familiar with the cross. It's not that I haven't suffered: giving up marriage, losing my family and so many sisters I have loved. But this is different."

Bob was able to explain to her that she needed to recognize it as a new stage of her life and deal with it. In consoling her, he told her he feels his own weaknesses, too, and that's what religious must expect. He spoke of his suffering. His hardest cross had come earlier, back when they first parted and he had entered the monastery. It was as though part of his heart had been torn out. She could see that those years had been more difficult for him than they were for her. It was a comfort to both of them to be able to share these feelings and then, as always, leave each other again and return to their work refreshed.

"What do you see as your work now?" I asked her. "You are no longer Mother Superior, so you've been relieved of some responsibilities."

"My main task now is to participate in keeping the spirit of Visitation alive. I love being with the students and playing in the orchestra for their musical performances, but my role is peripheral, not the same as when I was an actively teaching nun."

I had to respond to the expression of her influence as peripheral. "You still have more influence than you may think," I told her. "I've seen you with the students and they light up when you speak to them. They cluster around you like children at a story hour—even the graduating seniors run to embrace you and beg to have their pictures taken with you. And you are a kind of magnet to the alumnae; I don't think you recognize how precious your presence is to our gatherings. You are very much a part of keeping the Visitation Spirit alive."

"A lot of things work together to keep that spirit alive," she answered modestly. "It's ironic that we're at the lowest point in our community, but the school is absolutely thriving. It's never been stronger and it's growing. We don't have many sisters anymore, so our challenge is to nurture and grow that spirit."

She then described some of the steps they have taken to ensure that Visitation will continue even when there are no sisters at all, should that day arrive. They have hired a Director of Salesian Studies to coordinate the efforts of different groups dedicated to preserving the virtues of their founding saints. The Board of Trustees is composed of members who know the spirit of Visitation and who govern the institution from that ethos. There is a national network of laypeople who train teachers in each of the five Visitation schools to understand and convey the Salesian virtues. It is apparent to Sister Marie Thérèse that the instructors are modeling the virtues, not just preaching them.

Representatives from the five teaching convents meet and carry ideas and resolutions back to each school. The students know the Direction of Intention by heart, the same prayer that every Visitation nun has recited since learning it in the novitiate. It is the third article in their spiritual directory.

> My God, I give you this day.
> I offer you now all the good
> that I shall do.

I promise to accept
for love of you,
all the difficulty that
I shall meet.
Help me to conduct myself
during this day
in a manner
pleasing to you.
Amen.

"When I see all this evidence of the spirit at work, it renews my faith that we shall live on as schools. Our purpose has been to grow in grace ourselves while forming our students in that same life of grace." She smiled at me and then gave a little chuckle. "You know, God never promised us we'd be here in 2020. We mustn't assume that the ideals Jane and Francis taught won't survive even if we don't last as a religious order. The changes of Vatican II included the ascendancy of the laity, and it has enriched the church to have laypeople involved.

"The idea used to be that religious life was somehow superior to the secular, but we know that's not true. Each person must discern the right life and live that one. Everyone is gifted spiritually; it's just that some people don't know how to nourish it. Love is the answer. It's all in the gospels. Jesus didn't condemn the Samaritan woman, didn't judge her. He just said, 'I'd like to give you some living water if you'd be willing.' We need to be as He was, whatever our station in life: to be present and there for others."

As a parting gift, Sister Marie Thérèse shared with me some of the letters she has received from Bob over the years. He always begins his letters "Dear Edna Rose." Her name in religion is

Sister Marie Thérèse, but to him she remains Edna Rose, the woman he fell in love with nearly sixty years ago.

> *Dear Edna Rose,*
>
> *All manner of trials can come upon us, but neither of us should doubt God's mercy and love for us when He has given such a singular depth of love to us from our early years. It is stronger than death itself for it is a fruit of the cross and of the risen life of Christ.*
>
> *Life moves on inexorably and at some point will end here on earth. But... our true life awaits us just beyond that point. Our hope makes death seem more of a beginning than an end and that includes, for me, in a special way, our own relationship. We placed our hope in the Lord, not in this life, and He surely will not disappoint us at the end.*
>
> *The more we focus on our Lord and His interests rather than any bonds in the world of time, the more we will meet and be united with one another. This is the hidden mystery that gives meaning to our separation in this world. May the Spirit bring us to that deep knowledge in love where we are, already in a hidden manner, one, until we are united with Him—and so with one another—face to face.*
>
> *Love and Blessings, Robert*

As I read his tender words I was filled with wonder at the profound love that has guided their separate journeys. They have carried each other in their human hearts while resting with trust in the divine heart of the One to whom they have given their lives. In Sister Marie Thérèse one sees the heart that embodies the ideals of the Visitation Order: acceptance of the will of God as the touchstone of one's life.

She has transformed the love that has blessed her by extending it with a joyful spirit to the students she has mentored and nurtured. Touching evidence of their love for her is expressed, not just by the many Mendota Heights students who stay in touch with her regularly, but also, each fall, when the alumnae of Cardome gather for reunion. They unfailingly send their beloved former teacher an airline ticket so that she can join in their celebration and remembrances. And they, like the Mendota Heights girls, have nicknamed her "Sister Honey," from her lifelong habit of greeting every student she sees with a cheerful "Hello, Honey."

Sister Marie Thérèse continues to give freely to the community into whose life she has entered so fully. She plays the organ or violin for their devotions, as well as participating in every aspect of convent life. Whenever I mention her name to a student, an alumna, a staff member or one of the other sisters, their first response is a smile. At the age of seventy-seven, she continues to spread the light that has illumined her life.

SISTER MARIE ANTOINETTE

The name Marie Antoinette is most often associated with that of the hapless queen who met her death at the guillotine in eighteenth-century France. But Sister Marie Antoinette Hynes received her name in religion without anyone's having given a thought to that sad predecessor. When asked to consider family names that might symbolize her new station in life, she thought of one of her grandfathers, whose name was Anthony. Catholics love Saint Anthony, known for his scholarship, his kindness and his help in finding lost objects.

In Parkersburg, West Virginia, in 1937, Grandpa Anthony's name was feminized to Antoinette, paired with Marie, the name of the mother of Jesus, and given to the new novice in the Order of the Visitation of Holy Mary.

Her name before profession had been Daisy Hynes, one that represented her personality well. Daisies have long been known and loved for their simple beauty and fresh appearance, even after being cut and kept for days in a vase. They are hardy plants; they stand up well and survive neglect better than the statelier, more glamorous flowers like roses and lilies. The unpretentious daisy has staying power.

Little Daisy Hynes had known neglect of a type that might well have kept a less sturdy soul from blossoming. She was born in 1919 to young parents; her mother was only seventeen. Within two years, the young Mrs. Hynes delivered another baby, a boy named William after his father. Just a year later, the young couple had a third child, another boy, who was born dead. Looking back at the circumstances, Sister Marie Antoinette can see that her mother was overtaken by adult responsibilities for which she wasn't ready. But at the time, the little girl only knew that she was a frightening woman with an explosive temper directed equally at her daughter, her son and her husband. Whoever displeased her felt the force of her wrath.

Sister looked sadly at me as she recounted one of her earliest memories. "I learned to climb stairs before I learned to walk. I wanted to follow my dad everywhere to get away from my mother, and when he went upstairs I would crawl up after him. That made Mother very angry because it got my white stockings dirty, and she told me I mustn't crawl up the stairs. So I pulled myself up to my feet and, by grasping the banister and holding on to a spoke with each step, I could follow Dad upstairs without making Mother mad." She paused. "That says a lot about my mother, doesn't it?"

Daisy's clumsiness irritated her mother as much as her getting dirty did. "I tripped and fell over things constantly, and Mother was sure I was doing it deliberately to vex her. She thought it was awful that I was so awkward. When I'd fall outside, I'd get dirty and she couldn't stand to think the neighbors would notice my messy appearance. It was a poor reflection of her if her daughter didn't look clean. She disapproved of many things about me." For a moment she stopped speaking. "It wasn't until I went to school that I was discovered to be extremely nearsighted, and the reason for all my tumbles was that I couldn't see the things that were in my way."

"Wasn't your father able to protect you from her temper storms?" I asked.

She shook her head. "My dad was a very gentle man and couldn't really protect himself either. He would just stand there and look miserable while she yelled at him. The only way you could tell he was angry was that his ears would turn red, but he wouldn't say a word. He was kind and patient with William and me, trying to make up for the way Mother treated us."

Her father's unusual docility may have been a result of his own unhappy childhood. "In those days we didn't know terms like 'insecurity,'" Sister said. "Over the years in the monastery we've learned psychology and brought in counselors to help us understand ourselves, but there wasn't any of that then. My dad had actually been sent away from his home because his mother worried that he might grow up to be a bad boy if he stayed in the city where they were living."

His mother's fear stemmed from an incident that happened when William, Daisy's father, was only six years old. He had been outside playing with a group of boys when they spotted a Chinese gentleman coming down the street. The older boys began to torment him, singing out, "Ching Ching Chinaman eats dead rats," and the little boys took up the chant too. Instead of being intimidated, however, the Chinese man took after the boys, scolding and shouting at them. William was so scared he ran home and hid under the bed. When his mother found out the details of what had happened, she decided that he mustn't be allowed to associate with such ruffians any more. Country living was the solution to prevent him from growing up to be a tough city guy.

He was quickly packed off to live with relatives on a farm, where he attended a rural country school. Gradually, he began to adjust to his new home, but when he was twelve his uncle decided he wasn't doing well enough in the little school. Once again, he was sent away, this time to live with a newly-married uncle in Parkersburg. Little wonder that he feared any misstep would get him cast out again. He learned to control his feelings tightly and to duck out of the way of any trouble.

I asked Sister how she and her brother William got along. Were they friends or did their mother's anger spill over on to them? She said they liked each other most of the time, but came to loggerheads over the matter of his tricycle. It had a side car for her to sit in, which made her mad. She ought to be able to drive it at least once in a while. Her mother sided with her brother; not many women drove in those days, and she said it was appropriate that the boy should be the driver.

Daisy and William's childhood together did not last very long, so whether they might eventually have achieved equality between them was never resolved. When Daisy was six, her mother abandoned the family, leaving her husband to bring up the two small children on his own. This proved impossible. He tried for a year, sending them to the local parish school, run by the Sisters of the Poor Child Jesus.

"They were very good to us," Sister Marie Antoinette said. "They would take us into their convent after school and let us wait with them until my father got off work and could pick us up and take us home. You don't forget kindnesses like that; I will always remember them."

The sisters' kindness was not enough to hold the family together. A childless uncle and aunt in Parkersburg offered to take William and bring him up as their own. He was willing to go with them; they were the only relatives who had any money, and they could provide him with privileges he'd never known before. Daisy, age seven, was put into boarding school, also in Parkersburg, with the Visitation nuns. In theory, the family should have been able to see each other more than occasionally, but it didn't work out that way.

"I think my father felt beholden to the aunt and uncle; he didn't want to assert himself too much as William's father for fear of offending them. They were acting as parents, and he was reluctant to interfere. So my brother and I seldom saw each other, except on holidays at our grandmother's house. She was my mother's mother and she was glad enough to have us visit, but Dad wasn't very comfortable there."

"Were you unhappy to be the one sent to boarding school while your brother was taken in by the well-to-do relatives?" I asked.

"No, I really wasn't, because I had my dad. I loved my father very much, and I would never have traded him for my aunt and uncle, which is what William did. Of course, he was just a little child and didn't have a lot of say in the matter, but I could see the way it was unfolding. My father came to visit me at school once during the week and every Sunday afternoon, but he almost never saw William. He thought it was only right that William would see our uncle as his real father because he was doing so much for him.

"During the summers I went to live with my dad at the boarding house where he stayed; it was run by an aunt of his. I could see him in the evenings and I was just happy to be with him. I wondered about my mother sometimes, but I didn't really miss her. I was mostly glad she wasn't there to yell at me and be displeased with everything I did."

Life during the school years with the Visitation sisters felt safe and happy to Daisy too. Her activities were very regulated as the girls kept pretty much the same schedule as the sisters. Community was emphasized over individuality. The sisters addressed the girls as a group, as in, "Let us get ready for bed now," or "Let us all be sure to fold our napkins neatly when we've finished our dinner." Sister Marie Antoinette remembers often referring to herself in the plural. She would ask a teacher, "May we go out in the garden now?" even though she was quite alone.

Their games were supervised and there wasn't much free time, but when she was alone she loved to read, so she seldom felt lonely. And she had her father's visits to look forward to. Sometimes he was so tired from working two or even three jobs he'd fall asleep on the sofa in the visitors' parlor. She would nudge him and softly say, "Dad, wake up." He'd be startled then and smile at her, and they would just sit and be cozy together. She understood that boarding school was expensive; his working extra hours was a necessity.

Daisy decided when she was only in eighth grade that she would remain in the Visitation Convent all her life. "I didn't process it much," she told me, "but I experienced a feeling of inspiration. It was on a day dedicated to the Sacred Heart of Jesus—funny I can't remember which one when it was such an important event for me—but I can't. I only know that the decision felt firm. And it must have been, because I have never wavered. When I was older, I realized how limited my experiences in the world had been, but that never made me regret my decision. The Lord led me, I'm sure, and I followed Him."

While she was still in high school, before she had entered the monastery, her mother suddenly returned to Parkersburg. She was pregnant, though unmarried, and wanted to make peace with her family.

"That was quite a shock," Sister Marie Antoinette said. "I think she had experienced some kind of conversion, and she was very much a changed person. She wanted to do penance and make up for her sins. She admitted that she had been a poor mother; that it was Dad who had really brought us up even when she still lived with us. I felt sorry for her; I think we all did. But it was too late for us to trust her or be glad to see her. My father had had the marriage annulled by then and was not interested in taking her back. My brother felt himself to be our aunt and uncle's child, not hers, and I already knew that my home was to be in the convent. I believe we all forgave her as best we could, but none of us wanted to be with her much."

"What a difficult time for your family," I sympathized. "I can picture how hard and awkward it must have been for all of you, and for her, too."

"Yes, it was hard. She told me very clearly that she didn't want me to enter the convent. Not because I shouldn't be a nun some day if that was what I wanted, but she thought I was too young to make such a big commitment.

"'Look at me,' my mother said. 'I should never have married so young. I was too young and selfish to live up to my promises, and you see what a mess I've made of my life.'

"I knew she meant well, but it was hard to listen to her, of all people, give me advice. And she was probably right; seventeen *is* too young to either get married or enter a convent. But it turned out to have been right for me. Here I still am, and I'm eighty-six years old," she smiled.

"After you entered did your mother come and visit you?" I asked.

"She did and brought the baby with her, but I didn't really want to see them. I would tell myself that the other sisters didn't approve of her being there, because of her disgrace, but I can see now that I was even more judgmental than they. I think it made me feel less guilty about not wanting to be with her if I could believe that she wasn't welcomed there by anyone. I still feel some blame for that. She didn't come often; one can't help knowing when one is not wanted. It comes through, and so she stayed away."

Daisy's father was content with her decision to become a nun. She still has the letter he wrote to her saying he desired for her whatever would make her happy. If that's what she wanted, then that was what he wanted. Some of their relatives complained that it was selfish of her to leave her dad when he was so alone; a grown daughter should stay home and look after him. But his words assured her that she was right to follow her calling.

After she entered, he moved to Washington D C, and later remarried, removing all her concerns about his welfare. He and his new wife had a daughter named Donna, born in 1942, so now there was another half-sibling in her life. Her new stepmother also had a daughter, Charlotte, from her first marriage, much closer to Sister Marie Antoinette's age than Donna. It was between the two older girls that the closest relationship developed. The two women are still good friends and keep in touch with each other by phone and mail.

After William grew up and married, he reestablished acquaintance with his sister. He and his wife visited her often while she still lived in Parkersburg and were always available to drive her when she needed to go out for medical appointments. William died in 1991, shortly before Sister Marie Antoinette moved to Saint Paul. She stayed in touch with his wife until her death a few years ago and feels satisfied that she was able to be connected to relatives in spite of her family's initial problems and dysfunction.

"What was convent life like for you after you entered?" I asked her. "You had been at school there for twelve years and knew many of the sisters; did it feel strange to be on the other side of the grille?"

"The sisters and many of their routines were familiar to me, but still, it felt very different to be among them both night and day. I had no doubts about my vocation, but I always felt a little undercurrent of worry about whether they thought I really belonged there."

"Did you not feel genuinely accepted?"

"I wouldn't have called it that then, but years later when I visited the Saint Louis sisters, I perceived how much more warmly they treated me than the sisters in Parkersburg did. I tried to analyze the difference and thought that maybe because of my mother's bad reputation the Parkersburg community was worried that I might turn out badly, or that I might not stay. That may not be what they really thought, but that's the conclusion I came to. It was a gut feeling. I didn't talk about it. When I went back home, I continued to be aware of the difference between the two groups."

"Did you have a desire to leave Parkersburg and go to Saint Louis permanently?" I questioned. "And would that option have been possible if you had?"

"No, I didn't consider asking for a transfer. To me, embracing religious life means that you learn acceptance." She lowered her voice and said in a confidential tone, "You wouldn't believe the attitudes of some of the women who enter the convent and immediately begin to find fault, not liking things a certain way, saying they should be done differently. I believe that if you ask to join, you are supposed to do everything you can to fit in and follow the way you are shown.

"I suppose that's a result of how I was brought up. If you're in boarding school you might not like what happens, but you just go along, or else. You make do. There's no place in the world that's exactly as you want it. If you're going to live in a community that has rules, you need to obey those rules, not try to change them. I don't mind if people talk things over and come to an agreement, but when they insist that things be changed because they don't like them that way, that's wrong. When that happens it makes me angry."

She looked at me abruptly and asked, "Isn't that how it is in married life? You're married, Elsa. Couples can't just say to each other, 'I have to have my way,' all the time, can they?"

"Not if the marriage is to last," I assured her. We discussed the high divorce rate and speculated that much of it may be due to unwillingness to put up with any disappointment or hardship.

She sighed. "My mother didn't want to accept hardship, and so she was unfaithful and she left us. I'm sure my dad would have been willing to work it out; he was very liberal for his age and time and thought women should have rights. He didn't boss her around or demand that she do things his way."

With a little sigh, she continued on her life in the convent.

"I was assigned to teach in our school very early on. Before I got my college degree I taught first grade and later, second and third. I got my B.A. from Saint Mary of the Springs, a college run by Dominican sisters. At first they came to our cloister on Saturdays to hold classes, but in 1941 three of us were allowed to go to their college and study there. That was really fun; they were wonderful women and they were very thorough in the subject contents. I majored in social studies and that was what I taught in our high school."

"Did you enjoy teaching?"

"I liked it well enough, but I didn't love it the way a real teacher would. These past few years I've done a lot of reviewing of my life; when you get to be my age you know it's time to reflect on your past." She chuckled. "You need to get ready for where you're going next. I've asked the Lord to help me see things clearly, and I can see that there are many things I didn't give my students that I should have. I try not to blame myself because I know my foundation wasn't very good. In college we were taught subject matter, but we weren't taught how to teach, and I didn't have a natural talent for it. I never really figured out how to engage the students' attention and interest.

"The class I enjoyed most was one that wasn't required. The sister who taught typing and shorthand got sick, and I was asked to take over. I had never taken either one, but I enjoyed learning it along with the girls. It met after school, and we were all very relaxed together and had a good time.

"I wanted to be a religious, but I didn't necessarily want to be a teacher. Nowadays they work hard at discerning what kind of service you're best suited to, but back then you were just assigned. If there was a need, you filled it."

Sister Marie Antoinette was obedient to her superiors and faithfully taught social studies, but she let it be known that she did not want to teach religion. That was one subject she did not want to get near. I wondered why and found her answer very touching.

"It's because it's the most important subject there is, and I didn't think I was good enough to be trusted with it. I was afraid of the responsibility; afraid I might make mistakes and lead the girls astray. What if some girl didn't make it into heaven when she died, and it was because I had misguided her? I did not want that to be on my conscience. Thank goodness that in the thirty-six years I taught I never did have to teach religion!"

In the monastery of today a young woman with such damaged self-esteem would be given counseling and brought to understand her fears. Sister Marie Antoinette had to figure it out by herself over years of prayer and reflection. And she had done it. Step by painful step, she had examined her motives, acknowledged her weaknesses and gradually come to accept her strengths. My admiration for her grew as I perceived the courage she had shown. She always tried to do her best, even when greatly troubled by thoughts of her own unworthiness.

She had lived in the Parkersburg Monastery during the emergence of the civil rights movement. It was a major awakening in her life. Because she had grown up in a racially segregated southern state, it hadn't occurred to her that there was anything abnormal about it.

"Can you believe how ignorant I was?" she asked me now. "I had never had a bad experience with a black person in my life, and I had no negative feelings about them. I actually did not realize that there were laws to keep them apart from white society. Seeing them in the backs of streetcars and theaters had not raised any questions for me as to *why* things were that way. There were no black students in either my parish school or boarding school; I simply had experienced no contact with them. I had just gone along with it, not understanding I was acting out the prejudices of my era.

"Then, one day after I had been in the convent for some years, a black girl came to be admitted to our school, and the principal turned her away. If I had not happened to be on duty as portress that day, I never would have seen it or known anything about it. The incident was not discussed in community."

The girl had applied and been accepted through correspondence and the question of race had never come up. Now she was at the door with her mother—they had her uniforms and books, everything she needed to start at Visitation—but when the principal saw that she was black she told her she could not enroll.

"All I could think was how awful it must have been for that poor girl and her mother. To have come with the expectation of being admitted, and then to be rejected so cruelly… it worried me something terrible. I've never forgotten it. It did something to me. If only I had been brave enough to speak up to Mother Superior, to point out the injustice, but I didn't. It still makes me ashamed of myself and our community.

"We didn't know it, but around the same time there were sisters in Covington, Kentucky, who were making history. They started accepting black girls even though they were fined for every day they had black students in their school, but they didn't give in, thank God. Somehow they managed to come up with the money. I wish we had had the courage to act in the same way."

Vatican II brought more changes to the group in Parkersburg. They were confused about how to follow the new directives until Sister Mary Helen McMullen, one of the Saint Paul community members, came to help them out in 1967.

"She was wonderful. She knew just how to handle us; she could see right away that we were afraid of change and also afraid of making mistakes. She would say, 'Let's try this or that—we don't have to keep it up if it doesn't work.' She *led* us; she didn't try to *manage* us, and so we all loved her and followed her advice. We gradually learned to give up some of the old customs and accept the new, less enclosed way of life."

Once again, Sister Marie Antoinette leaned toward me as if to share a confidence. "You know the really inspiring thing to me about Sister Mary Helen is that I don't think it came naturally to her to guide us so gently. She was really quite particular about how things should be. I think it was a virtue she learned and practiced because she knew that's what our saints, Francis and Jane de Chantal, modeled for the sisters."

In the 1970s Sister Marie Antoinette retired from teaching, but not from working for the community. As well as helping with every kind of housework in the monastery, she was Procuratrix, a position in which she did purchasing and bookkeeping. She helped with the personal care of the nuns who were elderly and frail, a task for which she had volunteered and especially liked.

By the 1980s the Parkersburg house had dwindled down to twelve members. More sisters were aging and dying, and few young women of that era were choosing monastic life. Sister Marie Antoinette could see that closing was inevitable, even though some of the other sisters tried to resist it.

"The bishop stressed how impractical it was for us to remain. Our convent had been built in 1900 and it was three stories tall, four stories in one wing, as the offices and storage were in the basement. We were getting too old to take all those steps. The building would have needed extensive remodeling to bring it up to modern standards, and we didn't have the money for that kind of endeavor.

"Some people can't face reality, but I had learned how to do that when I was only a child, and I left in 1991, a year earlier than the others. I chose Saint Paul mainly because Sister Mary Helen was here, but I also knew Sisters Mary Denise and Mary Bernard, and I liked their spirit. They had come some time back to help us set up a Montessori program in our school. Only two from Parkersburg wound up here, Sister Rosario and I, and she is dead now."

When Sister Marie Antoinette came to Saint Paul, she was strong and well enough to devote her time to housecleaning. That suited her well.

"There are many who don't like to clean and only do it because they have to, but I'm one of those people who really like it. I was able to help with the cleaning a lot in the first years I was here, but now the doctor won't let me do any heavy work. It's hard having to use a walker to get around, and I'm so shaky that I can't even help with the dishes any more. I just get in the way when I try to."

She sighed and shook her head as she looked beyond my shoulder. "For instance, that window behind you looks streaky to me, and I want in the worst way to get at it right now and make it sparkle. Once I could have done that, but I know I just have to accept that those days are over."

"How *do* you spend your days, Sister?" I asked.

"I help out a bit in the business office, stuffing envelopes and things like that, and I read a lot. As you know, I majored in social studies, and I'm still interested in current events and social issues. I try to keep up with what's going on the world by reading newspapers and magazines."

As she has done all her life, she also spends a good deal of time in prayer. Some years ago she asked a retreat master to help her pray more maturely.

"My personal prayers were childish," she confessed. "All I ever seemed to say was, 'I love you, God,' and 'Thank you, God.' This priest gave me a book called, *The Cloud of Unknowing*, and it helped me learn how to meditate and speak to God from my heart."

Part of her prayer life consists of reviewing her past and thinking of its meaning. "I've never really questioned my purpose or wondered why God chose me for this vocation. Perhaps I should have asked more questions, but I didn't. I've just been grateful for the grace. Today, the emphasis is all on love, but when I entered it was more on obedience and adhering to the rules. I like the emphasis on love as I am a loving person. God commanded us to love one another, and sometimes I worry that I haven't loved enough. I think that I'm supposed to *feel* love, and I sometimes don't. Saint Francis said that was okay as long as our intention was to love, but that's hard for me. I want to feel it."

Sister Marie Antoinette worries that she and the other aging nuns who came to Saint Paul have been detrimental to the growth of the community. "We were all old ones who came. We have been so grateful for the gracious welcome we received, but I fear that we didn't do them anywhere near the good they did us. We were probably a hindrance to their attracting new postulants."

"Perhaps you helped them grow spiritually, if not numerically," I suggested. "You brought wisdom instead of youth and energy."

Sister answered slowly. "We have to trust in the Holy Spirit that that is true. I hope that my presence here has done some good. I have felt loved and accepted in this house. I especially love Sister Mary Denise—I admire her qualities so much."

"What do you see as the future of Visitation, Sister?"

"That's a difficult one. Here in Saint Paul we're holding on, but we're not flourishing. A community needs new members to stay fresh and to grow, and I fear that unless some new women come in, we will die away."

"Is this another case in which you just have to trust the Holy Spirit?" I asked.

She smiled. "That's kept us going for four centuries or more. I've never been one to question His ways so I won't start now. He has led us and guided us, and I believe He will continue to do that until we are all safely home in His arms."

Sister accompanied me to the convent door, her grey curls bobbing up and down with each careful step. It's not easy to hug over a walker, but we managed. As I walked down the familiar sidewalk towards the car, I thought again how much this woman, Daisy Hynes, is like the tenacious flower whose name she once shared. For nearly seventy years she has persevered in following the simple virtues espoused by the founders of her order. Like the daisy, she is humble and unpretentious, her face turned ever upward to God.

SISTER MARY DENISE

Ask anyone acquainted with Sister Mary Denise to describe her, and you will hear the same words over and over. Caring, centered, patient, efficient, practical, steady, serene. The same words come from her sisters in the community, old friends who have known her since girlhood, staff members at the Visitation school and even a former student who asked Sister Mary Denise to be her labor coach and then godmother to the baby. The litany of the same qualities is recited by those who know her.

When I first met her in 1955, she was Margaret Villaume, a student in a navy blue skirt and blazer like the rest of us. I had transferred from my high school in Minneapolis to Visitation in Saint Paul when I was a junior. Margaret was a friendly girl, slender and supple. We blended together into a group of identically dressed students, chattering and giggling about boys and dates. There was no way I could have guessed that her heart was already pledged to a love that was beyond human.

She grew up in Saint Paul, just across the street from the Church of Saint Luke. The church was an imposing stone building on Summit Avenue, a street famous for its fine old Victorian homes and sweeping boulevards. Saint Luke's and its school were the center of the neighborhood and of the Villaume family's life. They prayed there often, as well as attending Mass; church was as familiar to Margaret, her two older brothers and her younger sister as their home.

Home, church, school—they were all good places for her to be, but she didn't stay in any of them a minute longer than she had to. The outside was her arena, winter and summer. She loved to play and be active, whether on her bike or ice skates, in the alley and street playing games with the neighborhood kids and, in the summer, swimming and riding horses. Her family owned other property, a home on White Bear Lake and a small farm just outside Saint Paul. While at the lake, Margaret was in the water as much as possible, often for as much as seven or eight hours a day. At the farm she rode horses with her friends around Mendota Heights and Sunfish Lake and all over the territory that in the 1950s had not yet been developed. Having to go in for dinner was an interruption to be borne until she could get outside and be active again until dark.

"I wasn't a reader," Sister Mary Denise said, "so you can imagine what penance rainy days were for me. I was probably one of the least introspective children ever born. Happiness and having fun were givens, taken for granted. There was never a thought of the future or of anything that wasn't in the right now. Really, in many ways I'm still like that; I'm not a dreamer; I live very much in the present."

School was another unquestioned given, something kids had to do and grown-ups didn't. She attended Saint Luke's School and assumed she would be there through grade eight, but during the summer between sixth and seventh grade, she learned that she would be starting at the Convent of the Visitation School in September. One of her big brothers had noticed the order for her uniforms among the mail and informed her of the impending change.

"Weren't you horrified?" I asked her. I thought of what a shock it would have been for me to learn of such a major change in my life without being consulted. In my widowed mother's egalitarian household such a thing would not have happened.

"It probably sounds funny," she answered, "but I really didn't question it all that much. My mother and my aunts had gone there when they were girls, so I was familiar with it. I just accepted it. Parents in those days didn't talk over every decision they made with their kids. I think little communication from the top down was the norm, not the exception. That was certainly the case in my family."

The decision had been made and she was measured for her uniforms. In September she started school at Visitation, but not before suffering the first big shock of her life. Her brothers had graduated from college and been given a trip to Europe together as a present. The rest of the family was at the lake home, happily preparing for the boys' return the next day. That night her father had a heart attack.

"Just the day before, Dad told me that he had been one of the donors to the fund for an ambulance with oxygen for the city of White Bear Lake. The small town had owned an ambulance before that, but not one with oxygen. It was that ambulance that came screaming to our house in the night, and it was the oxygen that saved his life. Without it, he would have died on the way to the hospital."

The fear of losing her father was an awakening for Margaret. He was in the hospital for five long weeks, an anxious time for the family. Although the fear gradually dissipated after he came home, the awareness that he was living on borrowed time was always with him and with the rest of the family.

"Dad had great devotion to the Sacred Heart of Jesus and he credited Him with saving his life. In gratitude he donated a statue to the Jesuit Retreat House at Lake Demontreville, a beautiful place that offers spiritual retreats for men. He was one of the early founders of that institution; prayer was an important part of his life and he and my brothers made retreats there regularly. I know his faith helped our family return to a feeling of normalcy. Worrying about his health would not solve anything; we were to put our trust in God and continue living as usual."

Margaret began seventh grade at Visitation and quickly felt at home there. By the time she was a sophomore in high school she had started thinking that she would enter the convent and become a nun some day. She did not experience anything dramatic, just a recurring, persistent thought—and a very private one. Discussing it with either her parents or her friends did not occur to her.

"I really didn't even discuss it much with myself," she laughed. "The thought just kept coming to me; it was a very strong inner direction that kept getting stronger, and I didn't question it. I had no doubt that it would be Visitation. I had been with the Saint Joseph sisters from kindergarten through sixth grade, and they were wonderful women. But my vocation came to me while I was at Visitation, and I felt that was where I belonged."

"Didn't it concern you that they were a cloistered order and that you wouldn't have as much freedom with them as with the Saint Joseph's?"

"Honestly, I didn't give it a thought. There was zero brain involvement, just this incredible certainty that it was what I was supposed to do." She smiled. "Can you believe that at the going-away party my parents gave for me before I entered, one of my friends asked me what I was planning to do in the convent? Would I be a teacher or what? And I answered that I didn't know, didn't care. I would do whatever was asked of me."

The only uncertainty she experienced was wondering just when she should reveal her plan and actually enter the convent. After graduating from high school she attended Rosemont College in Pennsylvania for her freshman year. She went to Mass daily and pondered whether she should enter the next summer or return to college for her sophomore year.

"After Mass one day I made a visit to the statue of Mary in her side chapel. I looked up at her and said, 'I'll be back at three o'clock, and I'd like an answer. I want to know if I should enter soon instead of finishing college.' I came back that afternoon and knelt down and the answer was 'Yes.' It wasn't spoken aloud, but I heard it as clearly as if it were."

Now she needed to tell her parents, a task that she knew would not be easy. During her senior year of high school they had built a beautiful new home on the farm they owned. They did it mainly for Margaret and her younger sister, Janet, thinking what joy it would give the active girls to live in the country. Now she had to let them know she would live in that house for only one summer.

I told her I well remembered her going-away party in that lovely house. I had been there with our other former class-mates from Visitation. We all oohed and aahed and asked each other how she could possibly stand to leave such luxury for the austerity of the convent. Her parents had furnished her new bedroom in French Provincial fruitwood with a bed, matching desk and dresser and dainty chairs. It was a picture-book room, exquisite in each detail. "How did they take it?" I wondered now, as I had wondered then but hadn't dared to ask.

"It was hard," she admitted. "They were supportive but quite jolted that I wouldn't finish college first. Mother said that for a long time she had been feeling that I might become a nun, but not before I finished my education. They would have liked for that to have happened, but they didn't try to stop me.

"Mother and Dad brought me to Visitation at four o'clock in the afternoon on October 17, 1957, the feast of Saint Margaret Mary." She chuckled. "Or at least it was then; Vatican II changed it to the sixteenth when they started reforming the calendar of saints."

"Was the leave-taking emotional?" I asked. "Did you cry?"

She paused, remembering. "No, there were no tears. Not from me and not from my mother or father. Or, if there were, they weren't shown. We said goodbye and I went in. I shared a silent dinner with the sisters that evening; in those days there was no talking at meals. After dinner I undressed and went to bed, and in the morning I got up and put on the clothes of a postulant."

"So you were already dressed in black when your parents came to visit you the next day?" At that time, when a girl went in, there was a period called the Eight Days in which her family could visit her every day. Following that was a final goodbye, and then she was formally welcomed by the community as a postulant.

"Yes, they knew I would be. I wore a short black veil, a black skirt and a blouse that had no collar. A little black cape went over that, and it had a white collar that could snap on and off for washing. I sent my things home with Mom." She laughed. "I knew I wouldn't be wearing pink shorty pajamas anymore!"

As we talked, I kept thinking about how physically active she had been during her childhood years. I thought how much she must have missed riding her bike and swimming. Had she considered that all that was behind her now?

Again she said, "I really didn't give it a thought. A vocation is a calling, and when you embrace it, things that were once important don't matter the way they used to. At different times in our lives we are called to do different things and behave in different ways. It didn't seem unnatural to me; it was like going from grade school to high school; you don't do the same things at each level. Your life evolves and changes with time.

"And I certainly didn't suffer from lack of activity; there were lots of recreational opportunities. We played softball and tennis and took long walks in our big yard, and in the winter we ice-skated. We also had housework and school work—we were always plenty busy and I didn't feel like my muscles weren't getting a workout."

For the major part of her formation, her novitiate was shared by three other women. Two of them, Sisters Mary Frances and Katherine, are still members of the Visitation Order, but are now in the Minneapolis Community. The fourth, Sister Genevieve, was fifty-six years old and a former army colonel who has since died.

"We three younger ones got along well with Genevieve in spite of our age differences, and our novitiate years were happy. I was very busy, even during the first year while I was still a postulant. I was sent immediately to the classroom as an aide to Sister Jane de Chantal for a few hours every day. Then I worked in the wardrobe—in those days, with all the sisters in full habit, we maintained one black and one white wardrobe for the different parts of our clothing. The habits always needed cleaning and mending. I helped in the kitchen and dining room, took a correspondence course in English and had recreation twice a day. The rest of the time was spent in prayer. We said the Divine Office every day, as we still do, so I was in church a lot."

After a year, a postulant receives her habit and a white veil and is given her new name in religion. Then she retires completely from school activities and remains mostly in the cloister for a year. Margaret, now Sister Mary Denise, adjusted quickly and easily to her new life. Because she had not envisioned what to expect, there were no big surprises or disappointments. She went along contentedly. The hardest thing was the sudden death of her beloved father in 1960. The second heart attack was massive; there was no way to save him this time. She was in her third year in the convent.

"His death was such a shock, even though we had known for ten years that he had a heart condition. Within a period of three years, two of my dearest friends from high school had also suddenly lost their fathers, and it felt like the world was upside-down.

"My father's brother, my Uncle Gene, died a year and a half before Dad. They were the best of friends; they were born eighteen months apart and they died eighteen months apart. When Uncle Gene died, I, of course, couldn't attend the funeral, as we didn't go out in those days. Dad wanted so much to be with me, but he didn't want to ask for a special permission to see me because he was afraid it might replace my regular monthly visiting time. That year it fell on my birthday, and he didn't want to disappoint me by missing it.

"I didn't know it at the time, but I learned later that after the funeral was over, he came to the convent and parked outside, just to feel near me. He stayed there for two hours, sitting in the car even though it was January and very cold."

I could clearly picture her father's lonely vigil outside the door of his daughter's convent. That he found solace just in feeling near her presence was not surprising to me, knowing Sister Mary Denise as I do. Her composure radiates outward; the inner serenity she possesses has a calming effect on those around her. Though her demeanor is unruffled, her feelings are deep.

She spoke now of her father and how much she loved him. "He was a good man, a good father. Sometimes on his way home from work, he would stop and look over the convent wall to see if we were outside. I remember waving to him from the rink where we were skating, and he'd wave back and smile. He did a lot of charitable work with the money he made as president of his company. I knew about some of the gifts, like the ambulance for White Bear Lake and the Jesuit Retreat House, but there were many others. He was reserved about his accomplishments; he worked quietly and faithfully at whatever he thought was right."

Like you, I thought, but did not say. Instead I asked if it been hard for her to miss going to his funeral.

"I think it was probably harder on Mother than it was on me. She had not expected me to attend; we all knew the rules when I entered. But when Dad died the sense of loss may have been brought home to her more strongly. My brothers, Eugene and Walter, were grown up and gone from home, so after Dad's death there was just Mother and my little sister, Janet, alone in that big house. I was with my sisters, here, in our community."

Vatican II had not yet convened at the time of her father's death in 1960, but the Saint Paul sisters had already initiated several innovations on their own. Changes in society necessitated changes within the monastery, and remaining enclosed for one's entire life was no longer feasible. For years, doctors and dentists had come to the convent infirmary when the sisters needed attention, but now modern medical equipment was becoming too sophisticated and expensive for home care. The sisters began to go out for medical and dental appointments. The college professors, whose custom it had been to come and teach the sisters in the monastery, now found their time too constrained to continue the practice. The nuns started to attend classes at Saint Catherine's. Sister Mary Denise started taking classes there in her second year in the convent, as soon as she had taken temporary vows.

She was soon to go even farther afield. Before completing her undergraduate work at Saint Catherine's, she went with Sister Mary Frances to California to learn the Montessori Method of teaching small children. The community was excited about this new program in education and was pleased to add something new to their curriculum. The Visitation Sisters in Saint Louis had implemented the Montessori Method in their school, and Saint Paul soon followed suit. They admitted little boys to Montessori and, for the first time since its inception, Visitation ceased to be a "for girls only" institution.

Sister Mary Denise went to Saint Louis for a year to intern in their Montessori program and then returned to Saint Paul to teach. In spite of not having finished her college education, she was already an experienced teacher. She had taught first, second, third and fourth grade before going to California for Montessori training.

"No wonder it took me so long to finish college," she said. "I was so busy teaching I could only grab a class here and there. After we moved out here to Mendota Heights in 1966, I took a year off from teaching and finally completed my degree."

That she was able to proceed towards receiving her bachelor's degree at that time speaks eloquently of her ability to set her personal concerns aside and focus on the tasks required of her. In 1966, her brother, Gene, who was an expert sailor and swimmer, drowned in Lake Mille Lacs. It was a terrible ordeal for the Villaume family. He went missing on the fourth of June and his body was not discovered until the seventeenth. No one could believe that such an able sailor had actually drowned; wild hopes were held out for some other kind of explanation of the tragedy until the brutal truth was revealed.

Sister Mary Denise's eyes still mist when she remembers those anxious days. "It was Sister Mary Teresa Dougherty who foretold to me that Gene would be found," she said. "She reminded me that our family had always been especially close to the Sacred Heart, and she believed that the mystery of Gene's disappearance would be solved on His feast day. She was right.

We got the news on June seventeenth, the feast of the Sacred Heart of Jesus."

Struggling with her grief over the loss of her brother, Sister Mary Denise nevertheless completed her degree. Later she got a master's degree from Saint Thomas while still continuing to teach. In 1971 she became director of the lower school, which went from pre-school through sixth grade, and she remained in the Montessori program as well. She and Sister Mary Bernard went to other Visitation houses to help their sisters set up Montessori classrooms. It was a busy time.

While all this was going on for the sisters in Saint Paul, the bishops in Rome were drafting reforms and making changes in the structures of the Catholic Church. Some of the innovations were difficult for many of the sisters to accept, but Sister Mary Denise found it fairly easy to adopt new customs.

"For one thing, remember, I hadn't been in the convent all that long, so our religious customs weren't embedded in me as firmly as in those who had been professed for years. I left the monastery frequently after my postulancy to attend classes at Saint Catherine's and in Los Angeles; I interned in Saint Louis and then went to other houses to help with Montessori. I was already more emancipated than many of the sisters who had barely left the house in forty years. It was harder for them to start hearing Mass in English instead of the familiar Latin; to have the grilles removed so there was no symbol of separation between the sisters and their visitors, things like that.

"Our clothing was probably the hardest thing to change as a community. Some of our members were not comfortable discarding the garb that had been designed by Saint Jane de Chantal and worn for nearly four hundred years. The association was too precious to them. We talked it over and decided it was something we *could* do, but didn't *have* to do, as a unit. In some religious orders the word went out that they were to change on Thursday or whenever, and everybody changed. That would never happen here; it would create bedlam. Visitandines don't believe in behaving arbitrarily. So it came about that some of us changed our habit, but some didn't. We went through a phase of having to wear our traditional habit on weekends, but that gradually ended too."

Their clothing and other externals changed, but not their routines. Sister Mary Denise went to school and came home and went to work, and that remained the same. Sister Mary Regina was Mother Superior when they moved out to Mendota Heights and during much of Vatican II. The two events coincided. Then Sister Mary Louise was Mother Superior for the next period so these two women guided the community through the discussions. They would talk things over and, if it made sense to change something, they did. For instance, in the dining room they each had a particular place at which they kept their napkin and spoons. They gave that up when they started changing places in the dining room once a week. Then they went to self-service from a hot cart and just sat wherever they wanted to. The changes evolved; they weren't imposed on them.

Order and civility also prevailed when some of the sisters reexamined their vocations and left religious life. They didn't all go at once, but over a period of several years. Sadness, not bitterness, was the prevailing emotion. Just as each birth, each death, each growing up and leaving affect the structure of a family, so do they affect a community. It's hard on either a family or a religious community when members leave; the sisters understood that change is both painful and inevitable.

The other Visitation houses also lost members. Religious communities around the world experienced losses after Vatican II but, more distressing than that, was the dearth of new people seeking to enter. Society was changing, and it was affected by more forces than the Council in Rome. The women's movement, the civil rights movement, the sexual revolution and the emergence of the anti-war factions that eroded trust in government resulting in a lack of respect for any authority—all contributed to the widespread belief that religious life was an anachronism.

Various Visitation houses around the country began closing, and the individual members had to decide where to go. They had come to know the sisters in other communities due to councils, meetings and task forces that brought them together face to face, something that did not occur before the '70s and '80s.

Sister Mary Denise smiled as she thought of the early communication method the nuns had used before they started going out. "Each community wrote an *année*, an annual letter that was sent to each of the other communities. That was a good idea when most of us had only one telephone in the house and we didn't know our sisters in the other houses anyway. Some of the letters were wonderful and some were just awful. They might tell us which priest celebrated Mass on Christmas and who came and who the altar boys were, utterly boring details.

"Now we don't need the letters any more. We have telephones and e-mail and very regular council and federation meetings. We have standing committees in the federation and there are representatives from each house on them. They meet and report back so everyone knows what's going on. Every six years there is a Federation Assembly at which each superior has a vote and each house elects a delegate who also has a vote. It is a very democratic process."

The improved communication helped the individual sisters decide which place to choose when their house closed, as they had a good feel for the unique spirit that permeates each community. It's up to each sister to decide where she wants to go and, when she makes her decision, she puts in a request to go there.

"Did that ever become a problem?" I asked her. "Was anyone turned down after applying to a particular house?"

"No," she answered, "there hasn't been a single instance of refusal. Not in this house or any of the others. We're in a different position now though, than we were when we accepted several elderly sisters; we can't take any more in. A house can't do that if there aren't younger sisters to take care of them, and we don't exactly have a surplus of young sisters here."

"Do you think that will ever change?"

"I don't know." She paused and thought a bit. "I'm not sure I want to know; that's the way I am about everything. I suppose I could spend time building a picture of an ideal, but if it didn't work out that way I would be disappointed. And where would that get me? As I said earlier, I'm not a dreamer. I'm more of a practical person. I can respond quickly to things that happen and I can figure things out, but I try to live more in the present. 'Try to' isn't accurate. I *do* live in the present. It might be better if I did spend some time projecting a little bit, but I don't."

Once again I was impressed by her serenity, the utter practicality of her way of perceiving the world. She is like a steady ship in a turbulent sea. Other boats might bob up and down, frantically trying to struggle through the waves and wind, but in her the keel is deep and strong, the vessel undisturbed.

"But there is such a resurgence of interest in the spiritual life these days," I said. "Between the New Age myth-makers and the rigid Christian right there is a whole spectrum of people searching for truth, for answers to the complexities of our lives. Don't you think that some of these people might be led to embrace the contemplative life in these times?"

"I don't know," she said again. "The seekers today are the children of the generation that threw everything off. Many of them grew up in homes where faith in God was seldom discussed, let alone the importance of becoming a religious. That is a big concern to the church right now. Because people are hungering for a spiritual life, they may wish to be admitted to the priesthood or the convent for the wrong reasons."

"What kind of wrong reasons?" I asked.

"They may not be realistic about what constitutes religious life. If their picture is one of meditative conversations with God, they're going to be disappointed. A diocesan priest is out there serving people. He has to take care of the building and the school, if there is one, as well as tend to the souls of his parishioners. He will wish he had more time to pray, but there's a boiler that needs fixing and a board meeting to get to.

"Coming from the 'me' generation that thinks 'my' personal happiness is the be-all of existence, it's hard for them to put that aside and be willing to make sacrifices for the good of others. If you become a sister, you will live in community, and that will make demands just as living in a family does. Religious life has realities that need to be dealt with; it's a life based on giving and serving, not getting. That viewpoint is at odds with our culture."

Reluctant to surrender my hope that monastic life will again have meaning for today's spiritual seekers, I asked her if she didn't think that the search for purposeful living might lead modern women to consider religious life in spite of lacking the foundation of faith that our generation had been given.

Sister Mary Denise shook her head a trifle impatiently. "There isn't necessarily any more meaning and purpose in our lives in the monastery than there is for those who live in the world. Living a spiritual life is not limited to ordained priests and professed sisters. Sincere seekers will find it in whatever their calling is. We here can't really have a good idea of what married or single people go through and what sacrifices they make. I believe that unless you've experienced something, you don't know it very well. I find that the more I am familiar with a married couple and the sacrifices they make in terms of each other, or their children or their work, the better I understand what their obligations are."

The old belief that a religious vocation was somehow *higher, holier*, than a lay vocation, that nuns and monks and priests had a chosen a *better* life than the rest of us, is obviously fading away. Sister Mary Denise's words made that clear. The human task is to answer, "Yes," to whatever vocation God has called us, and to live that vocation faithfully. Saint Francis de Sales stressed again and again that we should live our ordinary lives extraordinarily well.

Sister Mary Denise appears to be doing just that. Fifty years have passed since she heard Mary's answer in the little chapel at Rosemont College, and she has not wavered from her calling. Whether praying, studying, learning, teaching, following or leading, she has lived the legacy of the patron founders of her order, humbly accepting each task that has come her way. She is currently serving as her community's elected Mother Superior for the third time and also is the director of finance, operations and health care. In the school she is on the administrative council and is director of the early childhood program. She serves on several boards of local institutions as well as committees within the Second Federation of Visitation Sisters.

She does all this in her unruffled, unhurried manner, finding time when she can to attend to her spiritual reading, visit her friends, ride her bicycle, watch a movie on television or graciously accommodate my interview request for this history. The longing to know the future that so many of us struggle with has no place in her acquiescent heart. Twenty-first century speech would say she "goes with the flow"; Buddhist mystics would say she "lives in the now"; and Saint Francis de Sales would simply say she has learned acceptance.

This acceptance has not been easy, as she would be the first to admit. Besides losing beloved family members, she has witnessed the death of dear friends both within and without the sisterhood. Archbishop John Roach spent some of his final years after retirement in the Roach Residence on the grounds of Saint

Thomas Academy, just next door to Visitation. He frequently said Mass for the sisters and came to know them well. He and Sister Mary Denise formed a special friendship, sharing many spiritual thoughts while she drove him to appointments, talking and praying together. She stayed with him for many hours during his final illness and was privileged to be with him during his transition from this life to the next.

Another friend, so close she describes her as a soul mate, was Sister Anne Ernstmann from Federal Way, Washington. Their relationship was formed over a period of many years as they worked together in federation assemblies, and it was profound and beautiful. Sister Anne died of ovarian cancer in 1993 while engaged in the painful process of overseeing the closing of the Federal Way Monastery. Sister Mary Denise flew out to be with her frequently during her last months, and the two women shared their remarkable closeness to the very end.

Sister Mary Denise's losses have been hard to bear, but she has endured them, strengthened by the same faith that led her to the convent door more than half a century ago. In 2009 she will celebrate her jubilee: fifty years as a professed sister. It's likely to be a grand affair; she has touched so many lives. The Archbishop is apt to be there, along with half the clergy in Saint Paul and Minneapolis, and other dignitaries. I, no doubt, will attend. Unlike this sensible nun, who probably hasn't given it a thought, I enjoy forming a picture of the party. I see her moving among the crowd of well-wishers, not staying too long at the head table receiving toasts. She will be making sure everyone is comfortable, asking if they need anything, inquiring after the health of their family members, whose names she unfailingly remembers.

I hope that the program will allow me to raise a glass and make a formal toast to her. I will say. "Here's to you, Sister Mary Denise. Thank you for sharing your gifts and teaching us to live in the present, taking no thought 'to what might happen tomorrow; the same everlasting Father who cares for you today will take care of you every day. Our good is found in the present moment which is today. Our life is the today in which we are living; we cannot promise ourselves a tomorrow." She will recognize the words from the teaching of Saint Francis de Sales, in whose footsteps she has so faithfully walked.

SISTER FRANCES

Sister Frances Betterman is the only member of the Mendota Heights community to have entered the convent after Vatican II. She was one of the "new" Catholics who had never learned the old Mass in Latin, never puzzled over the changing shape of the liturgies, never thought it odd that the priest faced the congregation instead of the high altar while celebrating Mass. The Lenten fast, with its mild regulations, did not feel like a penance to her. The Sacrament of Penance itself was called the Sacrament of Reconciliation and consisted of a friendly, guiltless chat between the little girl and her parish priest.

I told her about my First Confession, mumbled in a dark box to a nearly invisible cleric who must have been bored senseless listening to recital after recital of childish transgressions. Like most kids, I had written out a list of my sins, and my chief anxiety was that I would forget something and have to go back. I remember putting down that I had lied twenty-three times; how I cooked up that number to cover the first seven years of my life I don't know, but it must have seemed plausible at the time. My weary confessor certainly didn't argue with me.

Sister Frances and I laughed together, agreeing that the modernized Church is a lot more user-friendly now than when I was young. When she professed her vows as a Visitation nun, she was not asked to surrender her given name for a new one, nor did she wear a bridal gown and veil to signify her new identity as a bride of Christ. She did don a modified habit, a way of dressing that had been discarded by many other nuns. The monastery she entered in Federal Way, Washington, was one that had chosen to retain many of the older customs, including maintaining a strict enclosure.

"What induced you to seek one of the more restrictive communities," I asked her, "let alone one so far from your home in Omaha?"

"The answer goes back to part of the reason I became a nun in the first place. When I was nine years old, we visited my dad's relatives in Springfield, Missouri. One of my older cousins was a Visitation nun there, and one afternoon we went to see her. Her name was Sister Margaret Mary, and I loved her right away. We stayed quite a while and, when we left, she gave me a doll. Then she gave me an even better present. She said, 'If you write to me, I will answer.'

"I thought that was really something. Here's a grown-up lady who's actually interested in what a nine-year-old has to say! So we started a correspondence and it went on all through my school years and even into college."

"Did you write about religious topics and vocations?"

"No, I wrote to her about my classes, the games I played, my friends—later on my boyfriends—and she would just respond to my interests and tell me about some of the things she was doing from time to time. I didn't go back to see her for some years, but we kept in good touch by writing."

Frances was born in Omaha in 1957, the youngest in a family of three children. Her father had come from a prominent family of professional people; his relatives were bankers, lawyers and doctors, all well-known in the city.

"Dad shocked them all by breaking the mold; instead of choosing one of the professions, he became a firefighter. My grandfather and uncles tried to get him to go white-collar, but gave up when he married a nightclub singer. I think they decided it was time to accept that he had obviously chosen another way of life."

"Your mother was a nightclub singer?" I was astounded, although on reflection I could see that I must have my own stereotype of nuns. Their mothers surely couldn't be nightclub entertainers!

"Yes, but only until she married. After that, she didn't sing again. She said all that was behind her and she didn't want to do it anymore. She was a great mother; Dad was a wonderful parent, too, and I had a happy childhood. I loved to climb trees and roller-skate. I went to an all-girls high school and played varsity volleyball; you can see my athletic interests didn't die out as I grew older."

Sister Frances thought about her days in volleyball and started to laugh. "We had a terrible team. We were the worst team in the whole league. I was considered their star player; they called me their secret weapon, but it didn't do us any good. We had the distinction not only of never winning a game; we never even scored a point. We were the laughingstock of the other schools. You know, it's funny, but instead of feeling bad about it, it began to be a kind of honor point. We all just loved to play and had a great time in spite of always losing."

I could see another memory starting to sparkle in her eyes. She said, "I must tell you about the worst thing I ever did in high school. When I was a senior, we had a huge English project to do. It was a college prep course and the teacher was very strict— no velvet-glove type. We had a whole semester to prepare this project, but I was a great procrastinator and just wouldn't get at it. We were supposed to periodically hand in our intermediary work for her to assess in preparation for the big thing, but I never had anything to give her. I don't know why I was so stubborn about it; I just couldn't bring myself to do it.

"Finally, we only had about three weeks of school left and she called me in. She said, 'Miss Betterman, you are going to have to turn in your project or I cannot pass you in English. Do you realize what that means? Without this class you will not be able to graduate.'"

Frances was worried, but she still couldn't bring herself to do it. The week before school was to end, the instructor called her in again. "Miss Betterman, you apparently don't take me seriously, but I meant what I said. This project forms the largest percentage of your grade, and you will fail the class if you don't turn it in. I will give your name to the office and you will not be allowed to graduate." It was now five days before school let out, and she had done nothing.

"Did you tell your parents about the pickle you were in?" I wondered.

"No. I didn't say a word to anyone. And she wasn't the kind of teacher who would call home. She figured we were grown-up seniors now who should be able to handle our own responsibilities."

She went on to say that this was 1975, the year that Omaha suffered a huge tornado that ravaged the city. It was a terrible storm; the enormous main street was completely destroyed, and her high school was badly damaged. The roof blew off and water poured in. It was so bad the National Guard had to be called in to protect the neighborhoods from looting and other crimes. The administration of the school announced that anyone who had homework or projects outstanding did not have to complete them because of the tornado.

"Talk about divine intervention! I had been saved by the storm!"

"What an awful way to be saved!" I said. "Weren't you torn between relief and all that terrible wreckage?"

"I was such a brat that I wasn't sorry at all. The school set up a special stage so it could hold graduation exercises, and I marched across it and accepted my diploma just as if I had a right to. That poor teacher had to sit there and watch me do it too. I had no pity for her—I was awful," she grinned happily.

"Hmm," I answered. "So how did such an unrepentant soul wind up in a convent instead of a home for wayward girls?"

That long-ago visit to Sister Margaret Mary stayed in her mind. She thought about her cousin's life as a nun, and their correspondence had kept their relationship going. Also, as a student in Catholic schools, she was encouraged to be open to the idea of religious life. She said there was no big pressure, just the suggestion that the girls should not rule out the possibility.

"But I knew I had many options to consider about what I wanted to do with my life. I thought it would be wonderful to be a wife and a mother, and I also looked at the way my successful relatives lived in Omaha. I could see they had happy lives; they were financially secure and enjoyed their work."

Frances enrolled in at the University of Nebraska without a clear idea of a major, but was willing to look at different areas of study. She had always been a good student, her one foray into flirting with failure excepted. And she met a special boy there who loved her as much as she loved him.

"Randy and I were so right as a couple; we really were

perfectly suited for each other. He was a real gentleman, never once pushing me or trying to coax me into anything. One evening he offered to show me the most beautiful view in Omaha and took me for a ride to the top of the bluffs overlooking the city. It was a Lovers' Lane and there were a lot of cars parked there with kids making out, but we didn't do that. We just admired the view and drove back down. He wasn't the kind who'd bring a girl to a park with the expectation that they'd make out. He was such a wonderful person I could picture being married to him and having children, but I also had this vocation idea in my head that wouldn't go away. And I had read a book that influenced me greatly, *In This House of Brede*, by Rumer Godden."

"I know that book!" I exclaimed. "I can see why it would lead you to consider religious life. It almost affected me that way, and I had been long married when I read it." I well remembered how beautifully convent life was depicted in it. It was made into a movie starring Diana Rigg, and that inspired Frances to picture herself living as a nun.

"I knew I couldn't live both lives; I would have to make a choice. So I decided I should talk to my friend and relative, Sister Margaret Mary."

Frances wrote to her cousin, saying she would like to know more about religious life, and she was immediately invited to make a retreat at the monastery in Springfield, Illinois. She spent a week there, living with the sisters in the cloister, participating in their prayers, their meals and their recreations. It was unlike anything she had ever known before, but it felt utterly comfortable. It became more and more clear to her that she would have to go back. She belonged there.

"When I came home and told Randy, he was very dear about it. He said he always thought I might choose that life; he wouldn't stand in my way. It was my mother who took it the hardest. She didn't understand how I could do it. She wasn't

Catholic—my faith came from my dad's side of the family—and she thought nuns were strange creatures. She really loved Randy and knew he had a very good future; she wanted in the worst way for me to marry him and have children. My decision made her so sad. She always hated for me to tell this to people, but she actually cried for twenty-four hours, non-stop, when I told her my mind was made up."

I wondered how her father and brother and sister had handled the news.

Mr. Betterman was a man of very few words, so he didn't say much, but Frances felt that he was proud of her choice. His niece was a nun, and the idea of monastery living was not as foreign to him as to his wife. Her siblings had a typical reaction, saying she wouldn't stay, that she wouldn't last a year, that she'd be back.

"But I surprised them and stayed. I've been a nun for twenty-eight years now, and I still am."

"Did your mother ever get reconciled to your choice?"

"Oh yes. In time she could see that I was happy and that she wasn't really losing me after all. I would always love her and she could visit me whenever she was able. She and Dad were so okay with my decision that by the time I was accepted as a novice, they gave me a pair of roller derby skates instead of the usual bible or rosary. They knew that the things I had loved to do were not going to be choked off by convent life."

Frances was twenty-two years old when she entered the Visitation Monastery in Federal Way, Washington. She had planned to go to Springfield, but by the time she was ready, the number of sisters in the Springfield house had dwindled to twelve, and they had decided to close and merge with another community. Frances spent about a month in Springfield as an affiliate, meaning she could live in the community without being formally admitted. She helped the sisters pack up and get ready to move, running many errands for them. The twelve sisters in

Springfield joined the twelve living in Federal Way, so for awhile, they had a lively monastery of twenty-four nuns. Frances' cousin, Sister Margaret Mary, was among those moving to Washington, and Frances was delighted to be with her in the new environment. They remained close friends, as well as sisters, until Mary Margaret's death in 1997.

The Washington sisters had closed their school some years before the Springfield group joined them and had been dedicating themselves to providing weekend spiritual retreats for women. It was a fulfilling life for the young novice. Her novice mistress, Sister Mary Ruth, had had an unusually rich spiritual life, and she shared her experiences with Frances.

Sister Mary Ruth had originally been a Notre Dame nun in Omaha, but had felt called to leave her active order and enter one that was more contemplative. In the Visitation order she found the right match for her spirit. When the Springfield convent closed, she happily followed her community to Federal Way and was eager to guide Frances in her formation.

"It was the perfect environment for me," Sister Frances said. "It was a happy place, full of energetic sisters personifying our motto which is, as you know, Elsa, 'Live Jesus.' We really took that motto seriously, and let all our actions be permeated with the joyful spirit of Jesus. We had concrete benches out in our yard, and I used to jump over them—this way and that—just out of sheer exuberance. There was a huge asphalt drive and I roller-skated there. The newspaper came out and took pictures of the 'Skating Nun'; people in the city found it interesting to learn that we were real women who did things like that. Even though we were enclosed, we could go anywhere on our property, and that included a piece of the beach on Puget Sound. We were allowed to go to the beach and swim; we had neighbors on either side, but they were very respectful of our privacy and we never felt like we were being watched. I think they must have liked knowing we were having a good time."

She was happy with her new life in the monastery, but Washington was very far from Nebraska and she did miss her family. For the first few years, every woman who came for a retreat looked like her mother to her. That let her know she was homesick, even though she didn't always realize it. Her parents came to visit as often as they could, at least every year or two. They would have seen her more often had she located in Springfield as planned, but now that wasn't possible.

"I couldn't go to see them, of course. We followed the rules of enclosure so we only went out for necessary appointments. But it was great when they came to see me. We didn't have grilles in our community, as many convents did; we had what we called 'material separation,' which was a kind of railing or balustrade. We could reach over it and touch and hug, but we never went over it. It was one of the symbols of our separation from the world."

Her work kept her busy enough to hold homesickness at bay. She played organ and guitar for masses and daily prayers, eventually becoming liturgist for the monastery, and also worked in the archives. She enjoyed learning the history of the Federal Way house; the nuns had a school there for many years and even "adopted" several little girls who would otherwise have been in orphanages. They brought them up in the monastery, providing both schooling and parenting to the children.

Helping her sisters conduct the retreats was very fulfilling work as well. Theirs was a ministry that gave an especially generous service to women, particularly those of limited means. They charged as little as possible, just enough to cover the convent's expenses. For only thirty dollars, each woman had a private room and bath in the beautiful house for an entire weekend, and all meals were included. The sisters set up programs with priests who were retreat masters, shared their liturgies with their guests and gave them opportunities to consult and pray with the sisters individually. They continued this service as long as they could, but the order was aging and dying, and after fourteen years they simply didn't have the numbers to continue. They made the painful decision to close their monastery, deciding that each sister could choose where she wanted to go rather than trying to amalgamate again. There were only eight left, and four of them, including Sister Frances, opted to go to a second federation, or active, house.

"How did you feel about moving from the place that had been your happy home for so long?" I asked.

"The idea of a move actually felt good to me because change was exciting, but the closing itself was traumatic. Our Mother Superior, Sister Anne, was dying of stage four ovarian cancer and suffering terribly. We had to see her through that, and it was very hard. She knew she was dying and her monastery was closing; it must have been an awful challenge to her faith. She was very brave throughout, helping as best she could to direct all that needed to be done to close. She invited Visitation sisters from all the houses to come and choose things; Sister Mary Regina came from here and selected our beautiful statue of the Sacred Heart—the one that you see when you drive onto the property in Mendota Heights. It makes me feel good to know it's here.

"Sister Mary Denise was a great help to us. She and Sister Anne were very close and she came often to comfort her and pray with her. Knowing that she and Mary Regina were both here made Saint Paul/Mendota Heights an attractive place for me to come. Sister Anne died in March and we closed in July."

"And has it been a good place for you?"

"My choosing to come here was definitely a good thing, but the manner in which I did it proved disastrous for me. I didn't realize until much, much later that I hadn't given myself the time to process what I had been through. I didn't really grieve the loss of Sister Anne and how devastating and frightening that whole experience had been. I just put it behind me and assumed it would stay there."

Her coming to Mendota Heights shouldn't have happened that way; before the sisters left Federal Way, they each had a conference with a psychologist to get feedback on the choices they had made. Sister Frances talked to him about what she wanted to do, and he endorsed her plan with enthusiasm. He thought it would be great. So she jumped right in without making time for reflection, or for adjusting to the new expression of Visitation life that prevailed in Saint Paul/Mendota Heights.

She arrived at her new monastery in July and started classes at the University of Saint Thomas in August, planning to major in theology and minor in business. When she entered the convent in Federal Way, she had expressed a desire to finish her college degree, but because they were no longer operating a school they said she didn't need a degree to function there. She felt the new location would provide an excellent opportunity to continue her education.

She plunged enthusiastically into her classes, starting out well, but gradually losing both interest and aptitude. Her decline into depression was so slow that at first she didn't realize what was happening to her. A couple of years passed in which she grew steadily less able to enjoy or concentrate on her studies. She developed a negative attitude toward just about everything and withdrew more and more into herself. One day, she found herself walking in the meadow behind the monastery, thinking that she would just keep walking, going nowhere, but simply walking on; she realized that something had gone terribly wrong.

It was then that she saw how low she had sunk and it frightened her. She talked to the psychologist in the school, who suggested she consult a psychiatrist; maybe she had a condition that could be helped with medication or therapy or both. The school psychologist gave her the name of a woman she thought would be good for her, and Frances went to see her.

"I just fell in love with her; she had a strong, magnetic personality and I thought she was wonderful. That was a huge misjudgment on my part; she turned out to be the worst thing possible for me. She was very big on medication and not at all good at diagnosis. Within a year she had me diagnosed as not just depressed, but manic-depressive, obsessive-compulsive, schizoid and I don't know what-all other aberrations she said I had.

"This doctor started with anti-depressants, but when I told her they weren't helping, she would say, 'Let's try this.' But she didn't take me off the first one—just added to it. Some of those meds had horrible side effects, so she would give me more pills to counter the side effects, but still not take me off the one that was causing them."

Within a couple more years, Frances was on thirteen different medications. She was sent to several different psycho-therapists for talk therapy, but they didn't question the psychia-trist's opinion either. This well-known doctor enjoyed a very fine reputation among the medical community as a staff doctor and teacher at a highly respected hospital.

"What a dreadful experience!" I sympathized. "I can hardly imagine what it must have been like for you."

"And for the other sisters as well!" she added. "It was not only terrible for me, but think what a worry and disappointment I was to them. Here I was, their newest and youngest member— I was supposed to be this breath of fresh air bringing them new life, and instead I got steadily sicker and weaker than the oldest of them!"

The community and others became gradually more distressed, especially when they could clearly see that Frances was deteriorating to the point of being almost totally incapaci-tated. Her weight went up to 220 pounds—she had weighed

110 when she arrived. She could no longer play the organ or drive a car and even became incontinent, necessitating a move to the convent infirmary. The nurse would wake her up during the night and take her to the bathroom so she wouldn't wet the bed. Her vision became distorted so that she could no longer see a printed page clearly. She told the psychiatrist, who advised her to have her eyes checked.

"You're just getting older, Honey," she said. "You probably need to get glasses."

"Unbelievable," was all I could murmur. "Did you have any prayer life at this time? Could you ask God to help you through this?"

She laughed ruefully. "Prayer life? I had *no* life. I slept most of the time and had not only lost my awareness of God—I had lost my sense of self. I got so bad I developed Parkinson's-like symptoms and had to see a neurologist. He was pretty concerned—said he thought that the problem was that I was over-medicated and I should get a second opinion. He had me hospitalized, but my psychiatrist was on the staff of the hospital he referred me to, and her opinion prevailed over the neurologist's."

Sister Frances continued to deteriorate until 2004, when the decision was made to send her to the Mayo Clinic. All those who knew her were beside themselves with worry; they feared she was dying before their eyes. Mayo kept her for two and a half weeks, withdrawing her from all medications and observing her condition without them.

"They put me in detox because I was a junkie—as strung out on drugs as any addict. I went through withdrawal, which is a painful experience, believe me. But I became me again—I returned to myself! The doctors at Mayo, and I, found out who I was without any drugs, and we all liked me!"

"What did they say about your former treatment?"

"They couldn't understand what my psychiatrist had been

thinking. They told me I was toxic—my liver was affected and that I could have died if this had continued. They said I was not clinically depressed; I may well have been situationally depressed due to losing my monastery and to Sister Anne's tragic death, but they said I had never been clinical, nor did I fit any other of her many diagnoses."

The therapist who'd been treating her came to Mayo to visit her, filled with remorse for not having questioned the psychiatrist's judgment. She said she had kept thinking the doctor must know best, even though she could see Frances was getting worse all the time, not better. The school psychologist felt terrible, too; she, like everyone else, trusted this doctor's reputation and judgment. And Frances began to realize she, too, should have asked more questions about why she was given so many medications, but by that time she was so heavily into them she was really no longer herself. She didn't have enough will left to question anything; she just limped along in her miserable fog.

"What did your parents think of your state at this time? Did they visit you and see the changes in you?"

"They really didn't know how bad it got until it was all over. For the first couple of years I seemed to be pretty normal, going to school and getting involved in my new community. They could see I had gained a lot of weight and didn't think that was good, but they didn't put two and two together. Then during the next few years they could see I was very tired and out of energy, but they were aging and ailing themselves, and absorbed by their own health concerns. The last, and worst, couple of years I discouraged them from coming to visit me, so they couldn't see what a mess I had become."

"After you were released from the Mayo Clinic did you tell them the whole story?"

"Yes, I went to Omaha to see them and I told them everything. They were horrified. They felt terribly sorry that I had gone through such an awful experience, and they wished they'd known so they could have helped me. Maybe if they had known, something could have been done sooner, but then maybe not. Who knows? My mother was just entering her final illness when she learned of my situation. I'm so glad she was able to see me in my state of wellness before she died. She left this world knowing that her daughter had been restored to health."

Sister Frances now views her time lost in that fog as an incubation period and hopes that she is a better person for having gone through it. She does wonder why it took so long for her condition to be recognized and resolved.

I asked her if she had considered a malpractice suit against the psychiatrist. She said others have suggested she should file one, but she doesn't want to be involved in court proceedings that would keep her focused on the experience, wrapped up in the past and entertaining bitter thoughts, instead of concentrating on rebuilding the existence that has been returned to her. She feels that the life of prayer and service that she had so looked forward to when she moved to Mendota Heights was hijacked, and now that her feet are on earth again, she wants to resume that life.

She says she is really beginning to be a Visitation sister again. She's studying the organ seriously now. "And I can drive to my lessons!" she exclaimed joyfully. "I don't wet my pants—how's that for being a big kid? And another positive thing is that I have learned to have real sympathy for people who develop chemical addictions. I know how slowly and treacherously they can take over one's life, and how hard it is to recognize that you're trapped in them. That has helped bring me back to prayer; I pray for them and for their suffering." She paused. "But I am not spiritually prepared for true forgiveness yet; I still can't pray for the doctor. I hope to come to that. And I also hope that my doctors at Mayo wrote to her about my condition. If nothing else, it might protect other patients if it gets her thinking about what a big mistake she made."

Sister Frances does not plan to continue her interrupted college education, at least at this point. Rejoining the prayer life of the monastery and taking full part in the liturgies have been her greatest happiness. She is absorbed in her music and is also practicing yoga, experiencing the richness it adds to her spiritual life.

Learning to cook so she can be of help in the kitchen has been another pleasure. "Guess what?" she asked me. "I baked my own birthday cake this year and served it to the sisters. They thought it was wonderful! And I'm the new caramel sister too! When Sister Bernadette died, I took over her job. I make all the caramels that Visitation is famous for, the ones sold at the Merrie Market and other fundraising events, and I love knowing I can contribute financially through the sales we make."

Getting back to regular physical exercise as well as yoga has been another joy. Her roller skates got lost in the move so she doesn't skate anymore, but she bikes a lot. She walks every day in the lovely meadow behind the convent. She lost fifty pounds during the first year of her return to health and continues to work on her diet. She laughed and admitted she had to watch out for eating too many of her caramels or all that weight could come back to plague her.

"And I'm so glad to have my memories back; they were pretty much submerged in my drugged years. I think of Sister Bernadette and how helpful she was to me when I first came here. I had been wearing a habit for so long I had forgotten how to dress—how to choose clothes and fix my hair. She was such a loving, caring person. She gave me this sweater I'm wearing," she smiled, stroking the navy blue wool.

"I also think about Sister Mary Anthony a lot; she died during my illness so it didn't register strongly with me then. But

I admired her so much—she was one of those people who just do everything peacefully and perfectly. A sister once asked Mary Anthony if she had ever made a mistake saying the office. She thought a minute and said, 'No, I don't believe I ever have.' She wasn't bragging; it's just the way she was. That's unusual, I think, to be a perfectionist without being rigid or controlling. I'm so glad to be well again and able to remember the people who have been dear to me."

She looked sadly at me. "You lose more than just yourself when you're on drugs; you lose everyone else too."

Besides helping with music studies and cooking activities, she is pleased to have been appointed vocations director for the community. She has been working on creating a website, a vehicle for letting the world know more about the monastery. She is hoping, in time, to be more active with the students in the school, recognizing that it is an area one needs to enter cautiously.

"Young people don't like to feel that anything is being pushed on them. And I don't want to push! Goodness knows that's not how vocations are formed. My role would be to encourage them to keep their hearts open and their souls attentive. We all need to learn how to be aware of the Divine so we don't miss the whisper of God if He sends an invitation."

Sister Frances sometimes feels hopeful that women will, once again, see religious life as one of their options. At other times, she is deeply concerned that religious vocations may be a thing of the past.

"But would that be such a bad thing?" she wonders. "No one can read the mind of God, and it is possible that He may have other plans for ways to worship and serve Him in the future. If the time comes when there are no more sisters at our school in Mendota Heights, it will still be Visitation if the charism of Saints Francis and Jane persists. We are the only school in the country to have a director of Salesian spirituality; I think it's wonderful that we have put into motion the very mechanism to keep the Visitation spirit alive. I have more questions than I have answers, and I have concerns, but I do not have fears. The Holy Spirit will continue to guide us."

SISTER PÉRONNE MARIE

I approached my first interview with Sister Péronne Marie feeling oddly apprehensive. Not that she is an intimidating woman! She is warm and gracious, the epitome of courtesy. But I had long been aware of her intellectual brilliance, her scholarship, her archival research and translating work that have led to a significant number of publications. In 1996 she received an honorary Doctor of Letters from the De Sales School of Theology, and within the last few years I learned that she is also a gifted poet. Would I be capable of bringing her many talents to the page? Could I do justice to her complexities?

Sister and I became acquainted when I returned to Visitation in 1993 to become the upper school director. She and Sister Marie Thérèse guided me through the management of the school's traditions, including the graduation ceremony—a decorous, complicated ritual very unlike those in the public high schools my grandchildren attend.

At a Visitation graduation the girls *process* like brides, like debutantes, with measured, deliberate steps, each wearing a long white formal dress and carrying a bouquet of roses. "Girls," the sisters intoned at practice, "there must be no differentiation here. You are a class, a group, not individuals. You are to move in careful unison, like a lovely river flowing calmly toward the stage. Now, let's try again and this time, keep your eyes ahead and stand tall. No fidgeting or looking for your parents in the auditorium. You will greet them *after* the ceremony, at the reception."

It was my task to learn these words so that I could carry on the practice in the absence of the sisters. They were handing me the baton and relinquishing their place in the school. I could hear Sister Mary Regina's gentle voice giving my class the same instructions nearly forty years earlier, and it seemed like she was with me in the parlor today as I waited for Sister Péronne Marie to appear. "Don't be nervous," I chided myself. "It's just your friend, dear Péronne, and she will put you at ease as these sisters have always done."

I was not disappointed. Sister arrived and took my hand, saying that before we started she wanted to thank me for engaging in this work with them. "We are so grateful that you are here to help preserve our heritage," she said. "It means so much to us that you consider our vocation histories worthy of your time."

"And I consider it a privilege," I answered honestly. "I am honored that you trust me with your precious legacy."

She smiled brightly at me. "So, where would you like to begin?"

"At the beginning, why not?" I laughed. "Tell me all the things I didn't know about you when I worked here."

Born in 1923 and given the lovely name Laure, Sister Péronne Marie was the fourth of six children born to Joseph and Angeline Thibert. They were of French Canadian descent, as were many of the residents in their town of Fitchburg, Massachusetts, and they spoke French and English beautifully, a comfortable bi-lingual household. Laure's father was a dentist and her mother a talented pianist who did not perform publicly. Their first child was a boy, followed by two girls and then there were no more babies for several years. The Thiberts thought that perhaps their family was complete, but then another pregnancy came. It ended prematurely, and the family grieved the death of another girl. Laure arrived only a year later, so she was especially precious to them.

"In many ways I was an only child," she said. "After my birth, several years passed before two more boys arrived. They were born a year apart, so they formed one little grouping and the three older kids another."

"Did you mind being kind of alone in the middle?" I asked her.

"Oh no," she smiled. "Not at all. The older ones petted and loved me, and my little brothers were enough younger that I wasn't jealous of them. I had a very special place in the family—I was always Daddy's darling daughter."

She went on to tell me more of her past, emphasizing how fortunate she was to have had loving parents, grandparents, many friends in the neighborhood and no thought, ever, that anything bad could happen to them.

"We walked home from school at any time of the day or night; we never locked our doors. It was a security we never questioned. Now I look around me at our monastery and the school, and everywhere there are locks, bolts, identification badges." She sighed. "Those days are gone, but I don't forget that I was among the lucky generation."

Bathed in security and safety, the little girl gave scant attention to what future might await her. She lived joyfully in the present, attending the neighborhood parish school, going to Mass with her devout family and playing with her friends. She felt God's presence in her, but it was an almost unconscious awareness. He was simply *there*, His presence in her life as unquestioned as her breathing. She had no idea that there might be a religious calling cloistered within her spirit.

She also had no idea that a dark menace was hiding within her body, a condition that was to transform her from a healthy, rosy girl to an emaciated wraith, barely clinging to life. Until her seventeenth year, her life was uncomplicated, sweet and brimming with the unfaltering exuberance of the young.

She has happy memories of her high school years—at least the first three. It was a public school and not too big, just seven or eight hundred students, with a football team, yearbook and other activities. Laure was involved in many, especially drama. She wrote plays and skits for the school and also composed little poems from time to time. Certain images engaged her imagination, and she felt a need to write them down, to turn the pictures into words. Poetry was quietly finding a home in her soul.

"And there were boyfriends," she added, smiling. "Nothing serious, but oh, the thrill of being invited to Prom or Homecoming! I loved dressing up in pretty dresses and shoes, dancing and flirting a bit with my dates. Just being together with my friends was fun, and as I said, we could walk the two miles home from school without any thought of danger."

Laure was an excellent student whose good times didn't interfere with her studies, and she was excited about starting her senior year. After graduating she planned to attend Trinity College in Washington DC. And then everything changed.

As Christmas of that year approached, she became mysteriously ill. At first it seemed as though she had an unusually severe case of intestinal flu, but when it didn't go away her mother sent for the family doctor. Over a period of time he prescribed several remedies, including dietary changes, but Laure only became weaker. Unable to return to school when classes resumed in January, she attempted to keep up by studying at home, but it was difficult. She was not only weak, but in great pain much of the time. There were frequent hospital admissions, and life as she had known it ceased.

"I can still picture the big, burly boys from high school wading through the snow to the hospital," she smiled. "Every time I had a new crisis, the hospital called my school and let them know I needed another blood transfusion, and the football boys would come to donate. It was so precious of them to try to help me. My family and friends were wonderful to me through those awful times."

By spring she was living on blood transfusions and morphine, and it was evident to the family doctor that she could not continue under his care. Alarmed, he referred her to the Lahey Clinic in Boston in the hope that the mysterious condition could be treated. New sulpha drugs were being discovered, and each time one was introduced it was hoped it would be the magic that would cure her. But it never was. Laure was in and out of the hospital in Boston for most of the next year, undergoing tests and trying new drugs. She would improve for a little while with medicines and a special diet, but then the disease kicked up again and back she went to the hospital. The specialists recognized her condition as ulcerative colitis, an illness that causes painful sores and lacerations to develop along the length of the large intestine. Severe cramping, bleeding and weakness are its symptoms, and the accompanying weight loss can be perilous.

"What should have been my senior year in high school and my first year in college were so hard for me," Sister Péronne Marie sighed. "I had hoped to graduate normally and then go to

Trinity College in Washington, but instead there I was, shuttled between my home and the hospital in Boston. All my friends left for school, and I was very lonely and frightened. You have a lot of time for reflection when you're confined like that for a long period of time. There's no question I matured a great deal, but at what a price!"

By the following fall it appeared that she was well enough to try college, as long as she could follow a very restricted diet of boiled milk and strained vegetables. She did not dare attempt Trinity, as it was too dangerous for her to be so far from her medical team, so she went to Emmanuel in Boston with the Sisters of Notre Dame de Namur. For three years she boarded with a woman in Cambridge who was willing to provide her unusual diet. Having to board away from campus was a hardship, as she had to use four different vehicles to get to school: a bus from Harvard Square, then a subway into town, then another bus and still another.

"At least I became very familiar with Boston; I was determined to see this as an adventure, not a burden. I was just so glad to finally be on my way back to life, and my health did keep slowly improving."

When her diet became a little more normal, she was able to move to a residence called Student House, where she lived with about two hundred other girls from many different colleges. Only she and her roommate were from Emmanuel. The house was owned by philanthropic "Beacon Hill Bostonians," who provided elegant opportunities for the girls, even high tea every Friday afternoon.

"This was a very rarified atmosphere for me," she said. "There was nothing like that back home. Fitchburg was a paper mill town, a small city with its own hospital, good public and parochial schools and a fine public library. My father was a dentist there, very active in civic affairs, so don't think it was a backwater place with no cultural opportunities. It was good little city, but it was not Boston, and it was quite a switch from that life to be daintily sipping tea and having English scones with my new friends.

"You were either an Irish Catholic Democrat in one Boston or a Yankee Protestant Republican in the other Boston. The other Boston was, generally, of greater wealth. Many of the girls in the residence were definitely other Boston, and the nuns at Emmanuel did not approve of my living at Student House. The dean called me in and spoke to me, but I didn't change my mind. I loved learning about *both* Bostons and I wasn't going to pass up this chance. Most of my new friends were from the New England Conservatory so you can imagine the wonderful concerts I was able to attend."

Laure's health was better and she was enjoying life, but she still was not strong enough to carry a full load of courses. It took her six years to finish college; she was twenty-four when she graduated. That was more then okay with her; she had made it in spite of her health challenges and was looking forward to graduate studies, delighted to learn that she had been granted a Fulbright scholarship.

Then the bottom fell out of her life once more. After being symptom-free for two years, she suddenly experienced the cramping and bleeding again. The specialists knew that a sudden recurrence after a quiescence of two years often meant cancer. There was nothing to do now but submit to surgery, and she returned to the hospital.

It was a major operation during which her entire large colon was removed, and she realized that for the rest of her life an external appliance to gather waste would be attached to her body. The next months were the worst and hardest in her life. The first time she looked at herself after the surgery she was overwhelmed with grief. Removing the diseased colon had saved her from the threat of cancer, but the thought of living forever with a bag hanging from her side plunged her into deep sadness. She felt that she would never be a normal woman again. No one would ever find her lovely, and how could she wear pretty clothes with that *thing* attached to her side?

"A dear friend of mine, an older woman, counseled me when I confessed my terrors to her. I will always be grateful for her reassuring words. She said to me, 'Oh no, my dear, you must never feel that way. Your body is an alabaster vase, holding your spirit, and you will know you are as beautiful as ever when you remember that.'"

Her words would eventually penetrate Laure's despondency, but it took a long time. My heart ached for her as, nearly sixty years later, she described her pain to me.

"Those were profound years for me spiritually. I had to learn about acceptance. But it was so hard to *really* accept a burden of this size. Wasn't God asking too much of me? Then I gradually grew aware again that I was not completely alone in this; that God was present in that mysterious way He has always been.

"And the clinic was wonderful. This was before there were such things as formal support groups, but they brought together others who had had the same surgery so we could learn from each other how to handle our condition. This is a disease that hits young people and we were mostly students. We were lucky in that a new skin cement had been invented, and that made the whole thing much less disfiguring. We loved it because it allowed us to wear normal clothes and dress nicely." She smiled ruefully. "I was so young—still at an age when a girl thinks the most important thing in the world is a pretty dress. But looking back, I can see how the whole experience helped me see what really matters in life, and it is not appearance."

Laure and the other young patients were pioneers in forming a support group, and they started planning to make a movie. They wanted to show themselves swimming and dancing, doing all the things that young people love to do. Their film would give hope to others who shared the same trauma. When she first started with the group she believed she could never lead a normal life, but now she saw that she could live fully and help others do so, too. But before the film was completed, a thrilling opportunity presented itself to her—so good that she left her hospital group to start this new adventure, and the others made the film without her.

One of the ladies at Student House had taken a special interest in her, recognizing her unusual intellectual talents. She helped her get a job at Newton College of the Sacred Heart, run by the Religious of the Sacred Heart. Laure could hardly believe she had been accepted as a teacher. Just barely out of college and without even a master's degree, there she was, teaching drama and contemporary theater.

She admitted to one of the sisters that she feared she was only one page ahead of the students, but the older woman just laughed and said, "Never mind that. Just help us civilize them."

She lived on campus and loved being with the nuns, becoming more and more attracted to their way of life. God's presence hummed ever more steadily into her inner life, and she began to wonder if she might have a religious vocation. Perhaps that interior awareness of God she had known all her life had always been a silent invitation. She talked with some of the sisters, and they encouraged her to open her heart and listen to the noiseless voice within.

The Mother Superior who had hired her, Louise Keyes, was convinced Laure would make a perfect Religious of the Sacred Heart and arranged for her to be interviewed at the mother house in Albany, New York. Laure took the train up from Boston, her heart singing with the image of the bright new life she knew awaited her. Never before had she felt such a sense of such joyful anticipation that she was on the right path.

The experience was a disaster. At first the Mother Provincial who interviewed her was very warm and interested, but when Laure told her of the surgery she had had a couple of years before, she became quite distant. The Mother Provincial was called out of the room, leaving Laure sitting there alone and bewildered. When she returned, she told Laure coldly that she must not consider entering their order; her health would never permit her to lead the kind of life they did.

Laure was devastated. She had dared to believe that she was a normal woman, one who could meet whatever challenges were placed before her. She had so clearly pictured herself as a Religious of the Sacred Heart, but now, huddling miserably in her seat, she carried the wreckage of her self-confidence on the train back to Boston that very night. There was no point in staying in Albany to learn more. The rejection had been total.

"I always think of this as one of my many sagas of pain," Sister Péronne Marie said slowly to me. "I really had wanted it so much, and I had been decisively turned down. It felt brutal. When I returned to the Newton campus, the sisters were horrified at how I had been treated. They all said that a terrible mistake had been made, that they had it all wrong in Albany. They had seen how I performed and knew I could keep up with their activities. They felt almost as bad as I did."

Laure began going into Boston more frequently. She still taught her classes at the college, but it hurt to be with the sisters and know that she could never be one of them. She was welcomed at the old Student House, where she had lived before starting to teach, and she stayed there many weekends. Being there helped her recover from the rejection, and the fear that she would never be considered normal began to dissipate.

During one weekend, a friend invited her to go to Dorchester to hear a lecture. On the way home they had such a good time talking that she missed her subway stop and realized the error couldn't be corrected in time for her to make the house's eleven o'clock curfew. The friend suggested they get off at Brookline, where she knew a group of Holy Cross nuns who would allow them to stay overnight in their convent. The sisters were engaged in giving weekend retreats and invited the girls to come back in a couple of weeks, when they would be hosting a Capuchin priest, Father Gabriel Diefenbach, to lead a retreat.

The feeling that she had a religious vocation would not leave Laure's mind, but she was afraid to entertain it. The Religious of the Sacred Heart's rejection of her had been too painful for her to risk a repetition, and she thought that putting aside all thoughts of religious life was the wisest thing to do. Yet it seemed like something was telling her to go and meet this priest with the name of the angel who had come to Mary. Would there be an *annunciation* for her in this meeting? She decided to trust her interior voice and went back to Holy Cross to the retreat. The moment she met Father Gabriel she knew that voice had been authentic.

"It's very hard to explain," she told me. "When our eyes met, there was immediate electricity between us. I could see he felt it, too. Something extremely out of the ordinary was happening. The best I can do is to say it was like looking at the face of God for the first time and I was..." she searched for the word. "I was dazzled. I was aware that I was in the presence of great holiness. Something very strong spiritually was going on, and I realized this man was to have a great influence on my life. I couldn't think what it was to be, but I knew I should not lose contact with him. We exchanged addresses and agreed to keep in touch; our correspondence was infrequent but always charged with some new spiritual insights for me. I just knew something was to come of that meeting between us."

Still uncertain about her life's purpose, Laure began graduate study at the Bread Loaf School of English in Middlebury. She was attracted to both teaching and nursing as careers; she had

had so many hospital experiences that medicine was appealing, and she had been inspired by the great kindnesses of the doctors and nurses who had cared for her. But English was her first love, and she decided to start there. She was now twenty-eight years old. It was time to send up some trial balloons to look at career opportunities instead of longing for a convent she couldn't enter.

Bread Loaf provided the most intellectually stimulating atmosphere she had ever known. Gifted poets, essayists and novelists lectured there; Robert Frost lived right up the road, and his genius hovered over the campus, permeating it with creative energy. The pulse of literature was beating there and it invigorated the students. Laure resumed writing poetry.

Many of her classmates at Bread Loaf were from the Midwest. Meeting with people who were not from the East Coast changed her view of where she should be. She loved the mid-westerners, finding them refreshing, honest and intellectually curious. Marquette University in Milwaukee had a highly regarded graduate school, and one of her best friends had married a man who taught at Saint John's University in Minnesota. And, to make the Midwest even more attractive to her, one of her sisters was living in Chicago at the time. Laure applied at Marquette and was quickly accepted to the graduate program in English there.

"Middlebury could have been hard to leave," Sister Péronne Marie said to me. "Not only was the atmosphere exhilarating, but I met a man there with whom I was much taken."

"Ah," I responded. "I notice a sparkle in your eyes when you speak of him. Were you in love, Sister?"

She smiled. "It probably wasn't love, although it certainly felt like a convincing imitation of it at first. We were so *very* strongly attracted to each other—he to me and I to him—that I would just see him walking on campus and I would go weak all over. He was forty years old and a fascinating man; our attraction to each other was strong and compelling. And remember, I was not an eighteen-year-old feeling her first little heart flutter. I was twenty-eight with the capacity for the deep feelings of a grown woman.

"He was an exotically handsome man with the reputation of having any woman he wanted. I think he was intrigued that I was not willing to give in, in spite of my obvious desire for him. He wasn't used to being rejected."

"What kept you from giving in?" I asked.

She answered easily. "It was because even with the excitement, there was this ingredient that was missing, something that transcended my attraction to him even though it was so powerful. That pervasive feeling that I belonged only to God would not leave me, and he respected my belief, thank goodness.

"I look back on it as my 'pagan summer,' knowing now the Lord was protecting me for some amazing things yet to come. I escaped from the enchantment. But it was very good to have experienced it, because I know how easy it would have been to succumb, and then I would have missed the true life of my vocation. I knew what I was giving up in terms of sexual attraction and the whole thing, and it has been important for me to know that. I came through it by the grace of God."

Laure moved to Milwaukee, soon settling seriously into earning a master's degree. Marquette was everything she had hoped for in a graduate program, and she was able to visit her sister in Chicago frequently. She arranged her schedule to work two days a week in the hospital as a nurse's aide, thinking she could test her attraction to a medical career versus teaching. It soon became apparent to her that she was happier in an academic setting, so she felt that she had at least that certainty to sustain her.

"Where were you in your spiritual life during this time?" I asked. "After ending your romance and moving away were you still hoping to become a nun?"

"My desire to become a nun was still there, but I tried to put it away from me because the experience at Sacred Heart had taken away all confidence that I would be accepted anywhere."

"I can imagine it must have been confusing to keep thinking you had a vocation to religious life but no monastery in which to live it. Did you pray a lot during that time?"

"God was with me, but it's hard to articulate my prayer life for you. You know, I'm still not very great at devotions. I mean, they're fine, but they're somebody else's way, not mine. For me it's something very simple. It's just *presence.* God was just *there.* It was that knowing that made my break-up with my dashing admirer inevitable. Maybe someday I'll be able to express it better through poetry."

During that first year at Marquette she did a lot of spiritual reading and became acquainted with the writings of Mechtilde of Magdeburg, considered to be one of the greatest and soundest German mystic nuns of the Middle Ages. Her poetry was very significant for Laure. Péronne now showed me one of Mechtilde's poems that she had underlined more than fifty years earlier to illustrate the great impression the poet had made on her.

The Soul and God

> Your glory pours into my soul
> Like sunlight against gold.
> When may I rest within you, Lord?
> *My joys are manifold.*

Then she handed me her response, not written until October of 2001. It had simmered silently in her soul all those years, and then one day it asked to be put into words and released. Sister's first verse follows:

To Mechtilde of Magdeburg (C. 1207–1297)

I walked into your poetry
long years ago
as into a vast cathedral
—Cologne, perhaps,
I heard the organ roar
deep chords
that rumbled through my feet,
thundered in my throat,
—arpeggios leaping, pirouetting up, up beyond the
    spires, wild,
dizzy with delight.

It was evident that Laure had grown profoundly spiritual; she was thirsting to realize her religious vocation, but did not know how. Then, in February of that year, she received a letter from Father Gabriel saying he was coming through Milwaukee and had a couple of hours between transferring from his bus to a train. He hoped they could meet for lunch at the depot and talk some more.

"Everything between Father Gabriel and me was out of the ordinary, and the way that meeting came about was another instance of it. We agreed to meet, and I went at the appointed time and waited, but he did not show. I can't remember now if I waited in the bus or the train depot—they were right across the street from each other—but I finally concluded that we must have somehow got our signals crossed, and I came out of the station. Just as I came out the door, he was doing the same thing from the other depot, and we saw each other. It was like something out of a movie with our waving and laughing and running across the street to meet each other.

"Thank goodness, there was still time for lunch, and we had a wonderful talk. I told him I believed my 'vocation thing' must be over, but then I happened to mention that I was going to meet my college friend in Saint Paul over Easter break. The moment I said 'Saint Paul,' he said, 'You must go and meet my good friends, the Visitation sisters there.'"

Laure had never heard of the Visitation sisters and reminded him that she was trying to put all this "sister stuff" behind her. But he persisted, saying she had to meet this wonderful Mother Teresa Dougherty, who was Mother Superior at the time. Then he stopped speaking and a remarkable expression came over his face. He looked as if he were having a vision and he said, "Oh! If I could just see you there among them!"

She knew something extraordinary was happening to her again. It was that dazzling sensation of being in a holy presence that she had experienced the first time she met Father Gabriel face-to-face.

After that, she knew nothing would do but to follow his urging that she meet the Visitation sisters. She had an anthology called *Soul of Fire* that listed great religious leaders from Plato to the present. She got to F and found Francis de Sales, then to J and Jane de Chantal, and to M where there was Margaret Mary: the great saints of the Visitation Order. Intrigued, she went the next day to the musty old library stacks in the university to find a book on religious orders. There, in the smelly, moldy volume she read of Saint Francis and how he wanted to establish an order for women who wished to be nuns, but who had been rejected for being unable to follow the austerity of the rules. These women needed a monastery in which to live out their religious callings. Laure had never heard of such a thing and was excited to read that he did not consider perfect health necessary for inclusion. She signed the book out and began to look forward to meeting the Visitation Sisters of Saint Paul.

On Easter Monday, 1951, she approached the rather forbidding dark building at 720 Fairmount and rang the bell. A nun's face appeared behind a small, grilled panel in the door, regarding the visitor through its round glass peephole. The door swung silently open and she was invited to enter. It was formidable—almost spooky—and Laure shuddered at the austere formality. What was she getting into?

She was ushered into the parlor where she saw, for the first time ever, the grille that separated the cloister from the external world. It was the day after Easter so there was no school and the place was very quiet. She thought to herself how wrong the Capuchin priest had been about her.

"This guy doesn't really know me after all," she thought sadly. "Ugh," she almost said aloud, "this place is not for me."

Then Mother Teresa Dougherty, who was both charming and disarming, entered. They had been chatting pleasantly for a few minutes when Laure said bluntly, "Well, you know why I'm here. I've read that you could not dismiss me because of ill health."

The moment the words were uttered, she was mortified. How on earth could she have blurted out such a tactless remark? What must Mother think of her? But the Mother Superior appeared to take no notice of Laure's boldness and continued speaking with her pleasantly. Then she invited her to stay for lunch and meet a few of the community members afterwards. Talking with the sisters in a small group, Laure felt a sense of peace and belonging and realized with surprise that this feeling was what she had been seeking. The uneasiness that had dogged her for so long—the sense that something was missing—had disappeared.

"Once again, it's something I can't put into words for you," Sister Péronne Marie said softly. "It was an inner thing—I can't explain it—just a feeling that I was as sure of then as I am here, now, today. I had gone from 'ugh' to 'yes' by two o'clock.

I knew I belonged there. I *belong* here," she smiled, amending the tense.

"I told Mother Superior that I would like to quit school and come in right away, but she gently said, 'No, dear. It would be better for you to finish the semester and get your credits.' I was so naïve—of course they would want me to come to them as well-prepared as possible."

Now she had the task of telling her parents. Here she was approaching the age of thirty, and as far as they knew she had never had a thought in her head of becoming a nun. They knew nothing about her Capuchin friend, nothing at all about Visitation. What were they going to think?

She wrote to them and told them the whole story, beginning with, "Please sit down when you read this letter." It said she would be visiting her sister in Chicago the following weekend, and they could talk on the phone from there on Sunday evening. She wanted to feel ready and she wanted them to be prepared, too.

"My brother-in law made me a good, stiff drink to help me handle it. I was so nervous—I was sure my father would be beside himself. I was his little daughter, and how could I desert them for a cloister and on and on. I built myself quite a dramatic case, expecting the worst, but the response I got was beyond anything I could have imagined. The very first thing my father said to me was, 'How would you like to go to Annecy before you enter?' I was more than stunned; I was flabbergasted. I had expected this big explosion but instead, out of the blue, he was offering, not just Europe, but Annecy!"

When the Thiberts had received their daughter's astonishing letter, their first thought was to take it to their parish priest to ask him what he knew about Visitation. This priest was a very old man who had come from France many years before and, as it turned out, had been born in the Savoy region of France, the area of Saint Francis de Sales. He told them about Francis and Jane de Chantal and the Visitation Sisters, including the monastery at Annecy.

Joseph and Angeline could hardly believe this coincidence—no, it was more than a coincidence. The history of the Visitation Order had been laid in their laps. They saw it as the grace of God in operation and realized that their Laure had found her purpose in life. After going with her to Annecy that summer, they came to Milwaukee in the fall to pack her up and bring her to Saint Paul.

Laure entered the convent in the autumn of 1951 and made her first vows two years later. She was one of four in the novitiate, older than the others but finding them compatible nonetheless. The hardest thing was wearing the dress of a postulant—a schoolgirl dress and blouse with dark stockings and a short veil.

"I looked ridiculous! Here I was nearly thirty years old and dressing like a child in that horrible outfit. I was never so happy as when I shed those clothes and received my adult habit."

My own desire to be well-dressed made me sympathize with Sister's aversion to unbecoming clothes. Renouncing the world is one thing, but it shouldn't have to be done frumpily! Winking at each other, we shared the conspiracy of women who admire elegance in dress.

Besides knowing she looked ludicrous, she was given the task of helping out in the English and French departments with sixth seventh and eighth-graders. That was very tough for her; all her experience had been with college girls, and she couldn't get over how silly the sixth-graders were.

"And the seventh and eighth-graders were even worse! They weren't as silly, but they were smart enough to see how nervous and uncomfortable I was with them, so they made it their business to get to me in as many ways as they could. I remember one awful day when they somehow arranged to have all the window shades in the classroom fall down at the same time! I was so startled I screamed, and they laughed and laughed at my embarrassment. It was a humiliating experience. At the end of the first semester I went in tears to my novice mistress, Sister Mary Helen, and begged her to release me from that awful job."

"And did she?"

Sister Péronne Marie laughed at the memory. "No, she didn't, but it was only for that first year when I was a postulant, and it was only for a part of the school day. I was definitely happier at the end of each day when I could go back into the community and be with the sisters. And the next year I received my habit and settled into novitiate life, so there was no more teaching during that period. I became fond of the sisters so quickly. Sister Mary Regina and the others were amazing women—so bright, dedicated, devoted to their work and to each other. There is no question that the bonds of affection among the community members were strong and authentic, and our shared life was very beautiful. In spite of my initial troubles with teaching, I never wavered about my decision to enter. My vocation remained central to my life, and I happily made my final profession in 1956."

"That was the year I graduated from Visitation," I said, surprised. "I never realized we were there at the same time."

"That's because you were in the school and I wasn't teaching. In those days the paths of the cloister and the world didn't intersect often. After your class graduated, I did teach again in the high school, and those were much better times. I experienced the peace and belonging I had been seeking, even back when I didn't know what it was I was after."

In the years ahead, Sister Péronne Marie was to face more health challenges. She was diagnosed with the same breast cancer that ended the life of one of her sisters, and she returned to Boston to undergo a double mastectomy. As in the case of the ulcerative colitis that had plagued her young womanhood, her spirit prevailed and she survived the disease. The days and seasons passed quickly, and soon the '60s and Vatican II appeared on the horizon of the sisters' lives. Like all religious orders around the world, they began receiving questionnaires about their constitution and about updating. There was much paperwork and a lot of need for discussing the questions, and the Saint Paul house was also preparing for their move to Mendota Heights.

"Those were very turbulent times—we were so incredibly busy. Sister Mary Regina was Federation President at the time, and she was dreadfully overtaxed. We had so many decisions to make; for example, were we to have grilles in our new monastery or not. It looked as if we would not, but we had to wait until official word came down, so the parlors were fitted with them, and then we had barely moved in and had to have them taken down. Little stuff, but it could drive you crazy."

I asked her to tell me about the federations and how they came to be. She explained that after World War II, when many European cities had been bombed and convents destroyed, there was a great need for all sisters to help each other financially. Federations were formed within certain geographic areas to give mutual help in everything. In America, because it is such a large country, the Visitation Sisters were divided into two groups. Those who were strictly cloistered became the First Federation and those who had schools in an active apostolate became the Second Federation. The Mothers Superior of the various convents formed a federation council so they would have more unity in governance and procedures. Then, because of the many federations in Europe, a sister from Spain was appointed Mother General of the entire order, worldwide.

Sister raised her eyebrows. "*That* did not go over one bit, I can tell you. Saint Francis originally had each of our houses autonomous, and so it was very much *not* part of the Visitation spirit to have a central authority. Here was a Spaniard, living in France at Annecy, totally ignorant of most European and American customs and the many differences between them. For instance, the convent in Rock Island, Illinois, had never had grilles separating the monastery from the extern area, and now they were told to put shutters on the windows. She told us to do the same thing when she came to visit us, but we ignored her. Politely, of course, but Mother Jane Margaret was not going to be ordered around. That period of having a Mother General didn't last long. The French didn't like it and wouldn't put up with it either. We are not a docile order. I think the Spanish nun was relieved to have it over with too; nobody likes to have to give orders to those who resist them. Now, as we look back on it, it was hilarious, but at the time it was maddening and confusing.

"This ambiguous period lasted several years. We were trying to update as fast as we could, and because I was bilingual, I was constantly called upon to translate what our Spanish/French Superior was saying—what a mix-up! When Mary Regina was elected Second Federation President, everything had been terribly mixed up for years.

"We moved out here in 1966, and I was made Head of School. In those days that meant I had the whole piece. I was responsible for admissions, development, bookkeeping, college transcripts for the girls, Montessori, busses—everything! I began to see that it was all just too much; there would have to be delegation of responsibility into different areas. In some of the things I was required to do I had no competence. And besides, we were trying to get used to this huge new place. After dear little Fairmount it was like being in a big echo chamber, and we had to learn our way around the building. And in the meantime, I continued to translate all the stuff that was coming over from France."

"It sounds like a wild time," I said. "Was it then that you started to reorganize the school and select distinct duties for the various departments?"

"It was and that turned out to be very good for us. For one thing, it meant we had to hire more laypeople and that began to prepare us for turning over our control of the school. As you see, we are almost entirely staffed by laity now who do a beautiful job of carrying on the Salesian tradition. The spirit of Visitation is being expressed without our direct involvement in the classroom and that is wonderful. It gives us such hope for the future of our school."

During those busy years it was decided that there was to be the first general assembly ever of the order. Constitutions, answers to questionnaires, procedures—all had to be gathered from the different countries. This came down from the Vatican to all the religious orders, and Sister Péronne Marie was required, in the first year of being in the new home in Mendota Heights, to go to Rome. She was part of a small group of six or seven sisters from different countries who coordinated the materials and prepared for the first general assembly. Their commonality, besides being Visitandines, was that they could all speak French. Some of the European sisters didn't have much to say—they just wanted to leave things the way they were. But of course, the independent Americans had plenty to say and sent manuscripts outlining their many suggestions. On seeing all the boxes of written matter assembled in her room, she despaired of ever getting through all of it.

"I really couldn't see how I could accomplish the task, it was so huge. I thought, 'I'll never get out of here! Will I ever get home? This could go on for months and I'll *never* get back to Saint Paul!' But I got through it, of course, and was even able to help some of the others—we all stayed together at our Visitation Monastery in Rome; we still have one there—and it was wonderful being with all those sisters from so many different countries."

The following year, the first general assembly was called, and she was delegated to go back to Rome with Sister Mary Regina, who was Second Federation President. It turned out to be one of the best times of their lives. The two women were already close friends, but the shared experience strengthened their relationship and they had wonderful times together.

"Everybody loved her, of course. Regina was one of the most charming women who ever lived. But she bloomed and expanded even more over there. For one thing, the European houses always served wine at table, and she wasn't used to that. She'd have a few sips and just begin to glow! She was so engaging and endearing anyway, but with a little wine she became positively eloquent and even wittier than usual. I cherish the delightful memories of our time in Rome together.

"A lot came out of that first assembly, and it all had to be written down. I did much of the writing in French and English so that took a good deal of time over the next years. Then, sometime in the '70s, we called a second general assembly, and I was sent again. By then most of us here in Saint Paul had modernized our habits, and I could see that the Italian nun who had been so fond of me ten years before was scandalized. I had only a short veil and my legs were showing, and I think it took about a week before she could look at me."

As more changes were initiated, some sisters rethought their vocations and left religious life. During those years Sister Péronne Marie was assigned to help them discern their direction. She considered it a great privilege to assist in bringing these young women to their own truths.

"Of course, we felt sad when we lost someone, but I believed it was for the best because each person must find her unique way to God. And we had always been so careful of whom we admitted, that we perhaps lost fewer than some of the big orders. Those were difficult times, very demanding on us as it was such a drastic change from the way we had been before. Now when we lost Sister Mary Frances Reis in 1989 that was different. She didn't leave the Visitation Order; she left our community to help establish the Fremont Foundation in Minneapolis.

"I was very close to Mary Frances—I had assisted in the novitiate when she entered, and I was Mother Superior at the time she left. I missed her terribly, but I was fine with her decision. I have no doubt that she did what was right for her, and that is what we all must do."

With the new foundation set up in Minneapolis in 1989, life returned to something like its former pace. Smaller convents closed and new sisters moved to Saint Louis, to Georgetown, to Saint Paul and to other communities.

Sister Péronne Marie has long been involved in academic research and has written scholarly essays and books about the Visitation Order and its particular Salesian Spirituality. As she approached her seventieth birthday in 1994, she prepared an essay called *Journey to Integration* for the annual Salesian Conference that summer. It was a prescription for, and summary of, the well-lived life. When she delivered it to the audience of Visitation Sisters, Oblate Priests and laypeople, they were stunned by its beautiful simplicity and profound wisdom.

Her premise was based on the words found in a journal entry of an early Visitandine, a sister who was a close companion to Jane de Chantal. She had written, "The art of dying well is so difficult to learn that it takes a lifetime to learn it."

Sister Péronne Marie asked her listeners to reflect on the word, *art*, which implies that a level of skill has been reached; the apprenticeship is over and the artist now has the freedom to express within the medium. Living skills, like all techniques leading to mastery, must be practiced over and over. Their practice leads to the development of those strengths that grow out of adversities and sustain us in the midst of them. At last, the steps themselves no longer seem laborious, but have become a free and natural expression of creativity. Living is an art, and so is death, its mirror image. The fear of death will drive us, unless we learn to transcend it and understand that it is not an end, but a beginning.

I have included a special appendix at the end of this book to define, in Péronne Marie's words, the steps, or virtues that have had particular significance to her life's journey, especially as she travels towards eternity.

Research and scholarship are important to her, but poetry has been the mainstay of her spiritual life and feeds her soul. Like God, it was just always *there*, even when not actively pursued. She tells me she cannot summon poetry; that she doesn't trudge along in it the way she does in academic work. Even as a little child she wrote poetry and continued to do so on and off throughout her college days and her years in the convent. It's just something that has always been a part of her.

During the summers of 1962 and 1963 she participated in two seminars offered to teachers of French. A well-known French writer, Claire Huchet Bishop, moderated and mentored the conferences and, under her tutelage, Péronne found herself writing poetry again.

She said of those summers, "I didn't know myself where it came from, but I just kept writing and Madame Bishop thought highly of my work. She was the kind of teacher who touches a student's most sensitive spot and calls forth the very best. We stayed in touch through the years—she died about twenty years ago—and she could always tell which of my poems were worthy. They were all in French, of course, so they haven't been widely read, but it is a solace to me to know they are there.

"Earlier, when I became so busy translating documents from the Vatican, being Mother Superior, doing this and doing that, there would be long periods without poetry, but then something would light the spark and get me going again."

She told me that she had discovered the poetry of Denise

Levertov and had been profoundly affected by her work. The two women never met, but Sister Péronne Marie feels as though they are intimate friends, that their spirits have met at the level of poetry. With a smile, she opened a volume of Levertov's to show me her picture, saying that the first time she saw the photograph she had impulsively kissed it.

"When Levertov died in 1997, I felt as though I had lost a dear and personal friend. I still feel very connected to her spiritually, even though she is no longer here."

"Are you writing poetry at present?" I asked her.

"I want to be," she said eagerly, "but I am somewhat torn away from it by my latest interest, which is more academic. I am working on a study of Calvin's successor, Theodore de Bèze, a Protestant Reformation figure who lived at the time of Saint Francis de Sales."

About ten years ago she became acquainted with a French Canadian Jesuit scholar, René Champagne, at a research symposium. In 1998 he published a piece containing studies of contemporaries of Saint Francis, including de Bèze, and he sent Péronne a copy of his book. She put it aside and nearly forgot it, but last year she came across it and decided to translate it into English. She was already interested in de Bèze, having learned of him years ago while studying in the archives at Annecy.

Annecy contains a wealth of material on Calvinist Geneva, and Péronne Marie was fascinated to see how alike Saint Francis and Theodore de Bèze were in temperament. John Calvin was a stormy individual, but Theodore was gentle and compassionate like Francis, and she believes that if the two men were alive today, they would be friends, engaged in dialogue and ecumenism. They would reach out respectfully and try to understand each other, but in the seventeenth century they could be nothing but enemies, each regarding the other as heretical, and they competed with each other for souls. Theodore converted many Catholics to

Calvinism, but Francis was a check to him in bringing Calvinists back to Catholicism. Little is known of the man even in Protestant literature, and Sister Péronne Marie enjoys the challenge of delving more deeply into his life. It delights her at age eighty-three to still be able to make a contribution academically.

She would be further along in her writing if another serious health concern had not hampered her in the summer and fall of 2005. Surgery was required to correct a hiatal hernia, and complications developed that nearly took her life once again. She is gradually regaining strength and manages to accomplish a little more each day.

"You just keep on in the face of these awful health problems," I said with wonder. "I admire your courage and tenacity in the face of all the pain you have suffered."

"Maybe it is because poetry isn't far away," she answered. "It's very life-affirming and I hear it calling me. My latest spurt began in about 1995 when I went to the hermitage at Pacem in Terris, the place we sisters use for retreat. It was winter, and I was finally quiet again, ready to listen to my heart speak. During that time I wrote a series of Advent poems that a Jesuit priest at Saint Luke's Parish in Saint Paul printed in his bulletins and read at his services, so many people came to know my work through the publicity he gave them. I was quite honored.

"And just two weeks ago, another Jesuit called to let me know he had done a day of prayer with a group of women and used my poetry for meditations with them. Just when I'm having a dry spell and think perhaps my days of writing poetry are gone, I'll suddenly get something like this phone call, and a new idea springs to my mind. I can't force it—it's either there for me or not. My work on de Bèze is absorbing, and scholarship keeps bubbling within me, but there are two or three images sitting like yeast in the dough of my spirit, and I know I will have to do something with them."

"I would love to read more of your poetry," I told her. "I've seen your occasional pieces in the *Vision* magazine from the school, and you've shared your poem on Mechtilde, but I want to become acquainted with the rest."

She replied, "Well, here's a start." She looked through the small stack of papers she had brought to our meeting, and then handed me a little booklet called *Small Songs for Silence*. As I opened its front cover, I saw the words, "I 'heard' these small songs to silence in my heart during my retreat at Pacem in Terris. Péronne Marie Thibert, October 8-17, 1995."

As I took the booklet from her, I felt a kind of tingle pass between us. There was something alive in the pages, some vibration of spiritual energy. Hesitantly, I began to read her own work aloud to her. I read:

Small Songs for Silence

I
Some find you dull,
Dreadfully boring;
No, others say,
downright disturbing.
But I know better.

II
Shall I let you in today?
Let you see the clutter in my heart?
Let you hear the stupid din?
Of course, I shall! Come in!

III

You were my mentor long ago,
　　(did you know?)
Taught me to wait most patiently
When all was new,
Taught me to answer without fear
Whenever love drew near.
You were my mentor
And I grew still.
Empty, I learned to wait until
Love chose to fill me to the brim—
Sun-splash of laughter
And of song.
　　(did you know all along?)
You are my mentor now as then.
How do I thank you,
Precious friend?

IV

I learned to trust you, silence,
On the day you took my hand
And led me to a land
I'd never seen before.
We climbed a high, high hill,
And there you said, "Be still."
I listened and I looked about,
Not knowing what
You wanted me to see.
I listened and I looked some more,
And then I saw! Walking toward me
In a field of sun-filled grain,
The one I had been searching for.
I learned to trust you on that day.

V

Here is my last song—the smallest one of all:
You are the hollow reed
Through which I call.

The room was very still, and as I read, Sister Péronne Marie's face began to glow. These were not blushes in the usual sense; the skin of her face and neck appeared radiant, highlighting the strong bones underneath. As I finished, her face dissolved in brightness and she bowed her head for a moment. The room was very still, yet charged with the electricity of her brightness.

Then she looked up, moved her face slightly, and murmured, "To hear you read them to me…" but she did not finish her sentence. I couldn't speak either. Then we smiled and, at the same moment, reached for each other to embrace. Our souls had met at the level of poetry; the universal voice had spoken through her and touched us both. My initial fear of telling her story had vanished. I had become the hollow reed through which she called.

THE JOURNEY CONTINUES

This book would be incomplete without the inclusion of Sisters Mary Frances Reis and Katherine Mullin. They professed their first and final vows at the Saint Paul Monastery on Fairmount Avenue and moved with their sisters to Mendota Heights in 1966. Each made important and lasting contributions to their beloved community and to the school.

Sister Mary Frances left Mendota Heights in 1989 to join three sisters from Saint Louis in establishing a new Visitation Foundation in North Minneapolis. The four women, with the support and blessing from the Visitation Federation of the United States, had discerned a call from the Holy Spirit asking them to "Take the Visitation to the poor."

In the late '90s Sister Katherine began to experience thoughts and feelings leading her to wonder if she, too, were being called to join the Minneapolis Community. After much prayer and discernment she left Mendota Heights and moved to Minneapolis for two years, the time granted to each Visitation Sister trying her vocation in a new monastery. In 2002 she was formally accepted into the Minneapolis Community where she remains today.

The new foundation celebrated its fifteenth anniversary in 2004, and Sister Frances wrote these words for a booklet commemorating the occasion:

> *The Visitation Monastery of Minneapolis was founded in the fall of 1989. Years before, it was conceived in prayer and discernment as a desire to express the mystery of the Visitation in a new way—a commitment to be one with economically challenged and marginalized persons.*
>
> *We are present on the North Side to "live Jesus" by being part of this multi-cultural community—to share prayer, hope and God's blessings. Our friends are drawn into a circle of faith that brings us all to a clearer vision of the face of God.*
>
> *We recognize our need to protect and nurture the contemplative and communal quality of our life in order to witness more clearly to God's love through our ministry of presence.*
>
> *As we reach out to support and comfort others, we recognize our need to be supported and encouraged.*
>
> *We dream that the liberating spirit that is part of our charism will foster the "prophetic" in all of us. We will show gentleness and offer peacefulness to the community, if only for a moment.*
>
> *Our ministry is to LIVE JESUS in our urban monastery (where) we choose to reach out in a special way:*

1. *To companion and affirm those who are impoverished and lonely—those living on the fringes of society.*

2. *To support those committed to a ministry of peace and justice by sharing our Salesian Spirituality with them.*

3. *To educate and network with those who, in being materially secure, seek ways of growing in faith, hope and love by bridging with people in our multicultural community.*

4. *To provide spiritual formation for those affiliated with us in a variety of ways.*

In 1994 the Visitation Sisters of Minneapolis founded a lay community to help extend their ministry in North Minneapolis. It was first called the Visitation Neighbors as it was made up of laypeople living in the vicinity of the monastery. This group expanded and is now called The Visitation Companions since it consists of participants both from within and beyond the neighborhood. The members do not make religious vows, but they assist the sisters in their work.

In 1995 the community welcomed its first new member, and by 1998 it became necessary to purchase a second house to accommodate more entrants. By 2003 the community's membership had doubled.

The spring of 2008 saw the opening of Saint Jane's House, a rental property that welcomes visitors who wish to spend extended time with the community, gaining spiritual guidance from the sisters as they help fulfill their mission with the disadvantaged.

The final two chapters of this book contain the vocation histories of Sisters Mary Frances and Katherine. Through bonds of spirit and affection they remain deeply attached to their original Saint Paul/Mendota Heights Community, where their vocations were informed and nurtured. It was in that setting that they heard the voice of the Holy Spirit calling them to carry the Visitation to the poor. Like Mary, who left her parents' home to bring Christ to her cousin Elizabeth, they left their mother monastery to carry His extraordinary light and love to a new, ordinary place.

SISTER MARY FRANCES

The seventh-inning stretch of a Brooklyn Dodgers' double-header in Pittsburgh was interrupted by a loudspeaker booming the news of the birth of a baby girl to professional baseball player Bobby Reis. It was Father's Day, June 20, 1937, and Bobby had been eagerly awaiting news of his wife back in Minnesota. As a professional ballplayer Bobby traveled with his teams and was often gone from home. He had left orders with the hospital in Saint Paul to notify him as soon as his wife delivered their child.

It was an unusually public announcement for any birth, but especially for a girl destined to embrace a private life as a cloistered nun. Mary Frances was the third child born to Bobby and Gertrude Reis. The first, Bob, was born in Saint Paul where Gert had grown up, and the second, Susan, in Long Island, New York. The young couple had moved to New York to be together as a family while Bobby played, but they were not there long when it became apparent that Gert was too emotionally fragile to be separated from her former, familiar environment. She suffered from profound anxiety and the attacks worsened in places new to her. Bobby felt compelled to ask his brother, Vincent, to drive out and rescue her—thus did she return to Saint Paul with Vincent, eleven-month-old Bob and newborn Susan.

Gert was only two and a half when her mother died, and she and her older sister, Franny, were uprooted from their home and family. Their father, a carpenter, was tubercular, and the treatment at that time advised living in the cold woods of northern Minnesota. He felt such isolation was not a good environment for the motherless little girls, so they were placed with relatives. When Gert was five and Franny eight, one of their aunts became engaged to a wealthy lumberman. She said she would marry him only if he promised to send her two little nieces to Visitation Convent in Saint Paul. He was willing to do this, and the nuns took the girls into their boarding school where they lived until they graduated from high school. They returned to the woods to visit their father just once a year during the summers; Gert considered Visitation her only true home until she married Bobby.

The Visitation Sisters loved and nurtured the little girls, but in spite of their efforts Gert suffered greatly from separation issues. The move to New York was more than she could handle.

"I believe my mom was psychologically wounded from those early years," Sister Mary Frances told me during our first interview session. "She had a great fear of abandonment—she wasn't a fearful person as such—she could go out in tough neighborhoods and face things in general, but it was a deep down fear that kept her uncertain of her place in the world. She had very little self-confidence. Daddy loved her and was willing to live permanently in Saint Paul; he saw that it was a better environment for a family than being on the road with a team, and he also had a real affection for Saint Paul with its small-town atmosphere—small enough that you could run into people you knew, but big enough to be a real city.

"How did he earn a living?" I asked. "Did he give up baseball entirely?"

"No, he played full-time for the Saint Paul Saints until his retirement. He never went back to the big time even though his career had looked more than promising. I'm not glamorizing my father—his career is noted in baseball history. He was famous for having played not only all the positions in one season, he once played all the positions in one game. He played for the Brooklyn Dodgers and the Boston Bees and, I think, Toledo as well; he was a great utility player."

"Did your mother's emotional health improve when your family settled in Saint Paul permanently?"

"It certainly was better than in it had been in New York, but her anxiety never completely went away. She medicated her pain with alcohol, which made her even more unstable at times. We looked like a normal family to our neighbors and, you know, much of the time we were. That's what made it so unsettling for us; we never knew when anxiety would overtake her and everything would go upside down. Mom was a very loving, compassionate woman and she adored us kids. Eventually there were six of us, and she took wonderful care of us most of the time. She was a great cook and a really talented seamstress—she made every stitch we wore—even our coats and jackets. Our friends loved coming to our house because she was so much fun to be with. She was a wonderful listener."

Their father dearly loved his wife, and he treasured the good times the family had together when she was functioning well. He did not ignore the difficulties, but managed to focus on Gert's many positive qualities. She was so innately loving in spite of her problems that Frances feels the children emerged relatively unscathed. Having witnessed during her formative years her mother's anguish, she developed a deep compassion for those who suffer, a compassion that serves her well today. She rejects the stereotype that an alcoholic or an emotionally wounded person can't be a good parent.

"You see," she said. "I saw how she struggled. After I entered the convent I gave her holy cards printed with one of the prayers of Saint Francis de Sales. It's the one that says, 'Do not look forward to what might happen tomorrow; the same everlasting father who cares for you today will care for you tomorrow.' Mom was so anxious she had that prayer posted in three different places in the house—on her bedside, the TV and on the refrigerator. She would say it every fifteen or twenty minutes some days, trying to keep her panic at bay.

"What a combination of love and suffering she was! She was flawed, as we all are; we are all blessed and we are all broken. I identified her suffering love with that of the heart of Christ; I saw how love and hurting can go together."

Even as a small child, Mary Frances had a special affinity for the Heart of Jesus. It was He to whom she prayed on the nights she cried in bed after a particularly hard time with her mother. She felt that He heard her, comforting her by a very real sense of His presence.

During her first year of college at Saint Catherine's, she also received some practical, psychological help. In a psychology class she was introduced to Dr. William Glasser's psychiatric self-help primer, *Reality Therapy*. Glasser's thesis is that we choose much of the misery that comes to us by continuing to repeat the same ineffective behaviors over and over. He asserts that we get unconscious gratification by believing we are victims of our circumstances. When we deliberately change our attitudes, the circumstances may not change, but our ability to handle them does.

"The book changed my life," Mary Frances told me. "I had never read anything like it before, and for the first time I realized I could *choose* the direction of my life. I could be a victim of the dysfunction and pain caused by my family situation, or I could choose not to let it drag me down. It was a great gift—it gave me the power to take charge. It taught me that while one cannot change events, one can always choose how to deal with those events. I chose joy."

The choice of joy was a natural one for a young woman who had always been prone to search for the positive in situations. If her mother were still sleeping when she got up for school, as happened frequently, she would get ready quickly and head for Saint Luke's Elementary School, frequently staying late to postpone returning home. There she could just be Frances Reis, not Frances Reis who came from a dysfunctional home situation. She got along well with the Sisters of Saint Joseph, who were her teachers, and loved being with her friends and classmates. She didn't try to be an exceptionally good student—just good enough to get by. Having fun was more important.

Art was one subject she took seriously. She remembers how wonderfully special she felt in first grade when the children were assigned to draw a mural of the Stations of the Cross for Lent. Sister announced that all the students were to take part, but in each station only Frances Reis would be allowed to draw the face of Jesus.

"You can imagine how special that made me feel," she laughed. "Only *I* was good enough to draw Jesus. But I got my comeuppance in third grade when I wet my pants in class and was humiliated. Sister was busy at the blackboard with a project, and she had ordered us to take out our math and work without a sound until she was finished. We all knew she meant business, and it would probably mean staying after school if we interrupted her.

"I didn't dare tell her I had to go to the bathroom, and the urge kept getting stronger until I couldn't hold it any longer. I let go. There I sat in my puddle and it began to drip onto the floor. Billy O'Rourke noticed and called out in a loud voice, 'Sister, Frances Reis wet her pants!'

"Sister whirled around and yelled at me in front of the whole class. She said, 'Frances Reis, you go straight to the janitor's closet and get a bucket and mop and clean up your mess!'

"I was completely mortified, as you may imagine. You don't forget those lows in your life. Years later I ran into Bill at a wake and he said, 'Do you remember when you wet your pants in third grade and I told on you?' We laughed about it then, but it wasn't funny at the time. One good thing that came out of it was that when I started teaching, I never, ever refused a kid permission to go to the bathroom."

While still in elementary school, Frances sometimes felt drawn to the convent. She remembers telling her sixth-grade teacher that she thought she might like to be a nun someday. Sister was very pleased and said she would make a wonderful Saint Joseph sister. Frances immediately corrected her, saying that her choice would be Visitation, not Saint Joseph. She didn't even know the Visitation Sisters yet, but she thought they must be wonderful. Gert Reis was a gifted storyteller, and she often entertained her children by telling them about her old boarding school days.

One story Frances especially loved hearing again and again was of the time the day students made a secret feast for the boarders and delivered it to them at midnight. The boarders tied knots in the sheets and lowered them out the window, where the day students placed the many baskets of treats to be hauled up. But they had neglected to include utensils, and Gert was chosen to sneak down to the sisters' kitchen to get them.

Tiptoeing up the stairs with knives and forks, she was

caught by Sister Jane Margaret, who had heard noises and went to investigate. She charged up to the boarders' quarters with the guilty Gert in tow and was astonished to find an enormous quantity of food laid out, the knotted sheets still lying on the floor. The girls expected to be scolded, but to their amazement, Sister just stood there and then started to laugh.

She said, "Well! I've never seen anything to beat this. I guess anyone who goes to this much trouble to have a party deserves one." She turned and left, and the girls fell on their midnight feast, giggling with delight over Sister's forgiveness of their mischief.

This and other stories lived vividly in Frances' imagination; what came through to her was the *humanness* of the sisters. Visitation sounded like paradise. Saint Luke's was okay, but in her heart she wanted to attend Visitation Convent School. They were not a poor family, but they weren't affluent, and to attend both elementary and high school at Visitation was out of reach. Gert was determined, though, that her daughters would go there at least for high school, and she convinced her husband that they could afford the tuition. She would save money because she wouldn't have to make the many different outfits needed for public schools. The same uniform could be worn for an entire year.

Susan enrolled there, and when her father saw what a positive effect it had on her, he was convinced his wife had been correct. Frances was delighted as her future was now assured.

"I loved Visitation," she said. "I made good friends there, and I followed my old pattern of staying late after school many days, just hanging out with the girls and the sisters. I wasn't particularly pious, although I loved the Mass, Benediction, the hymns and the whole Catholic culture. It was seeping into me— although I didn't think seriously about being a nun again until my senior year.

"One day when I was on a ski trip, a really close friend told me she thought God was saving me for something special. That started me thinking again, but until just before my freshman year in college at Saint Catherine's, I didn't talk to anyone about it. During the summer before I started college, I met a guy at Saint Luke's summer camp where I was a water safety instructor and counselor. This guy was one of the other counselors. He had been in the seminary, but he had dropped out and he became very interested in me.

"We saw a lot of each other that summer and after school started, and I told him some of my thoughts about maybe having a religious vocation. He was a wonderful guy, and I really liked and admired him, but he wanted a serious relationship and I just wanted to be friends with him.

"Then one Sunday in October of my sophomore year, while I was at Mass at Saint Luke's, I received what seemed like a message. It's hard to describe because it wasn't audible, but it was very, very real and I heard it in my heart. It was almost what my friend had said on the ski trip. The voice I heard said, 'I want you for myself.'

"I knew I had to talk to someone right away, and I thought of Father Quintan Kennedy, who was saying Mass that day. We knew each other well because I had a part-time job in the rectory, helping serve meals and clear dishes. I told him I really had to talk to him and he said to come to the rectory at 12:30 that day. Equipped with cigarettes for courage, I went and I stayed for nearly three hours."

Father Kennedy knew that Frances had a special relationship with the camp counselor and assumed that she wanted to talk about him. Instead, she spilled out all the inclinations towards religious life that she had experienced on and off for years. As she talked, what she had to do became very clear to her. Later she told Father she owed the articulation of her vocation to him, but he said, no, he had only listened.

Frances went to see Mother Jane Margaret, the same Jane Margaret who had caught Gert with the silverware so many years before. She said she was ready to come in if they would have her, but admitted to having one big concern. Because she had been in their school for four years, Frances knew all of the sisters well, and there were a few she didn't much like. She asked Mother Jane Margaret if she had to like them all. Jane Margaret laughed and said that would be impossible. "You can't like everyone, my dear. You just have to *love* them. They are two very different things."

In January of 1957 she was accepted as a postulant at Visitation in Saint Paul.

When Frances told her mother she planned to enter Visitation Convent right after New Year and would not be returning to Saint Catherine's for second semester, Gert Reis was astonished and bitterly unhappy. She could not understand why her daughter would leave her family to live in a cloister.

"Why do you think she was so opposed?" I asked Sister Frances. "She lived in that convent for twelve years herself and couldn't say enough good things about it."

"I know," she answered. "It was hard for me to understand then, too. My sister Susan has told me since that Mom was sad because becoming a nun meant I would never have a family of my own. But I also think that Mom had many guilt issues about the chaos her condition caused for all of us. I think she wanted to deny that, but to have a daughter choose to separate herself from her made her face some of her own flaws and worry that she had been a bad mother. And that is really sad, because it wasn't at all the reason I was going. I didn't see myself as leaving my family; I saw it as a going *toward*, not as a running *from*.

"I asked her not to tell Daddy; I wanted to find the right time and right words to do that myself, but she didn't honor my wish. I discovered that one night when he and I were sitting on the couch together watching TV and he said to me, 'Frances, why would you want to lock yourself up for life?'

"That was the first and last word from my father about my vocation for ten years. He wasn't exactly against it; he just didn't get it. He didn't try to talk me out of it—he believed in a 'live and let live' philosophy—if that was what one wanted to do, well, do it.

"After about ten years, though, he called me to tell me a buddy of his had cancer and asked me if I would be willing to pray for him. That was the first time I saw he realized that nuns do have a purpose—praying for others is one of our jobs. I knew then he was proud of me. He always supported me, came to all my events, but he never understood the life. Back in those days we were so separated from our families. They could come to visit once a month for one hour. He hated that."

"How did the ex-seminarian boyfriend take your announcement?" I asked.

"He was disappointed, but he understood. He had experienced the tug of a vocational call too, and he realized I had to answer mine. On Christmas Eve we went to Midnight Mass together and stayed out until five in the morning talking. I slept all Christmas Day until late afternoon and was horrified to see the time when I woke up. It was my last Christmas home, and I had slept through it! That was really awful."

Frances had hoped to enjoy her final cigarette on the drive to the convent, but the whole family went to see her in, and they drove in two cars. With all the shuffling to get everyone in, she wound up in her father's car—not what she had intended. He hated cigarette smoking, and the girls never smoked in the house; he wouldn't allow it. Her plan had been to ride with her more lenient mother, but she landed in the other car instead.

"Tough luck," I commiserated. "The prisoner is supposed to get a final meal before execution, and you wanted a final smoke before entering."

She laughed. "That's exactly how I felt. But I did get a last smoke many years later. The day before my aunt, Fran Reis, died, I visited her in the hospital. She was a lifelong chain smoker and didn't plan to give it up on her deathbed. She asked me to give her a cigarette, but when I placed it between her lips and lit the match, she was too weak to make it draw. I took it from her and put it between my lips and stepped behind the door. I lit it there and dragged on it enough to get it started for her. Then I held it for her and she was able to finish it. So I did get my last smoke, years after I lost interest in smoking. Aunt Fran would have enjoyed the irony, had she realized it."

Frances loved her new life in the convent. The old traditions were still in place and her romantic heart found beauty in them. The silence at meals, the gracious gestures and the singing of the Divine Office behind the grilled wall in the chapel infused her soul with devotion. She described her first year as feeling like a honeymoon; everything was perfect. During her second year she was hit by homesickness and cried often, but was not tempted to leave. She knew the homesickness would pass, and it did.

She continued her college classes both at the convent with visiting professors and at Saint Catherine's. This was still pre–Vatican II, but the sisters were allowed to go out for instructional purposes. She also was active in Visitation's school even before completing her degree. Teaching Montessori and primary school were personally rewarding to her. She did this until 1980 while also attending summer school to obtain a master's degree in theology.

After Vatican II the rules of cloister became more flexible, and the sisters began to travel beyond their home city for educational reasons. Sister Frances chose Saint John's University in Collegeville, Minnesota, for her studies in theology, after which she left her beloved little children in the lower school to teach religion in the upper school.

"Those were tumultuous years," she mused. "So many good things happened, but change does not come easily and there were hard times, too. I was among the first to change from the traditional habit. The first day I came out of the chapel in my new outfit—worn with permission after community consensus—one nun called me aside and told me that I was no longer a Visitation Sister. That hurt.

"We went through a phase where we had to wear the full habit in the chapel—I was constantly changing clothes. It seems almost humorous now, but at the time it was very confusing and upsetting. What kept me going were the Jane Margarets, Mary Reginas, Mary Patricias. It was their humanness that bore me up in spite of the difficult sisters and the arguments over customs.

"One day I took one of our elderly sisters, Mary Consolata, for a walk in the garden. She was so far gone into Alzheimer's by then she could hardly put a sentence together anymore, but she must have intuited my inner turmoil. She said to me, 'You would never be happy anywhere else.' I considered that an oracle straight from the Lord. *Walk in the garden. Keep walking in the garden.*"

With more freedom to move about in the world, Sister Frances began to see that while the cloister had provided great opportunities for spiritual growth, there were things that were not good about it. She saw how removed she had been from her family and how that had affected them. Her younger sister, Mary Jo, had been only seven when Frances left home; Cindy was five. On one occasion Mary Jo told her that she had never really considered Frances part of the family. That was painful to hear.

When her father lay dying, she was allowed to visit him in the hospital, visits that reinforced how wounded he had been by her absence. One day as she sat with him, she said, "Guess what, Dad. I got to go home yesterday."

He answered, "Frances, does it take your dad dying for you to come home?" She had thought her news would please him but instead it only heightened her awareness of the pain he had suffered over her absence from the family.

On another visit, she saw that he needed a shave and offered to do it for him. He looked disgusted, saying, "What could you possibly know about giving a man a shave? Susan will shave me when she comes—you couldn't possibly know how."

Frances had believed that it was she who had made the sacrifice when she entered the monastery; now she perceived how much the people she loved had to sacrifice. When her father died, she was able to attend his funeral and was profoundly grateful to participate in grieving with her family. In 1973, with her mother and her siblings, Bob, Susan, John, Mary Jo and Cindy, she stood at her father's grave. She was the first member of the community to venture out for a family funeral.

Her eyes misted as she described the pain she had witnessed when Sister Mary Denise's father and, later, her brother, died. "She bore it so bravely," she said. "There was no complaining, but I could feel her loneliness at being separated from her family at those times. She could neither give nor receive the comfort they all needed—it was time—and past time for these old rules to be amended."

In spite of the challenges of change and the flaws she saw in the cloistered life, Sister Frances was happy with her teaching assignment and her life in general. She taught religion to the upper school students and eventually chaired the religion department. Campus ministry was a new concept, one that wedded belief to action, and she embraced it with enthusiasm. Instead of confining faith to the classroom, with abstract discussion of how it could be realized in daily life, campus ministry emphasized tangible outreach. She founded the first campus ministry program at Visitation, setting up opportunities for the girls to participate in community projects to assist the poor. She also organized trips to Haiti, where they could see personally the havoc that dire need creates in the lives of those facing it. They worked among Haiti's poor, helping in clinics and schools, and returned home with increased awareness of a world beyond their own.

Meanwhile, in Saint Louis, two Visitation Sisters were simultaneously experiencing puzzling feelings. One day in 1978, as Sister Karen Mohan knelt to pray, she heard a voice saying, "Take the Visitation to the poor." These words began to come to her frequently, and she finally confided in one of the other sisters, Mary Margaret Mackenzie. Sister Mary Margaret asked her if she had been talking to Sister Virginia Schmidt, but no, Karen had mentioned this to no one else. Virginia had come to Sister Mary Margaret with the identical words. She too had received this message.

Sister Mary Margaret was not the superior at the time, but she was recognized by her community as a kind of "wisdom woman," and it seemed natural to go to her with this kind of thing. She brought Sisters Karen and Virginia together and said, "I think the Holy Spirit is trying to get something through to us—we had better pray."

These three sisters began meeting on Sunday mornings for an hour of prayer. They were all interested in social justice and had responded with joy to a formal church pronouncement titled *Pastoral Letter of the American Bishops on the United States Economy*. In the letter the bishops strongly urged that more attention be paid to the economically deprived. It spoke of a "preferential option for the poor," meaning that the plight of the marginalized must be publicized and addressed.

For nearly ten years these three sisters prayed, asking the Holy Spirit for guidance in responding to the message they were hearing. They visited other individuals who were working to better the lives of the poor. For three summers they spent two weeks living in the inner city of Saint Louis, where the economically challenged people accepted them as neighbors, never questioning why they were there. It was becoming clear that they were not being asked to start a new school or a hospital or a food shelf, but to take the *spirit* of the Visitation to the poor. They were to go and live their lives of prayer and community among the neediest members of society.

These three sisters were on the Visitation Federation's task force on social concerns. Within the order it was commonly known that Sister Mary Frances Reis of Saint Paul/Mendota Heights was also interested in these issues, and she was invited to be on the task force with them. Together, after much prayer and study, they made a two-pronged presentation to the Federation. One was a set of guidelines for each one of the monasteries. The other was the announcement of a need for a new foundation of the order.

Creating a new foundation is a major undertaking for any religious order. It means demonstrating the need for its existence, getting permission from the bishop to leave one's community, receiving an invitation from the bishop in whose diocese it is to be placed and building or finding a new monastery. Usually, when a new foundation is made, it is done by the members of one monastery. This was no longer possible due to the diminishing numbers of sisters; it would create a great hardship for an order already short on personnel.

Nevertheless, the superiors met in the fall of 1988 and voted to establish a new foundation. Mother Philomena Tisinger of the Georgetown Community was the president of the federation, and she felt strongly that the Holy Spirit was guiding this inspiration and must be answered.

It was made known that any sister who was interested could apply. The federation president and four council members were appointed to assess the suitability of the applicants to ensure they were healthy, both spiritually and psychologically. One needed to be strong and stable to live in an environment of poverty and violence.

There were a few sisters who went through the interview process, and four were chosen: Mary Margaret, Karen and Mary Virginia of Saint Louis and Mary Frances of Mendota Heights/Saint Paul.

"What caused you to apply to be part of the new foundation?" I asked. "You were happy in your community of origin and with your work in the school where you could see the difference the campus ministry was making in the lives of your students."

She thought quietly for a bit. "You know," she answered, "it was very much like my first call to become a Visitation Sister. I felt a silent but strong, message asking me to become part of something bigger than myself. The day it all came together I was at Mass in the monastery in Mendota Heights, sitting on the side of the chapel where the organ is—you know how you always remember exactly where you were at significant moments in your life—and I went up to receive the Eucharist. As I took the cup I got an intuitive message that said, 'I have prepared a contemplative heart in you, Mary Frances. Now take it to the poor.' That was my moment of confirmation. So although I loved teaching and I loved my community, it was like all of that was preparation for this.

"Even as a little child, I remember having a real affinity for the poor. Maybe it was because we were kind of poor—not poor like they are in this neighborhood, but poor compared to some of our neighbors and my classmates. And the dysfunction in my home gave me compassion for those who feel different, less privileged than others. That was a preparation for this, too. If we only ask the Lord what it is that we are meant to learn, we always gain enlightenment from the things that cause us suffering."

Feeling confident that she was meant to be part of the new mission, Sister Frances and the others clearly saw that the question was no longer *if*, but *where*. Together with the five federation council members and a facilitator who was well-versed in the discernment process, they made a retreat in the countryside near Saint Louis.

After studying how to come to a decision via spiritual discernment, they went off separately and prayed, each taking along a little slip of paper on which to write the revealed answer. When they reconvened and shared the results, there were six for Saint Paul/Minneapolis and three for Saint Louis. This was something of a surprise, as there were three sisters there from Saint Louis and only one from Saint Paul. The facilitator instructed all to go off separately and pray to the founders, Saints Francis de Sales and Jane de Chantal. When they reconvened, it was unanimous—all for the Minnesota Twin Cities location.

After that, things progressed rapidly, with the four sisters receiving help from the many friends of the community who wanted to be of assistance. One group studied demographics to determine which city, Saint Paul or Minneapolis, should house the new monastery. Their conclusion was that North Minneapolis should be ruled out; it was too dangerous. But the sisters felt they still needed to examine all options—it was the Holy Spirit who was to guide this, not a committee.

Other friends took them to visit the churches and social service agencies in the areas they were considering: Frogtown in Saint Paul and the South and North sides of Minneapolis. The sisters went on midnight rides with the police in each district, listening to their descriptions of the crime statistics and poverty levels.

They went to the hermitage *Pacem in Terris* (Peace on Earth) often used by the Visitation Sisters when they need a secluded place to pray for direction.

"Now," Sister Mary Frances said to me with excitement, "this feels like the time to tell you of some of the signs and wonders that accompanied us on our search. Things happened that we could not just dismiss as coincidences. On the way to establishing ourselves here in North Minneapolis, we received encouraging affirmations from each of our three saints.

"As you know, our order venerates three special saints, Francis de Sales and Jane de Chantal, of course, and also Margaret Mary Alacoque. She was a Visitation Sister in France in the seventeenth century who experienced visions from Our Lord. She is known as 'the Saint of the Sacred Heart' because she received revelations from Christ that she was to be His instrument in spreading devotion to His Sacred Heart. Our order has always had special devotion to the Sacred Heart of Jesus.

"Our first sign did not come from her though, but from Saint Francis, speaking through Sister Péronne Marie, who was our superior at the time. Sisters Mary Margaret, Virginia, Karen and I made a retreat during which we were to come to a final decision on our location. We had such trouble coming to unanimity that we prayed to the Holy Spirit for a dream—we even went to bed with pencils and little slips of paper under our pillows, but no one had a dream. We kept coming up with three votes for North Minneapolis and one for Frogtown. We had a majority, but not consensus, which was deeply disturbing to us. Finally, the sister who believed she was hearing the message that it was to be Frogtown said that she would cast her vote with the others. It was the only way to resolve the impasse, and she felt the Holy Spirit must be telling her to change.

"We were relieved to have reached a decision, but our hearts were heavy, not ready to celebrate and rejoice. Because we had wanted consensus, we felt disappointed and unsure. We had brought a special recording of the *Magnificat* and a bottle of wine for when the great moment came, but none of us felt like it had arrived. Still, I called Sister Péronne Marie, as arranged, with our decision but, before I could give her the news, she said, 'Oh I'm so happy you called. Tell me your decision, and I must tell you about the most phenomenal dream I had last night!'

"At her words, I began to cry, and turned to the others and told them that Péronne had received the dream we had prayed would come to one of us. Then they all started crying—you should have seen us—so happy we were laughing and crying at the same time.

"'You had a dream?' I exclaimed, almost dropping the phone. As we told her our decision, she was not surprised. She said, 'Your decision was my dream. I kept hearing over and over again these words: IT WILL BE NEAR NORTH. Then I saw the four of you coming closer and closer. You looked so tired, as if you had been through a long and tedious struggle. Then I looked up, relieved it had only been a dream.'

"We then told her how we had implored God for a dream just the night before. A sense of awe and of being in the presence of mystery gradually came over all of us. There had been a dream given, just not to us. We told her that at this moment we had not been very elated, and she responded, 'Of course, that's the cross.' And we remembered 1 Corinthians 1: 18–19, which we now realized would become one of our foundational scriptures.

"Now we could drink the wine and play our music; it was just magical, the way our spirits were elevated and ready to rejoice."

Further evidence that the message was from Saint Francis was that Sister Margaret Doyle happened to be in Sister Péronne Marie's office when the call came in. Sister Péronne Marie had turned to her and said how astounded she was that the answer had come through her dream. Sister Margaret had smiled calmly and reminded Péronne that Saint Francis had instructed the sisters to listen to the heart of their superior when they wished to know the will of the Holy Spirit, who would speak to them through their elected leader. It was a strong reminder to the four sisters that their Holy Founder continues to guide them with the words he wrote nearly four hundred years ago.

Before continuing with other signs the sisters received from their saints, Sister Mary Frances thought of another "coincidence" that did not feel like a coincidence. She told me about a police officer, Sean McKenna, who had been on the night beat in their neighborhood for about ten years before the sisters started investigating the area. Sisters Mary Margaret and Virginia rode in his squad car when they went out on the nighttime visits and they became good friends instantly. He said to be sure to let him know if it was his beat area they chose as he would like to help them find a house. At that point they hadn't known where they would locate, since it was before their discernment retreat.

After the decision was made, they were driven to the neighborhood one bright morning by one of their benefactors to start looking for property. They had barely entered the neighborhood when they spotted a squad car, and Mary Margaret saw it was Sean driving it. They flagged him down and asked him what he was doing there.

"I wish I knew," he answered. "I'm supposed to be on the night beat, but for some reason they told me to take the day shift today instead."

He told them to follow him around, and he showed them some blocks he advised against—too much violence there. Sean knew the neighborhood so well, he could tell them where there was poverty but less violence, and he guided them to Fremont Street, where they chose their house. He came to the commissioning of their house, and later, at Christmas, presented them with a gift: a framed collage that included the invitation, a small holy card printed with a quotation from Saint Francis de Sales and a picture of the house drawn by Sister Jane de Chantal of Mendota Heights.

"I see what you mean by another non-coincidence," I said as I admired the picture.

"Saint Jane de Chantal's turn came next," said Sister Frances. "We had selected the Fremont House and were eager to close the deal because it needed a lot of work and renovation before we could move in. But the closing date kept getting changed—one day a realtor couldn't make it, another time it was the banker and then the owner—I don't know how many times it was set back, but it was frustrating. When we finally closed, the date turned out to be August 17, the day when we pray the first vespers of Jane de Chantal. It really felt like another sign that, through no choice of our own, we gained title to our new monastery on the eve of her feast day."

The final confirming sign came from Saint Margaret Mary. The foundation of the house had begun to sink and needed to be hoisted up with heavy machinery to get it level. The workmen discovered a space between the bottom of the bookshelf and the floor, and from that small space they pulled out a piece of paper. When the sisters arrived that day to see the work, one of the men held it out and said, "Boy, have we got something to show you!"

It was a holy card picturing the Sacred Heart and the twelve promises He had given to Saint Margaret Mary. Frances smiled and said, "You can see why we've never doubted for one minute that we were led to be here."

"And how has it been for you?" I asked. "Now that you've been here eighteen years, you must have some extraordinary stories to tell."

"We all have," she answered. "You could talk to any one of us, and you might hear some repetitions, but it is just as likely that you would not. You see, when we came to Fremont, we didn't have an agenda. We had discerned that God wants the Visitation to be here and that our agenda would become apparent when the doorbell rang. It has never stopped ringing.

"We can't take care of a homeless family, but we can call Mary Jo Copeland down at Sharing and Caring Hands and someone there will see that their needs are met. Or someone comes to the door and has to get into treatment; all we have to do is call Turning Point and ask if we can bring him over, and they will take it from there. We funnel services to those in need.

"We're not a food shelf, but we are neighbors and we share what we have. Many benefactors give us food, knowing that there is always someone near us who is hungry and out of money. And the local merchants know us now. Each month we buy four hundred dollars worth of Cub gift cards to share between the two houses. We don't give cash to people, but we give lots of groceries and bus tokens and vouchers."

"How is all this funded?" I asked.

"We have a group called the Friends of Fremont, who have established an annual giving program, and we're very careful about how we budget. We live on alms and we use the money we're given to meet our own expenses and for our ministry to children and families: the Windsock Program, field trips, summer camps and even tutoring and scholarships sometimes."

I knew that Windsock had been initiated very soon after the sisters moved into the house on Fremont. The children in the neighborhood learned quickly that these new neighbors were unlike any they had seen before, and they were drawn to visit them frequently. The sisters played games with them, read stories aloud, provided snacks and listened to their concerns. The needs of these children were endless, and the sisters realized they would have to set some boundaries or they would be overwhelmed. They began hanging a windsock outside their front porch as a signal to the children that they were welcome to visit.

"Kids are so flexible and resilient," Sister Frances said. "It didn't take them at all long to learn the rules, and they really respect them. They wait for the windsock to appear, and when we tell them it's time for it to come down, they go back to their homes without complaining. The next day they're back, of course, and we're always glad to see them.

"We realized early on that we needed some time to fully live our monastic life, which is not just about service, but also about prayer and contemplation. Our concern was how to keep the contemplative balance while dealing with so much chaos. We began to look at how to do this.

"At first we had Windsock six days a week; now we have it Monday, Wednesday, Friday and Saturday. And then we thought, how about if we take just one Thursday a month as a quiet time, so we put a sign up on the door saying, 'The sisters are not available today.' It was so helpful to us we started doing it two times a month, and then we advanced it to three and, finally, to four. The neighbors accept it and understand that we are just not open. We put the sign up, we turn off the phones and we re-collect ourselves.

"We aren't necessarily on our knees in the chapel all Thursdays—there are so many things to do that sometimes we're still incredibly busy. For instance, yesterday was a Thursday, and I took one of our sisters to physical therapy, compiled the lists of recipients for the hundred and fifty Thanksgiving turkeys that the school in Mendota Heights contributed and went to our other house to make cookies and cider for the people who help us deliver the turkeys."

Sister Frances wanted it known that the helpers are not made up just of members of Friends of Fremont and campus ministry students from Mendota Heights; many are people from the neighborhood. Their relationship with the sisters is not one of recipient to benefactor, but friend to friend. Those who receive help understand that the majority of those who give to them are not rich people—just ordinary men and women who want to make a difference in someone's life.

The sisters also make sure that neither the donors nor the recipients are anonymous. This requires a lot of time, but is very important to the Visitation charism of relationship. The Minneapolis Sisters are not an agency; they are a *presence* in the community. If seven hundred names come up for Christmas stockings and people call to say they would like to sponsor a family, one of the sisters will talk to the family to ensure they want to be included. They ask if the family would like to meet the sponsor and make that possible if they do. Everyone who gets a basket or a gift knows it in advance, because they are in a relationship with the sisters. There are no surprise rings at the door with a Santa Claus showing up. Many of the recipients help deliver to all.

I asked her about the place called Turning Point. She explained that it is a holistic treatment center for men, providing services for those who wish to recover from addictions to give themselves a chance to reintegrate into a crime-free, drug-free life. The sisters have founded Circle of Sobriety, a program that includes the wives, significant others and children who have been affected by the men's' drug abuse. Among other things, the counselors at Turning Point bring their clients to the monastery.

They say to them, "Now I just want you to sit here and be silent. This is serenity; this is what you're in treatment for, guys. There ain't no rappin' here, there ain't no boom boxes here, there ain't no TVs here—and you just stop and let it sink in. This is what you're in treatment for."

"It's very interesting," she mused. "The guys don't realize it, but they are being asked to find God in their inner stillness. They tell us they can't get over how peaceful it is here."

When I asked Sister Frances to tell me some individual, personal stories, she smiled and thought for a moment before answering.

"Just today, a man came and needed bus tokens. I gave him the tokens and also asked him if he would rake the leaves for a guy next door who had just had surgery. He was willing and did it right away, glad to get the tokens and glad to help someone else.

"And then there is this dear little girl. She came the other day while we were at prayer, so she stayed and prayed with us. What she had come for was a screwdriver and a battery so she could fix the Easy Bake Oven that we had given her for Christmas last year. So I went home with her—there you see it's the time thing again—and I helped her with it. I'm not very mechanical, but I got it to work, thank goodness, and she was very grateful. The whole time I was there her mother was out cold on the couch—didn't even know I was in the place. It's so important for us to love them, because they often can't get it from home.

"It isn't just us doing the giving either. A widower whose wife loved flowers brought us a beautiful cactus in memory of her. The people give us gifts from their hearts. We don't neglect to look beyond the beauty of a thing to its giver and to its Creator."

Sister Frances paused as she remembered another personal story. She said this one would be hard to tell.

"One day—October 4, the Feast Day of Saint Francis of Assisi—Karen and I were the only ones home, and we were getting ready to go on a retreat when we heard gunshots. We looked out the window and saw a man lying on the boulevard on the side of our house. Our first response was to dial 911 to get help there fast. Then we ran outside to see what we could do for the man. We could see that he was not only hurt—he was dying. He had been shot in the head; there were at least three, maybe more, bullet holes in the side of his head. He was bleeding profusely.

"We knelt and gathered him into our arms, Karen on one side and I on the other, and began to say the prayers for the dying. He was unconscious but as we prayed aloud with the wails of the sirens beginning to sound in the distance, he moaned, as if in response. I have heard that with the dying the last thing to go is the sense of hearing, and we hoped that he may have heard and been comforted by our prayers. Then the police and ambulance came screaming up, and they took him away. The next day we learned that he had died.

"A couple of days later we were on the front porch and suddenly this group of men walked up. They were members of his gang. And they came right up the steps and the leader said, 'You the ladies that give the last rites to Lulu?'

"And we said, 'We didn't know his name, but we helped him as much as we could.'

"He said, 'We appreciate it.' And he asked if we would pray with them. Or maybe he asked if they could pray with us. They wanted help in dealing with their loss. We invited them into our chapel, where we made a spontaneous prayer for Lulu's soul and for their healing, asking for God's merciful light to shine down on all of us. They said, 'Thank you.' And then they went away."

"Did you ever see them again?" I asked, feeling a shiver of fear. I wondered if I could ever have acted as bravely as the sisters did that day when a man named Lulu lay dying on their lawn. I feared that I wouldn't have had the strength to go out to the yard—that I would have called the police and huddled in the closet until they came.

"No," she said. "We didn't see them again. They just went away, but we had connected. That's life in the 'hood.'"

Her eyes seemed to look into the future. "It just grows and grows. We have a kid at De La Salle and another few at Ascension Grade School. Karen teaches guitar and I do massage for women who have experienced violence, either physical or emotional. There is no end to the needs. That's why we have to have boundaries, or our wells would run dry. But, you know, my prayer life is more intentional here—more direct. In many ways I'm feeling more of the contemplative life here than I did in my former monastery in Mendota Heights. We are building community here constantly, with each other and with our neighbors. It's as though a big picture is growing out of our many small connections. We are knitting, not unraveling."

Recently, the sisters started hosting dinner dialogues with neighborhood groups to provide an atmosphere of warmth and spirituality where people are safe to share. Twelve teenagers came to the first meeting for a pizza supper and then formed a circle in the living room.

"The best part," said Sister Frances, "is that *we* are not leading the meetings. We provided the initiative and the pizza, but the real work was done by three African-American men, one of them a former gang member. The way he got those kids to open up was amazing.

"He had his daughter with him, and he asked the kids how many had fathers in the home. Not one. His daughter was the only one. He asked them how that felt, and they poured out their concerns to him. Just as when I taught religion at Visitation and formed circles of prayer, the kids prayed for their parents. The teen stereotype is that they don't want adults around, but they do. They don't want to be preached at and disapproved of, but they want them there. The adult presence was very important to them that night. We will listen to the Holy Spirit to see how to stay with these kids and serve them. The meetings will move to another level, but we can't let this group down. We can't be just another set of adults who feigned interest, but didn't follow through."

Local neighbors have gathered together with the sisters and formed a group called A Circle of Collaborative Leaders. They are working on a long-range plan to foster communication and cooperation within the community. Forty years have passed since Vatican II, and Sister Frances believes that the Church is just now really beginning to understand the idea of the giftedness of the laity; the future Church will include the laity in a way not comprehended now.

"And what about religious life?" I asked.

"It's not going to look like it does today," she answered with certainty. "I can't predict what form my community or others will take. I read an article written by a nun whose name, unfortunately, I can't remember. It dealt with the future of religious orders, and her position was that some orders will die, but with dignity. They will simply cease to exist, satisfied that they accomplished their purpose in the time they were given. Then she said some will swing back to the old ways and live much as we did before Vatican II. Others she called 'sojourners,' saying they will incorporate different faiths like Buddhism or Protestantism into their Catholicism. The final group she mentioned will choose reconciliation: uniting religious and laity."

It is clear that the Minneapolis Visitation is one of the reconciling communities. Sister Frances smiled when she told me that nuns from other religious orders have told them that their monastery is light years ahead of the movement within the Church in general in terms of empowering the laity to embrace leadership.

"If we are ahead," she said, "we should be—that was what Saint Francis de Sales was all about. After all, he wrote the very first book of devotions for the laity because he knew that *all* are called to the spiritual life, not just consecrated religious. Four hundred years ago he and Jane de Chantal saw that. We, as a church, are finally beginning to practice what he preached."

Sister Mary Frances, like the other Minneapolis Visitation Sisters, remains as fresh and enthusiastic in bringing the Visitation to the poor as when their monastery opened eighteen years ago. Saint Francis de Sales left a legacy of wisdom and holiness that sustains her and them as they live their daily lives in trust and peace. He said, "Let us belong to God… in the midst of so much busyness," and they have followed that dictum joyfully. She blessed me when we parted; our time together had ended and she needed to keep an appointment to help one of her neighbors. In the midst of busyness she is not rushed, knowing the peace of Christ rests firmly in her heart.

Sister Jane de Chantal helps Carol Hilger '69 and Kitty Montgomery '68 to discover their own creativity.

The Sisters chant the Little Office of the Blessed Virgin in the Choir at 720 Fairmount. ca. 1965

Sister Péronne Marie gives a manners tip to Marie Villaume '65 and Jeanne Mullaney '65 in the student refectory where eating becomes one of the fine arts.

Sister Mary Frances and two young neighbors in North Minneapolis. 2008.

Sister Mary Denise and a delicious thumb provide comfort
for a Montessori student.

"How can I keep from singing?" Sister Marie Thérèse
praises God at the organ.

Is this a "Coup de gras?" Novice Sister Brigid Marie mows the lawn
outside the cloister porch. 1962.

Kathy Mullin prepares to ride and sing through the neighborhood.

Sisters Mary Denise and Mary Paul (Paula) keep their hands
busy as they chat at recreation on the screened porch.
Sister Mary William (now Katherine) is not sure that she has
the talent for fine embroidery. ca. 1963.

Not quite the Super Bowl, but high competition at croquet from Sister Marie Thérèse. ca. 1970

In the monastery community room Sister Péronne Marie stokes the fire.

Sister Katherine demonstrates "all through love, nothing through constraint," with kids from the neighborhood.

Front row, (L to R): Sisters Marie Antoinette, Péronne Marie, Marie Thérèse, Margaret, Immaculata. *Back row (L to R):* Sisters Mary Denise, Dorothy, Mary Paula, Carol Ann, Brigid Marie, Jane de Chantal.

SISTER KATHERINE

The Mullins of Edina were a godly family. Without a trace of self-consciousness, Sister Katherine used these words when I asked her to tell me a bit about her background. "We were a godly family." Coming from almost anyone else it might have been braggadocio; from Katherine it was a simple statement based on observation and memory. She might have been announcing that the grass in the Mullin yard was green, the snow that covered it in winter, white.

We were meeting in the Fremont house, the first of the two Visitation Monastery settings in Minneapolis. Before arranging ourselves in the living room with cups of tea and my recording paraphernalia, we stepped into the chapel to ask the Holy Spirit to guide our thoughts and words that afternoon. A godly behavior; a godly habit.

"I don't mean that we were especially devotional," Katherine said. "We didn't say the rosary together every night as some families did or attend all the prayer services at church. Sunday Mass, yes, that was a given and was never questioned. Our faith was taken for granted—it was a natural part of us like our Irish heritage. We were an ordinary Catholic family.

"The godliness was evidenced more by the integrity I witnessed daily in my parents' actions. Dad often talked about business at the dinner table; it was so apparent that he abhorred any kind of dishonesty or what he called 'fast dealing.' And my brother, Bill, was a lawyer—it was obvious to me as he and Dad talked that they shared the same values."

Bill was six years older than Katherine and had left home to board at a Catholic high school in Iowa when she was only eight, so he was already quite grown up and studying law by the time she began to pay serious attention to the adult conversation at the table. The two men discussed business ethics, and Mrs. Mullin frequently contributed her informed opinions as well. She was educated and intelligent, a generous community member who organized clothing drives for the poor and volunteered many hours at Saint Mary's Hospital. Young Katherine understood that her family's financial resources were gifts meant to be shared, not hoarded. Those living in poverty were to be helped, not scorned.

Four children were born to Edward and Mary Mullin: Bill, the eldest, followed by Mimi, Katherine and Rick. Bill and Mimi were close in age, so they had already established a close brother-sister bond by the time Katherine arrived in 1940, three years after Mimi.

"I think I wondered what my place in the family was," she said. "The two older ones paired together a lot, so I could have been lonely if not for my mom. She had really good instincts, and I think she realized that I took on the 'middle child syndrome.'

She gave me extra nurturing, and that gave me the strength to become my own person. I made my own friends and didn't try to force my way into Bill and Mimi's world, so there really wasn't much rivalry among us. We went our separate ways without animosity, but without real closeness either. At that time, anyway—we are close now.

"When I was six, a new baby, Rick, was born, and he immediately became my special interest. I adored him, spent a lot of time taking care of him when he was tiny, and played with him when he grew older. I taught him how to ride a bike and to play ball and all the other games little kids enjoy. Bill and Mimi helped him too, but I was happiest when it was Rick and me. I never thought of him as a pest the way some kids considered their little brothers; I was crazy about him." She laughed. "I still am. We're really good friends."

Sister Katherine has mostly happy memories of her family life and childhood. Materially, they had all they needed and wanted: a spacious home in a safe and beautiful neighborhood, good clothes and plenty of toys and books. Mr. Mullin, Katherine said, took providing for his family very much to heart.

"Dad had a strong personality," she continued, "a great combination of seriousness and fun. He entertained us during Sunday brunches with his gift for mimicry, taking on everyone from the president of the USA to the priest who said Mass that morning. He was never mean about it—just funny. I think I inherited a feel for mimicry and for making people laugh from him, and I have always been grateful for it. Laughter is *so* healing, and we often need it to put life in perspective.

"His sense of humor was delightful, but he wasn't always good-natured. He had strong opinions and so did I. I was often sassy. There was nothing funny about the way he dealt with my defiance. He was passionate about politics, and his views were presented as morally correct; other viewpoints were not worth considering. Being young, I didn't know that I could disagree and still be accepted. He did not have the parenting skills needed to match my constant resistance to his vehemence, and I didn't know that he had doubts or questions about anything. That was hard because it taught me to think in terms of black and white, absolute wrong and absolute right, which takes a long time to undo.

"It was many years before I was able to tell him how he had affected me, and he was genuinely startled. He said that he had had no idea of how difficult it had been for me to deal with him—just hadn't seen it. He told me he was sorry, and that was very healing for me. I'm so glad we finally discussed it, and I could begin put it to rest."

When the Mullin children were very young, there was no Catholic school in Edina, so Mimi and Katherine were sent to Northrop Collegiate School for girls. It was a very good institution, but her parents felt uncomfortable that faith was not emphasized there, so they transferred the girls to Most Holy Trinity School in Saint Louis Park. Katherine attended third grade at Most Holy Trinity, and it was there she had her first experience with an order of teaching nuns.

"It was wonderful for me: I loved my third-grade teacher, a Benedictine named Sister Leeann. We still keep in touch, so strong was her influence on me. I remember thinking that I would like to be like her. She handled discipline firmly, but so fairly—the boys couldn't put anything over on her, but they loved her and knew that she loved them. She was my earliest role model of a lovely nun, and the idea germinated in my head that being a nun could actually be a life. These ladies with the funny-looking veils maybe had something to offer that was valuable."

Whether her sense of the presence of God within came from that first encounter with the Benedictine sisters or from the quiet, abiding faith of her own family, she does not know. She felt a dim but very real awareness that God lives in every person, and it kept her from being self-centered. She clearly remembers the joy she felt riding her bike through her neighborhood, stopping to visit grown-ups at their open garage doors, pausing to play with various younger children who were out in their yards, and waving hellos into backyards. She pedaled along, often singing the popular song "I Believe" at the top of her voice.

"Do you remember that song?" she asked me. How could I not? It was on the radio often during the 1940s. We started, first humming, then gaining momentum and singing the words, together. "Every time I hear a newborn baby cry, or touch a leaf or see the sky, then I know why-i -yi-yi-yi I believe."

"Oh yes!" she laughed. "I loved those words and the melody too. Not just any popular piece would do for my bike rides; it had to have meaning. That was important to me."

By the time Katherine was ready for fourth grade, her parish in Edina had opened a parochial school. It was staffed by sisters who were less warm, more distant, than the Benedictines. Being a nun was still an attractive idea, but she knew she didn't want to hold herself aloof from others the way they did. She felt closest to God during warm and fun encounters with others, and the cool demeanor of these sisters disappointed her.

After completing eighth grade in 1954, she started high school at Visitation Convent in Saint Paul and once again experienced nuns who were warm and welcoming. She felt completely at home there; she was with sisters who accepted her for who she was, and the attractiveness of religious life was reaffirmed for her. Because she commuted from Edina, a considerable distance in those days before freeways, she boarded during the week and came to know the sisters more personally than if she had been a day student. By 1954 the boarders lived in a house directly across the street from the school, rather than in the same building with the sisters as they had in previous years.

"Sister Mary Patricia frequently was in her classroom after dinner, correcting papers and preparing for the next day's lessons. When I saw her light, I would dash over just to hang out with her. We didn't talk about vocations—I just enjoyed her companionship. It didn't occur to me that I might be interrupting her work; she was so gracious, I felt like a welcome guest. The thought of staying on at Visitation and joining their community was so attractive to me. It felt like it would be a natural next step in my life."

"Did you have other interests besides school and your affection for the sisters?" I asked.

"Oh yes! My social life was fun—I had lots of girl friends and many boy friends—I was constantly falling in and out of love. But somehow I knew it wasn't for me—I was to lead a different life."

Sister Katherine looked thoughtful for a moment. "It was after my Confirmation that I first realized this. It didn't seem like a big deal at the time—all catechism and memorized answers—not much different from the rest of eighth grade. I went home after the ceremony and took a plate of cookies downstairs to watch TV. And suddenly I had a moment—just a moment—of understanding that I had God within me in a new and special way."

It was a startling moment, but it passed, and being a kid, she went back to her TV and cookies. But she never forgot it—it was the first time she had felt a real relationship with God, not just an awareness. The experience stayed with her, sleeping quietly just under her consciousness. That silent presence influenced her feelings and softened her encounters with others.

She said, "I didn't think of it as a special thing at the time, but now I hear frequently from the younger brothers and sisters of my classmates how kind I was to them. They liked to hang around with me and I liked having them there. Somehow I knew that they, too, carried God within them. It has always been through people that I see God embodied; it is through them that I reach Him."

At the end of her junior year, Katherine was elected student council president and was sent that summer to an all-state conference for student leaders. At first she took the meetings lightly. Having fun with other kids was her idea of how to enjoy the experience, and she kept them up late at night, giggling and mimicking the counselors and the way they gave assignments. Then one of the counselors surprised her by taking her aside for a private talk. He told her she had special leadership qualities that she probably didn't recognize. Hadn't she noticed how the others followed her, joining in her pranks and escapades? He intuited that in spite of being a fun-loving, outgoing kid, she had a quiet, reserved space within, a place that asked her to listen. The counselor told her she had the ability to influence others, and she should use those qualities, not squander them. It was an affirmation that affected her deeply and helped her take her role as student council president very seriously.

"It also encouraged me to give some real thought to the religious vocation that seemed to be calling me. I realized I should break up with the boy I had been dating, because I knew he really liked me and it didn't seem fair to let his affections go too deep.

"So I spoke to him after we had been out one evening. He told my friends how I had done this—standing on my front steps and breaking his heart. I didn't want to break any hearts! He was a really nice guy, and I knew he was sad about my decision, but I told him I had been asked to follow a different path. Our group was so warm and loving; I could just picture how they listened to him and comforted him."

Sister Katherine smiled as she talked about her friends. "I was blessed with wonderful friendships, women who are fun, enthusiastic and loyal. Loyalty really defines them. I shouldn't say 'was blessed,' because I still am. I met with some of them just last week in planning our 50th Visitation class reunion. They have stood by me all this time—even during those first years in the convent when I couldn't communicate with them. But there they were at my first profession and again at my final one, and it was like we never skipped a beat in life together. They never questioned me about my decision, just wanted to be supportive and helpful. If I felt it was right for me, then it was all right with them, and, looking back, I can see that their attitude helped considerably.

"But I saw that I had to speak to my parents—it wouldn't do to have them hear about this from my friends. During Easter vacation of my senior year in high school I told Mom and Dad of my desire to enter Visitation. They weren't too surprised, but they said I was too young, that I must go to college first. Sister Mary Regina agreed with them. A true vocation would not disappear in college; I should continue to pray and be open to God's voice within me."

Katherine went east to Marymount at Tarrytown on the Hudson, a women's Catholic college whose beautiful campus was located near an all-men's Catholic college. It was a built-in dating situation, and students of both schools took advantage of their proximity to socialize frequently. Katherine joined in the fun but was careful to cause no more heartthrobs; she didn't want to disappoint any more boys. She knew *her* heart was back in Saint Paul with the Visitation Sisters.

She began to see the campus minister, a Dominican priest, to discuss her dilemma with him. Each time she went to his office, it was with the same question: not *if*, but *when*, she should enter. After many such visits he asked if she would like to settle it that day.

"Yes!" she answered with enthusiasm.

He said, "OK, sit down," and then, to her horror, he reached in his pocket and pulled out a coin. "Tails says you enter now, and heads says you finish college and enter then."

Katherine was appalled by his choice of such an irreverent symbol to decide her future. That was up to the Holy Spirit, not a coin toss. He started to flip, but before it was in the air, she cried," No! Don't do it—I know—I know—I want to enter now!"

The priest laughed and put the coin away without looking at it. "You don't need me or a coin to decide," he said. "You know what you want."

"Do I ever!" she answered.

Leaning back in her chair, she looked directly at me and said, "That was so important to me—to know that I *really* did know; that God's will comes from within. No outside voice can lead you to it, much less a clever gamble."

She came home for Easter, just a year after having announced her vocation to her family. This time they didn't say she was too young. Seeing a little something different in her, they hoped that she really knew her own mind. They did not want to stand in the way of God's will.

Only her older brother questioned her decision, and that was not to dissuade her but to ascertain that she really knew what she was doing. He said, "Hey, Kathy, what will you do if you decide you don't want to be a nun but you've already made your vows?"

It was unthinkable to Katherine that her choice could be in error, but she was touched by his caring, knowing that he didn't want her to miss the mark. Her eyes misted as she recalled his words and the brotherly concern with which he had spoken them.

She began preparations for leaving home, taking a trip to Colorado with a close friend whose mother wanted to ensure that Katherine would at least get to see mountains once before renouncing the world. The mother crouched in the back seat of the car while the girls maneuvered it over the high, narrow roads, laughing and giggling without letting on they were just as terrified by the treacherous curves.

"You can see from things like that how surrounded I was by wonderful people," she said. "We could even make a fun adventure out of shopping for the special clothes I would need in the convent. One of the girls and I cooked up a skit in the shoe store, persuading the saleslady that I really preferred black granny shoes to the red high-heeled pumps she wanted to sell me."

Though convinced that entering the convent was the right thing to do, she was not as well-prepared to face the reality of the cloister as she had thought. She sighed. "I no longer could come and go as I had. I was really going to be separated from my family. My mother knew, but I didn't realize that she knew. On the morning I left home, she made up an excuse not to go with me. My dad and siblings drove me; I learned only much later that she hadn't wanted to break down in front of me.

"That part was so hard," she said sadly. "I was very happy when the cloister rule changed after Vatican II. It made sense in another day and time, but in our world it was hurtful to families and to those of us in the monastery."

Although feeling the pain of separation, Katherine adjusted to convent life and was happy to be there. She couldn't really picture what she would be doing, but trusted that her life would unfold well in a community that was filled with intelligent, devout, fun-loving and prayerful women. She was not disappointed.

In her first year as a postulant she was sent to help in the classrooms, a move that proved right for her. It fed her relationship with God by connecting to His presence through contact with the students. During her novitiate she was out of the classroom and very much into nature, which strengthened and nurtured the other side of her spirituality, the awareness of God through His creation. Sister Jane Margaret, her novice director, had just the right mix of playfulness and seriousness for Katherine's personality. Her formation seemed geared to exactly the right environment to further her growth and integration as a person and as a Visitation Sister.

When she made her first vows in 1961, she was called Sister Mary William in recognition of her father. Her dad was proud that she carried his name, but when she had the opportunity to change it back to Katherine after Vatican II, he gave her his blessing to do so. He said, "Hey, Kathy, you know what you want to be called. We baptized you Katherine because we wanted you to have that name. When you had to change it, we accepted it, and I was pleased that my name was the one given to you. It's fine with me if you reclaim your original identity."

The years that followed Vatican II were among Sister Katherine's happiest at Saint Paul and later Mendota Heights. She had finished her interrupted bachelor's degree at Saint Catherine's. Now she was free to travel farther afield and pursue graduate studies. She loved teaching the children in the lower and middle schools, and received a master's degree in reading from Cardinal Stritch College in Milwaukee.

"Those were wonderful years for me," she said. "I realized that I was my own person outside of the monastery; it felt good to know that I could be confident without the presence of the community around me. And this was also the time when we were allowed to go for home visits! I could stay with my parents for two nights before boarding the train for Milwaukee. It was just so good to be with my family again! We would make popcorn and watch football games together just like old times."

Sister Katherine had been teaching for nearly twenty years at Visitation when she was asked if she would be willing to work in the admissions department. Someone needed to take charge of the process to make it more systematic and consistent. She agreed to give it a try and discovered she had a flair for it. Would she be willing to take it on permanently? Yes. In 1983 she left the classroom to handle admissions full-time.

It was a job that suited her outgoing nature well. Associating with people had always been life-sustaining for her; it was through others that she most often found God. Person-to-person contact was the core of the admissions program.

As director of admissions Sister Katherine had the opportunity to observe the overall structure of the school with an objectivity not provided by classroom teaching. With other sisters she reviewed the student population and noted that it was quite homogenous. There were a few students of color, but the majority was white, upper-middle class kids from Saint Paul and its surrounding area. She wondered how well the children from poor families were being served; what percentage of minority students had an opportunity to attend a virtues-oriented, college-preparatory school like Visitation?

Establishing scholarships for minority students became a special interest for her. She could see how the school benefited from embracing more diversity, and she actively encouraged students of color who were interested in education beyond high school to enroll. Empathy with and concern for others had been seeded in her consciousness during her earliest years; she understood that privilege, whether financial or educational, was to be shared, not exclusively retained.

"I really loved being in admissions," Sister Katherine said. "So many dear students came and went, all of them passing through our department. From my vantage point, I knew everyone in the school, some less well than others, but I had at least some contact with all of them."

During my tenure as upper school director at Visitation, Sister Katherine directed the admissions program, and we became good friends, working together on the often difficult selection process. It was hard to turn anyone down when so many wanted to come; we did our best to assess the likelihood of success of all the applicants. I noticed how clearly she presented Salesian values to all who applied and how friendly and welcoming she was. The lively girl who had loved her friends' younger siblings and reached out to all the kids in the neighborhood years ago in Edina was still apparent in the mature nun.

Concurrent with her work in admissions, Sister Katherine was deeply involved with the recently formed Ministry Network. Aware of the diminishing numbers of sisters, the federation had wisely concluded that its main goal should be to ensure that Salesian Spirituality would be passed on to future generations even if the sisters were no longer present in the schools. This awareness coincided with a movement within the Church at large to recognize the importance of the laity. Vatican II had inspired many reforms, one of which was to take a look at the role the laity had played in the formation of early Christianity.

The Ministry Network was established to include laypeople in living and modeling Salesian Spirituality; Visitation school board members were the first to be introduced to the concept via retreats that focused on Salesian virtues. The sisters formed committees of representatives, lay and religious, from each school. Sister Katherine was active within the ministry and became the second leader of the group at the national level.

As leader, she was able to assist the federation through her natural ability to inspire people to support a good cause. She said, "Spreading our charism came naturally to me; I was already comfortable and fairly successful doing it through my admissions work. I prefer to team up or co-chair with someone, as opposed to acting alone, so I asked my colleague, Margie MacNeill, to work with me.

"We saw our task as putting together teams of laypeople at Visitation Convent Schools to study our spirituality in depth and then have age-appropriate activities, curricula and gatherings that would involve all levels of the schools. At Mendota Heights our team started out small, maybe five or six of us, and later we would have as many as a dozen members in a given year. We met every month to plan events, workshops, dinners, prayer services, plays—everything to bring Salesian Spirituality alive for our school community. Annually we called together the teams that were functioning at all the schools to share ideas, work on projects and pass on 'best practices.' We held these meetings at each others' schools."

Because of the foundation laid by the Ministry Network, a solid system is in place in Visitation schools to continue fostering Salesian Spirituality among the faculty, staff and student body. The school at Mendota Heights has been the first to implement, as a paid position, a director of Salesian Studies to coordinate a mentoring program that ensures that Salesian principles are understood and followed. Specific Salesian themes and virtues are emphasized each year. Learning is not left to chance: discussion sessions between mentors and mentees are scheduled regularly; together they explore formal and informal issues in work that is both academic and reverent. Sister Katherine left a living legacy that is still growing.

As much as she loved both Ministry Network and admissions, she became aware of a desire for something else. After seventeen years of steady involvement in these two areas, she could fell her energy beginning to wear down, and she did not want to run low on enthusiasm. She believed her assistant was capable and ready to replace her, and she started to get her ready to become director, in case the day came when she felt she should leave admissions.

She said, "It must have been the Holy Spirit who suggested that I had been long enough in admissions. I had entertained no thoughts of what else I might do, but it was very shortly after I talked to my assistant about taking over that the idea of entering the Minneapolis Visitation occurred to me.

"Going there to visit and help was not new to me. From the time they opened in 1989, I often went there for a day and just fit in with whatever was going on. At that time it was just a useful and fun thing to do. I missed Mary Frances from the old Visitation and I loved the Saint Louis Sisters, so I fit in very well with their community. Now and then I stayed overnight, but I had never felt a call to join them."

Sister Katherine, who had for so long felt anchored to the Saint Paul/Mendota Heights Community of Sisters, now began to feel herself afloat and wondering what she was to do. To begin with, she kept thinking that her place was in Mendota Heights. She loved the students, the community, the school—she felt she must be wrong to be thinking so much about Minneapolis. Her certainty was that she would never leave her community. But the idea kept recurring until she knew she had better look at it. Was the Holy Spirit speaking to her?

In 2000 she resigned from her admissions position and asked for a two-month sabbatical to help her decide what to do next. She would spend her sabbatical with the sisters in Minneapolis to discern the will of the Holy Spirit in this matter.

Sister Katherine has usually experienced God's will by following what seems natural for her to do. If a task feels like a good fit for her, if it allows her to be her best self and she is comfortable with it, then it seems right for her to continue with whatever it is.

"And I was so comfortable here that summer! I did everything the other sisters did, followed their schedule, joined in their work—it all seemed a perfect blend for me. I realized more than ever that they were on to something here, that they were creating something new to Visitation.

Once again, I noticed tears escape her eyes as she told

me of her departure from the Minneapolis sisters when her sabbatical was up. She told them that this was a very serious time for her; she needed to discern if this were a genuine call to join them. Would it be okay with them if she felt she were directed to come in? *Would it be okay?* They let her know that it would be much more than okay for them to receive her as a community member.

Sister Katherine returned to Mendota Heights to pray for guidance while she helped out in the school, supervising the student dining room and working on a vocations team with Sister Brigid. They went together to a retreat at Mercy Center in Colorado Springs to study the vocation discernment process.

Again, she seemed to be getting affirmation from the Holy Spirit that she was on the right path. A faculty priest there was teaching skills for vocation workers on how to evaluate their own vocations, before working with others on discerning theirs. It was exactly what she needed.

She visited the priest privately and told him of her situation: she had been in a community she loved, happy and productive with her work, but was now perhaps feeling a new, disturbing call. How could she best handle this?

He gave her some exercises to do, instructing her to write two letters to her community. The first would tell them that she had been thinking about joining the Minneapolis group but, on reflection, had seen that her true life lay with them and she would be staying. The second letter was to explain the same thing but would have a different ending: she would leave them and join the group ministering to the poor in Minneapolis. Neither letter was to be sent, but the act of writing would help her reach clarity of purpose. Very soon into the process she saw that she was, indeed, receiving a new call.

As she wrote the first letter, it was very hard to express a commitment to staying. There was no energy in her thoughts or words. But when she wrote the second letter, there was real passion—a spiritual energy—behind it.

Returning to the priest to thank him for providing the means to make her decision, she felt her heart sing with joy at the vision of her new life ahead. She knew it would be very hard, not only to tell her community that she was leaving, but also to face the reality of actually leaving them. It would be difficult for them to hear her news. She had empathy for her sisters, feeling their grief at losing her, and she grieved for leaving them. And yet, she understood the call and was firm in her intention.

On a Saturday morning in December of 2000, she made her announcement to the Mendota Heights Community, after first seeing Sister Mary Regina privately in her room. Regina had become very hard of hearing by then, and Katherine did not want to risk her not hearing the message clearly. Sister Marie Thérèse was the superior at that time, and they went together to break the news.

Sister Katherine wept softly again as she recounted to me the meeting with her old teacher and mentor. Wiping her eyes she said, "Mary Regina was heartsick; she loved me, as I did her, and the thought of having me leave was devastating to her. And she was well aware of the shrinking numbers in the monastery, and to lose another member was of real concern. But she had so much courage and faith—she couldn't ask me to stay, no matter how much she wanted it—because she did not question the will of God. I cried, but she did not, although she may have cried later, alone."

Then Sister Katherine met with the rest of the community, conveying her thoughts and feelings to them. Their response, prayerful and generous as always, was loving. She remembers that Sister Jane de Chantal embraced her later, saying, "How could you do anything else? How could you do other than follow the Holy Spirit?" Not one sister made her feel as though she should not be doing what she felt she needed to do.

She entered the Minneapolis Monastery on June 13, 2001. When any Visitation Sister makes a transfer to another monastery, she is given two years to try it—to live that life and see how it feels—before it is finalized. The members of the community she enters must also be satisfied that she is truly called and that she fits in well with them before her incorporation can take place. In her two years of trying out Minneapolis, the new location never once stopped feeling right to Sister Katherine. In June of 2003, in a simple ceremony during Morning Prayer in the chapel on Fremont Avenue, she was formally accepted into the new monastery.

"And has that feeling of things being right continued for you here?" I asked. "You've been here seven years now. Have there been disappointments as well as joy?"

"Oh, of course, there have been some disappointments," she quickly answered. "No life is without them, but that doesn't mean one rejects a whole experience in the face of a few discouragements. I had a lot to learn about dealing with the culture of this neighborhood and the sisters here helped me do that. Although people are people and are alike in many ways, there are noticeable differences between the African-American community and the people I grew up with, different from the sisters whose lives I shared in Saint Paul/Mendota Heights."

"Can you describe some of the differences to me?"

Sister Katherine thought about that for a minute. Then she said, "One telling example has to do with how much more open they are about their personal troubles than are the people I've been used to dealing with. They come right in and lay out some of the most private details and problems of their domestic lives; if they're talking to me and another sister enters the room, it doesn't faze them, and they keep right on going as if no interruption had occurred. They can tell us about betrayals of the worst kind, about abuses they've endured, about their worries for their children—issues that my family or yours would have kept tightly wrapped and covered up from the neighbors.

"And yet, when it comes to business—topics my family and their friends often talked about more openly—most African-Americans are very unwilling to discuss it. That's the part of their lives they don't want known. It takes time and sensitivity to adjust to those differences, to avoid asking questions that could be perceived as prying, while at the same time talking with them quite openly about matters that are taboo in my culture.

"Their interpersonal difficulties are different from those familiar to most of the families I knew at the school. Economic challenges can be enormous, and they often cause major disruption to their families' stability. They face eviction notices—they may have to move suddenly and don't dare tell anyone where they're moving because the bill collectors may not be far behind. They get their gas and water turned off; for the people living on minimum wage or even lower, just one big bill like a raise in rent or a medical emergency can mean the difference between their making it that month or not. Very few of them have the kinds of safety nets we have built into our lives.

"Their problems seem almost insurmountable, and yet they are generous with each other; they not only share their material goods, they make room in their homes for any who are displaced by illness, death or imprisonment. They also share their faith in ways that are beautiful to see. In their churches they put great emphasis on the gospels and scriptures and their religious demonstrations are a wonder to behold. Both the African-American and Hispanic cultures have deepened my faith by sharing in their spiritual expressions.

"The Hispanic community holds processions, which are among their ways of honoring God. Grown-ups, teenagers, little kids—they process together to make a point about injustices they want to see addressed, but also to celebrate a saint's day—especially Our Lady of Guadalupe—or even a secular holidays like Cinco de Mayo. In spite of their many issues and concerns, not the least of which are the immigration policies that never seem to get reformed, they maintain and express their faith both personally and publicly. They are wonderfully demonstrative, and they provide a great lesson to us tight-lipped, white Minnesotans to smile more and loosen up."

In bringing the Visitation to the Minneapolis poor, the sisters see the gospel story of Mary and Elizabeth played out over and over. A family near them was evicted in the middle of winter, and they came to the sisters' door in desperation, a mother with two small children who didn't know where they could sleep that night. The sisters had just learned of a unit open in an affordable housing development, and they were able to borrow a van and help the family move into it.

Two years later, that mother came back to let them know that their help had provided the encouragement that led her to turn her life around. Her two children were newly baptized, and she has a steady job in a bakery. She comes to visit now from time to time, bringing rolls and muffins from the bakery.

"Do you see how like the Visitation story that is?" Sister Katherine asked me. "We give, we comfort, we help; and then we are given back comfort and help in whatever form is possible at the time. We never expect to be repaid—that is not within our belief system—and yet, we frequently receive gifts from people because we have a relationship with them. The exchange becomes mutual. Saint Francis de Sales and Saint Jane de Chantal modeled our Visitation Order after their own beautiful relationship, which was of the heart. It was about knowing God through sharing and embracing."

Just as when she was a child on her bike in Edina, Katherine still wanders through her neighborhood, getting to know people and making friends. She goes on foot now, but she continues to meander around the blocks and through the alleys, greeting adults and stopping to play and joke with the children.

One day several years ago, she was strolling along when, out of the corner of her eye, she saw something in an alley she was crossing. Stopping for a second, she realized it was a man and a woman dumpster diving—digging into garbage cans and pulling out trash. She had witnessed this from her car window from time to time, but never while on foot, never so close. The sight repelled her and she hurried past, shuddering. Then she felt something calling her back, something telling her not to be so hasty.

With her stomach churning, she entered the alley, approached the couple, and saw that the woman was pulling tin cans out of the garbage bin while the man crushed them with his feet. She hesitantly came closer and smiled a hello to them.

"Do you wanna help?" the man asked, cheerfully.

Everything in her screamed, "No! I don't want to help—I want to get away from here!" But then that "something" stopped her and she thought, "Why not? I could do that."

She wasn't quite willing to put her head and hands into the garbage bin, but crushing cans with her feet was not beyond her. Timidly at first, but then with more vigor, she helped the couple flatten their cans, and they struck up an acquaintanceship, exchanging names and telling each other a bit about themselves.

The woman, her English heavily accented, told her that she collected cans and sold them to a recycling plant to buy gifts for her grandbabies. She had emigrated from Liberia. Katherine told her she tutored a girl from Liberia, and they smiled at finding something in common.

Sister Katherine said to me, "I could tell this was a lady with great dignity. I could have judged her unkindly—once maybe would have—but I am so glad I stopped instead. I knew we sisters had a sack of crushed cans on our porch waiting to be collected, so I invited her to come over and get them.

"Then about three weeks later, I was out walking and I spotted her again. I called her name and she turned around with a happy grin of recognition. 'Kafferin!' she called, 'I know you!' She remembered my name. It reminded me of Mary, recognizing Jesus after the resurrection. She and I have remained friends all these years, and after I don't know how many times coming to our porch to pick up cans, she has finally begun to accept my invitations to come in for a glass of lemonade. She has taught me so much; I am grateful for all the opportunities I have to be spiritually strengthened here."

Because the sisters' houses are right on the street, both the wonder and the messiness of life come directly to them. Shortly after Sister Katherine arrived at Fremont, the doorbell rang on a chilly fall afternoon, and in came a crying child. She was a sixth-grader who had come home from school to find the door locked and her mother not home. She needed badly to use the bathroom, so she walked ten blocks from her house to the sisters because she knew they would help her. In her urgency she had wet her pants, and was mortified, fearing it would make her look like a baby. She cried and cried, saying she had tried so hard to make it but she just couldn't.

The sisters helped her clean up, finding dry clothes for her and assuring her they understood. They phoned her home every twenty minutes, but still no mom. Because it was close to supper time, they invited her to eat with them, and she stayed until her mother returned home later that evening. They were relieved to know that the mother had not abandoned her child; her lateness was due to a communications mix-up. Sister Katherine happened to have a book about a young girl who had acted courageously, and she gave it to the young girl, with each sister writing an inscription. Another relationship had been forged.

Not all the stories have happy endings. The sisters have worked with an expert in community advocacy, seeking direction in how to deal with severely troubled families. This advocate talked to them about the need to document cases of real neglect and/or abuse. For the sisters, it is a very painful area to consider, because their relationship with their neighbors is built on trust. And yet, there are times when help beyond what they can offer is needed to protect the children. The results of the sisters' work is not always seen or appreciated, and that is okay with them.

"Are you discouraged at times to see the scope of the problems you encounter?" I asked. "So much pain, so much suffering, must be very hard to witness, day after day."

"It is hard," Sister Katherine acknowledged. "But I am never troubled by not being able to take care of all the needs that I see. My life with my sisters—our prayer, our community living—doesn't allow us to be out there forty hours a week. I am comfortable with what I can do, and I do it as well as I can. That's what the spirit of Saint Francis speaks about: to be what we are, and to be that well.

"We never expected to fix everything, and the lady of the trash can helped teach me that. I can't do it all—don't ask me to put my head or my hands into that garbage—but I can crush those cans. God has given me gifts, and I will share what I have."

"How do you picture the future?" I asked, as I had asked each sister when our conversations were coming to a close. "What do you think it holds for you, and for the Visitation Order?"

Sister Katherine did not have to think for long before answering.

"The future?" she said. "I am concerned, but not worried. I have no fear. We Visitation Sisters believe a valid lifestyle like ours will continue to maintain and sustain the community we dwell in. What exactly is going to happen—what texture, shape or form—we do not know. But we know this spirit will not die. It has persevered for nearly four hundred years, and it will continue to live in some way.

"Look at the school, for instance. Without sisters it is flourishing, and I mean flourishing in Salesian Spirituality, not just academically. The young people there want to work for peace and justice. We have strong connections with Saint John's and Saint Benedict's colleges, and the Youth in Theology and Ministry Program are strong rays of hope. The kids are learning great theology, and they are learning service."

Sister Katherine is the vocations director for the Minneapolis Monastery, and she acknowledges that the future might look very bleak when viewed through the lens of past expectations. Women are not coming to join. They show great interest in helping—in giving of themselves—but not as a lifetime of vowed commitment.

Always an optimist, she believes that people who seek to be connected spiritually are expressing a new kind of monasticism. It is one that may not require living in community in a defined geographical space but, instead, will become a monastery of the heart. These new monastics will lead lives of prayer and service that may or may not include vows of poverty, obedience or celibacy. They will discern, with the help of the Holy Spirit, what form their services are to take while they build and nurture places of adoration and contemplation within. That the current hierarchy of the Catholic Church has difficulty accepting non-traditional ways of worshipping and serving concerns her, but she trusts that they will come around in time.

"The Church as a governing authority," she smiles, "is not famous for moving quickly. But the Church as a people is burgeoning with lay leadership; they take part in our ministry and pray and serve with us. We see it all the time in this neighborhood. Saint Francis de Sales was the first to say that *all* are called to a religious vocation, because we are all meant to be holy, whether in a monastery or not. Some serve in a monastic setting, but others follow different paths to holiness. When we love others we recognize the light of Christ within them and they reflect it back to us."

Sister Katherine entered religious life as a cloistered nun, ready to spend her entire life behind the walls of a monastery. When the grilles were removed and the walls broken by doorways, she stepped out of her enclosure to participate more fully in the world. In 2000 she took another step, away from the quiet suburb of Mendota Heights and into the streets of North Minneapolis where she engages daily with society's marginalized members. There she embraces a sphere in which her eyes see not just poverty and pain, but the beauty, faith and courage within her neighbors. They are eager to be welcomed into the warmth of her embrace and she feels her spirit grow in the power of their love as they, in turn, embrace her.

The Minneapolis Visitation Community sees their neighborhood as their cloister where they engage daily with God through their ministry to the poor. Like her sisters, Katherine is a gentle presence in a world that may often be violent but also contains integrity, redemption and hope. Throughout her life she has experienced the presence of God most fully in her relationships with others; her second vocational call placed her in a landscape of humanity where interaction occurs repeatedly. She embodies the spirit of the Visitation by carrying Christ within her, bringing His love to all she meets and affirming their innate dignity. Carrying Jesus in her heart, her soul daily magnifies the Lord and her spirit rejoices in God, her Savior.

EPILOGUE

Writing the stories of the Visitation Community has been a deeply moving experience. Many times I found myself marveling at the intensity of the Salesian spirit that lives so tangibly within each sister. I wanted to see where it all began, to walk where Saint Francis de Sales and Saint Jane de Chantal walked, and to feel the spiritual energy that I was sure must still inhabit the place. I knew I must go to Annecy.

My intuition was rewarded. Annecy was vibrant with reminders of Visitation's Holy Founders, and my spirit soared as I recognized places I had only seen in photographs. The Basilica of Saint Francis, built in 1911, is a magnificent memorial to the two saints. Their bronze effigies, which are also reliquaries, are set on either side of the main altar, softly illuminated by banks of vigil candles. Stained-glass windows at the back of the edifice depict major episodes in the lives of both Francis and Jane. The monastery of the Visitation Sisters of Annecy is adjacent to the basilica; the nuns have lived there since it was erected with the basilica in 1911.

Less grand, but perhaps more fitting to an espoused life of simplicity, is *La Galerie*, the first dwelling that housed Jane de Chantal and her small group of nuns. The house represents the thrust of the Order: to practice ordinary virtues with love and humility, thus making them extraordinary. The modest chapel has been restored and preserved, as has Jane's humble bedchamber. Sisters of Saint Joseph live there now; they are completely familiar with the history of the house and are most gracious in conducting tours.

Situated below *La Galerie* and the basilica, an imposing statue of a seated Saint Francis looks out over beautiful Lake Annecy with its gliding swans. As I stood there I pictured him crossing the lake on one of his many journeys to and from the 600 parishes of his diocese, his barque disturbing the surface's mirrored image of the snow-capped French Alps.

I felt anointed with Salesian charism and thought of the *thin places* to which Sister Brigid had referred, "Those moments when the barrier between heaven and earth seems very thin." Heaven did feel unlocked in Annecy, almost close enough to touch while I silently prayed. I thanked Frances and Jane for giving me the courage to compile and to honor the histories of their remarkable spiritual heirs and for guiding me to this holy place.

Flying back over the Atlantic Ocean, I leafed through the pages of my manuscript, pausing at each nun's story when the lines brought back a memory from our interview.

Here is Sister Brigid Marie, the shy, sensitive child who found God in the night stars, in the beauty of the natural world and among its living creatures. And, also, in her community of Visitation Sisters, where she has lived her vocational calling for forty-nine years. Since I wrote her chapter, she has completed her work at Sacred Ground and is now a certified spiritual director. It is work well-suited to her, being both personal and relational. Listed among the seven gifts of the Holy Spirit are understanding and counsel; Sister Brigid Marie has been blessed with both in abundance.

Next, Sister Mary Paula, whose personality has as many facets as the roster of names she has worn all these years. Abruptly robbed of the support of her father and grandmother, the two people who knew and understood her best, she struggled to express her extraordinary intelligence and wed it to God's will. How was she to discern her purpose in life? Although her prayer was answered on Christmas Eve during her freshman year in college, it did not bring her peace quickly. She persevered, enduring difficult times in the novitiate by anchoring her soul in the genuineness of her vocational call. Happiness found her at her profession of final vows. Her life has been spent exploring a variety of occupations and duties that have included praying, studying, teaching, writing, publishing and organizing groups and ministries of students and adults. Currently, she is preparing to lead tours to Annecy in preparation for the four hundredth anniversary of the founding of the Visitation Order in 1610. When I last spoke with her, she was excited about the perspective that geography gives to experience, seeing how it could shape her interpretation of the Annecy pilgrimages. I wish I could follow you, dear Paula, to see how much more I could learn from you than I did on my own.

Now I turn to Sister Margaret Agnes, the runaway nun, baldly admitting that she is "a difficult person." She has celebrated her 100th birthday, marking seventy-one years in the convent, each day spent in praising God. My gift to her was an outsized box of candy bars in memory of the little home-built booth from which she peddled her goods at 100 percent profit more than ninety years ago. She sent me a gracious, handwritten thank-you note, saying that this time she would *give* the bars away, foregoing the profits for her great occasion. Her intelligence is undiminished; her adventurous soul looking to eternity, but she is in no hurry to get there. What fortitude! She perseveres through her daily devotions, still murmuring, "Not yet, Lord, not yet."

Sister Jane de Chantal, whose baptismal name, Marie, was exchanged for that of the original Mother of the Visitation Order. I see her eyes glow with wonder as she describes the rumbling from the ceiling in the chapel at Saint Catherine's on the day she received her confirming summons from God. Though often unhappy with the direction her community has taken as it adapts to modernization, she remains steadfast to the bedrock that lies underneath. She is living proof that life in a monastery is not always ideal; there are disagreements among community members just as in ordinary families. The difference in finding solutions lies in consensual group adherence to the guiding virtues of humility and obedience. It doesn't solve everything, but it keeps the members united in a belief that all seek the common good. Sister Jane's piety and perseverance hold her steadfast in the belief that all will work out well in the end.

My page turns to Sister Mary Immaculata, and I hear her chuckling ruefully over her lack of worthiness to receive the exalted names. Yet her obedience to the order she embraced encouraged her to believe that the superior must know better than she. To have disputed Mother Jane Margaret's choice for a name would have been presumptuous. Her vocation came to her in mid-life; she understood that when the soul is ready, and not before, God will make manifest His will. Her life as a professed sister was profoundly rich and happy—she told me that she never doubted for even a moment that she was in the right place. She regarded her improvident youth with some regret, but confessed to retaining an extreme fondness for Manhattan cocktails. At her funeral I met her nephew and was delighted to hear him reminisce about taking Immaculata out to dinner when he visited. The meals were invariably preceded by Manhattans, startling the other patrons, who were unaccustomed to seeing a ninety-plus-year-old, nearly blind nun, in full habit, enjoying cocktails. When slowed by the aging of her body, she acquired a scooter that gave her mobility without using a wheelchair, and she loved to whisk through the monastery on it, visiting her sisters while wielding a mop to dust the floor and sideboards. The beloved scooter is parked now, the mop rests in its corner, her laugh silenced. Her body joined those of her sisters in Resurrection Cemetery on April 12, 2007, but I have no doubt that her soul flew straight to heaven.

Next, Sister Mary Dorothy, another embodiment of steadfastness and humility. Debilitated in body and mind by early childhood illnesses, she remains strong in faith and has been an unfailing example of acceptance, patience and endurance. Recently she celebrated her fiftieth jubilee, enjoying the company of her religious community and her family. Many relatives came for the weekend, attending her religious ceremonies and honorary dinner, but also taking her to their hotel for Yegge family reunion parties. They had such a good time that, on the Saturday night of their visit, Sister Mary Denise had to pick her up for evening prayers. A pair of her beautifully embroidered dish towels, painstakingly stitched by her one working hand, now blesses my kitchen, but I cannot bear to put them to the homely use of drying pots and pans. I cherish them as totems: objects of remembrance, respect and reverence for an ordinary life lived extraordinarily well.

Sister Carol Ann, a complex woman whose strong desire to serve God in a monastic setting is troubled by questions, not of *whether* or *when*, but *where*. Her vocational call lay dormant during the years she spent working professionally and caring for aging parents, but was awakened by a "chance" letter inviting her to attend a discernment session at the convent that first led her to picture life as a religious. She professed her first vows with the Mendota Heights Community, but has not felt ready to make permanent profession there. Within the last several months she has moved to another Visitation Monastery in Brooklyn, where she continues to pray for the peace of clarity of place.

Shifting in my uncomfortable airplane seat, I come to Sister Marie Thérèse's chapter. Lost in the poignant beauty of her story, I soon forget that my legs are cramped. Her life has been one of great sacrifices and many losses, and yet she fastens her attention on God's blessings and gifts, making each day one of joyful optimism. The beautiful strains of her violin have graced the community and the school, and her radiant spirit somehow manages to combine both playfulness and reverence. Just being in her presence is uplifting; love and happiness radiate from her eyes. I think the students call her "Sister Honey" because they recognize her innate sweetness. She, of course, modestly insists that it is only because she addresses each one of them as "Honey."

Sister Marie Antoinette. I can't look at her name without seeing the lovely gray curls that bob up and down on her head. "It's a wig, dear," she whispers with a grin. I think of her gentleness and acceptance, her patience and kindness. Though not warmly embraced by her original community, it didn't occur to her to ask for a transfer. Her ideal was to live in peace, accepting whatever God sent. She is often smiling a welcome as I come through the convent's front door. Still a true Salesian at eighty-nine, she performs ordinary tasks to the best of her ability, making them extraordinary in the eyes of God.

And now, Sister Mary Denise, my friend and former class-mate, who has steadfastly remained her patient, efficient and serene self amid the many changes and challenges that have confronted her. Elected Mother Superior still again, she must address the concerns and needs of an aging community, its diminished numbers complicated by increasing physical frailty among its members. Instead of regarding the future with fear, she strives to live in the moment, remembering that we all are in the hands of a loving God who will continue to care for us today, as every day. Like her sisters, she faces life with the assurance, the special charism of Saint Francis that reminds her to keep her focus on living in the present, each moment, each hour, each day. And to do it as well as she can.

Next, Sister Frances, the once happy, energetic nun whose life was so brutally interrupted when the drugs meant to heal her depression nearly killed her. When I interviewed her for this book, she was cautiously beginning to find her way through the recovery process, still stunned by the astonishing magnitude of the incompetence of her care. She tried to immerse herself in the life of the monastery, working on her music and working as vocations director. Later, she decided she needed some distance from the entire experience and requested a leave of absence to discern her life's purpose in light of all that had happened. She is currently living near her father, completing her college education and praying for guidance.

Sister Péronne Marie, whose sensitivity to "truth and beauty, beauty and truth" grasps the glory of God and expresses it through prayer and poetry. Since our interview, she has published her poems in a book titled *Gentle Fidelity*. I see in her a soul of great strength: feminine, wise and devoted to scholarship. She met the sudden loss of youthful health and vigor with faith and courage, continuing her education and the spiritual search that led her to Visitation. Sisters Mary Regina and Péronne Marie guided their religious community through the chaos of Vatican II and its aftermath. By translating and interpreting the early chronicles of the Visitation Order, she enhanced the wealth of Salesian literature and imparted a wider understanding of its special spirituality. The virtues she delineates in *Journey to Integration* stand out like arrows slashed on the trees, marking the trail we must follow on our way to eternity. The woods are often dark and frightening, the distance uncertain and the end not clear, but the reassuring arrows give us courage to follow them to safety.

Last, I come to the sisters from Minneapolis, Mary Frances and Katherine. I think of them as the "double vocation" nuns, each called twice to leave the familiar and follow the Holy Spirit into an unknown place.

Dear Mary Frances, I can almost hear her tender heart beating beneath her dress as she describes her love for the people of her neighborhood. And Katherine with her sparkling eyes and ready laughter, telling of her adventures among her new friends. Though living in an often violent environment, they, like the other sisters, reach out with peace to all who come to their door. In the nineteen years since the Minneapolis Foundation was commissioned, the *relational* quality that defined the vision of Saints Francis and Jane has gently permeated the area. Fearful people construct barriers around themselves, but since the sisters took up residence, many of those barriers have dissolved. Theirs is a ministry of presence. Whether tutoring children, participating in ceremonies, bringing neighborhood discussion groups together, holding prayer services or hosting parties, the sisters are fully engaged in "taking the Visitation to the poor." Leaving Mendota Heights was wrenching, both for Sisters Mary Frances and Katherine and for the community. But they never doubted that the Holy Spirit would only lead them to where they were most needed. They continue to share their contemplative spirits and communal life with the underprivileged people whose neighborhood they share.

If I were an artist I would paint or sculpt two representations of the Visitation presence in the neighborhood. One would be "Our Lady of the Trash Cans," modeled after Luigi Poletti's famous sculpture of the Immaculate Conception that stands in Rome's Spanish Square. His Lady stands atop the globe of the world, around her head a starry crown and a serpent crushed beneath her heel. Mine would show the Lady dressed in the bright colors of Africa with a circlet of children's faces around her head and crushed cans beneath her feet. The other would be a kind of *pietà*, with the Lady kneeling beside a dying man on the grass, his head on her lap, the Cross of the Visitation on her breast. She would be gazing sadly down at his face and holding his hand in comfort.

Those and other images I can only keep in my head, limited as I am to words. I hope that they have succeeded in portraying the stories of these fourteen remarkable women who so graciously allowed me to enter the sacred spaces in their hearts. These women are a microcosm of the thousands of Visitation Sisters who preceded them, each with a unique story to tell. But no matter how different in detail, all would share a common, unifying spirit, for each would have heard, and accepted, the invitation of the Holy Spirit to follow Saint Francis de Sales and Saint Jane de Chantal.

Mary Frances, Katherine and all the sisters in Mendota Heights, you tell me how you have been nurtured and enriched by your interactions with the people you came to serve. You have thanked me for listening to you and recording your vocation histories. I hope you know that being with you, first hearing and then writing your stories, has deepened my awareness of God's eternal presence.

In wonder and gratitude I thank God for guiding me to this task, and you, my dear sisters, for helping me fulfill it. You changed my life, giving me spiritual strength to keep my focus on the present day, not looking forward to what might happen tomorrow, because the same everlasting Father who cares for me today will take care of me every day. May you continue to teach and inspire us to know that we can never love our neighbor too much. We are all called to holiness, and there is nothing small in the service of God. You have tended the flame of Salesian Spirituality that has glowed for four centuries, living in its light and sharing its message. Thank you. *Vive Jésus.*

APPENDIX

In addressing the qualities needed for a well-lived life, Sister Péronne Marie employed the metaphor of a wagon wheel to represent an individual's life as it travels down the road to its ultimate destination, physical death. It seemed more appropriate to her than a modern tire, which rolls easily on smooth, paved interstate highways. A wagon wheel suggests pioneering and slow travel down dirt roads that are often unmarked, bumpy and filled with holes and hazards. It speaks of honesty and staying in touch with reality.

Sister's wheel happened to have sixteen spokes, so she focused on sixteen virtues for humans to practice. There is no magic number of virtues, or order of importance, and there are others besides those cited here. These sixteen are among the qualities that have had particular significance to *her* life.

Prudence. The ability to judge and to act upon that judgment, it contains much more than caution. It includes a quality called *memoria.* "Memoria characterizes the person who remains open to his or her past without retouching it, falsifying or glorifying it. Such openness makes possible the wholeness of integrity. Don't confuse it with the tendency of the elderly to wander endlessly in the past. That tempts us to nostalgia or remorse" (May 29).

Remember-ability. Citing artistic license, Péronne Marie coined a name for a virtue she views as indispensable to the well-lived life. Remember-ability is connected to our social, cultural, religious and ethnic heritage. One must use it as strength to keep moving forward, and not dwell on the past. Without a conscious effort to maintain a healthy perspective on the past, humans can easily remain stuck there in a profitless, wistful, sometimes bitter invocation of ghosts. The past can imprison one with guilt, anxiety or despair over what one did, or had, or was. It is tragic to identify only with productivity, wealth or lack thereof.

Forgiveness. A very important spoke if the wheel is to be balanced. Long before one reaches old age, this should be learned. Even if it takes professional help or specific spiritual direction, it must be done. Only an individual can hold up to God's healing light that which must be forgiven. In forgiving others, the self must not be neglected, for it needs forgiveness too.

Gratitude. Belongs with forgiveness, for both are integral to remembering, and to essential wholeness in consideration of the past. Humans need to be grateful, not just for the good things that come their way, but also for the hardships that shape and help them become who they are. By accepting and enduring these hardships, one becomes fuller and more authentic. They are, like battle scars, tough reminders of life's struggles and successes.

Gentleness. The charism of the Order, the spoke without which the others would not exist. Once humans have learned to forgive and to be grateful for their past, then they are able to move forward on their journey into the present. Here they reach out to others with the respect and graciousness and courtesy that are inherent in the virtue of gentleness. Graciousness begins with respect for another's dignity and for one's own as well. From this attitude comes authentic courtesy, and not merely a self-serving politeness.

Docilitas. The English word, docility, does not convey the same meaning as the Latin *docilitas*. Docility signifies the tameness of one who is easily managed or handled. *Docilitas* is alertness, an ability to be attentive to the moment. It is the capacity to be silent, to be still and thus to truly receive and absorb the words of others. Garrulousness in old age sadly deprives the elderly of the companionship of others. But the garrulousness of the young, or middle-aged, self-important bore is sadder still. *Docilitas* has everything to do with being teachable and having the ability to learn.

Listen-ability. Listening to others and thus entering into their suffering. It is very close to compassion, to suffering with another. Pity is not compassion. Pity does not share. It is not mutual. When humans remove the distinction between young and old, they will have compassion with the suffering of the elderly and be able to share the common burden of aging. They need to relate to each other not as the strong and the weak, not as the caregivers and the cared for. Sharing the suffering of others leads to the next virtue.

Commonweal. This spoke represents the relational quality of Salesian Spirituality: responsible citizenship or public service. To separate partisan politics from this moral responsibility is not easy, but humans must be courageous and not see themselves as other than part of this. Courage is not fearlessness. Courage means keeping one's fears, one's distastes, one's laziness, under control for the sake of the common good. It goes hand-in-hand with public service. All must find ways to serve the common good.

Benignity. Kindness. Benignity is one of the moral marks of old age. It is generous, liberal. Benignity does nothing to damage the dignity of another. Avarice is its opposite: holding, grasping, managing, manipulating. As death nears, one must be constantly alert to the sometimes inordinate attachment to things.

Humility and Simplicity. These virtues go together because they are so alike. Humility implies a modest sense of one's self-importance. Simplicity suggests the absence of pretentiousness and luxury. They both keep a soul from taking itself too seriously, and to help it shed its preoccupation with ego. With the years, one can so easily become righteous and presumptuous. Humans can be too sure of what they will do in the future when faced with moral challenges to faith or behavior. As they grow in simplicity and humility, they begin to "travel light."

Hilaritas. Ability to see ironies, farce and the light side of situations. Hilaritas is the final virtue that medieval monks associated with old age. It may seem out of place in the elderly, but it is a kind of celestial gaiety of those who have lived a lot, done a lot and have acquired detachment. Holy laughter heals and redeems.

Faith. The umbrella that encompasses all virtues, including trust, creativity, patience and vision; the ability to let go and to stop trying to control. It is essential to spiritual life and to the creative process. All humans need to place their trust in God, for if they believe they have all the answers and know everything, they are in danger of missing the many truths that may be breaking forth around them. They will never have the capacity to be surprised if they believe only in themselves.

Acceptance. Frailty and strength are known as the dialectic of aging. They are experienced in sharp antagonism to one another. It is hard to come to the acceptance of these polarities if one has made no effort along the way to accept the ambiguities and contradictions that life presents. When physical strength is sufficient for the attainment of one's aims while engaged with the world, one is not apt to give much thought to the intensity of the life force at work within. It is taken for granted. But when the inner vitality of the soul surpasses the capacity of the body to communicate, it is critical to come to terms with what is happening. One can defensively deny the finitude of the body, or become totally absorbed in physical deterioration. In either case, the spirit is stymied and turns others off. One needs to accept fragility and begin to see it not just as a limit, but also a freedom, as paradoxically containing the potential for new life and energy. Frailty becomes essential to the making of a self. Far from being an indignity in aging, it becomes a source of intensity, without which no self is whole.

Endurance. Synonymous with patience and long-suffering. When sickness, sudden loss, protracted pain or the impaired movements of old age bring all the bustle of the middle years to a halt, one must become centered in living as a purposive being. It has been noted that Beethoven produced the String Quartets during a period of great suffering. They were the fruit of his contemplation during a suffering that was an important piece of his creative ability. He finished the work and died at peace.

Hope. The last spoke. Aging can become a growing vision of light instead of a diminishing tunnel of darkness. Darkness is what humans will leave behind when they die, and lightness is what they will perceive as they enter eternity. They will die as they have lived, either ready and confident, or unprepared and fearful.

Sister Péronne Marie concluded with these words: "When certainties fail us, hope is the voice that consoles and tells us we will come through our crises, just as we have before, and will again. To those who are approaching, and perhaps fearing old age, it is a time of discovery. Of what? We must each find out for ourselves. Otherwise, it won't be discovery."

GLOSSARY

basilica. A large church, comparable to a cathedral, but without the bishop's chair.

cell. The bedroom of a religious.

cloister. Space in a convent that is restricted to the sisters or monks or the lifestyle that is characterized by a withdrawal from the usual busyness of daily living and is devoted to silence and prayer to deepen one's relationship with God.

convent. A community of priests, religious brothers or religious sisters, or the building used by the community, particularly in the Roman Catholic and Anglican Churches. In modern usage, it almost invariably refers to a community of women, but in historical usage they are often interchangeable" (Wikepedia).

The Divine Office. Communal prayer, often chanted, that includes psalms, readings and prayers. The sisters gather at different times throughout the day to say specific portions of the Office.

Federations. While each Visitation monastery is autonomous, the federations were formed in the early fifties to provide mutual support and help to monasteries.

> **First Federation.** In the United States comprised of monasteries that are strictly cloistered.

Second Federation. In the United States comprised of the monasteries that are involved in an active apostolate, as are the schools or the near North neighborhood of Minneapolis.

grilles. Structures with slats placed perpendicularly to each other creating small squares or open windows through which the sisters could converse with visitors.

habit. The distinctive clothing worn by religious that signifies the specific community of membership. The Visitation habit was patterned on the widow's garb of the seventeenth century. After Vatican Council II, many of the sisters chose to wear more modern clothing.

holy card. A small, pious card printed with a picture of Jesus, Mary or another saint and a prayer.

little virtues. Designated by Saint Francis de Sales as the hallmark of his spirituality, they include humility, gentleness and simplicity These and other virtues characterize a spiritual life grounded in the ordinariness of daily living rather than grand deeds.

Magnificat. Mary's words recorded in the Gospel of Luke, wherein she praises God and extols her humbleness before the Creator and the gift she has received: to be the Mother of God.

monastery. The living quarters of men or women religious who live in community to work and pray.

mother superior. The elected leader in a community of women religious. Once she was addressed as Mother, but the Visitation Sisters in Minnesota commonly address her as Sister.

novice. A person who has completed postulancy and who has not yet taken the vows of commitment to the community.

novitiate. A period of training, often one or two years, for a person who is entering a religious community. One of these years is traditionally cloistered.

nun. Originally referred to women who lived a completely cloistered life in community. It is often used interchangeably with sister but applies more properly to cloistered sisters.

Oblates of St. Francis de Sales. Founded in the nineteenth century by Father Louis Brisson and Mother Marie de Sales Chappuis, this religious community of men lives Salesian Spirituality and often fosters it in schools and parishes.

portress. A female receptionist, especially in a Visitation school. It derives from the ancient monastic order of porter, one of the first positions given to an aspiring monk.

postulant. A person who enters the first year of training as a religious. This period gives the individual a chance to live the community life, allowing the person and the community to see how compatible they are before the more serious training in the novitiate.

professed. A person who has taken temporary or final vows of commitment to the religious order of choice. Often the vows are poverty, chastity and obedience.

profession. The act of taking the vows required by a particular order and committing oneself to a religious community.

Procuratrix. From the Latin, to care for, this title once referred to the nun who conducted the financial business of the community, overseeing purchases and paying the bills.

religious. As a noun, a person who has joined a religious community. As an adjective, the quality of living the tenets of a religion.

reliquaries. Containers for religious relics.

rosary. A traditional Catholic prayer to our Lady, prayed with beads that become the device for counting the prayers. The rosary consists of five decades, each one beginning with an Our Father, then ten Hail Marys

and concluding with a
Glory Be to the Father.
Each decade is based on
a religious mystery, often
Gospel-based, to be medi-
tated on as the prayers are
said. These mysteries include
the following: Joyful,
Sorrowful, Glorious, and
Luminous.

Salesian Spirituality. Developed by Francis de Sales
and Jane de Chantal in
the seventeenth century,
this spirituality stresses the
joy of Christian living in
the present moment and
in one's vocation, whether
religious or lay.

sister. Originally referred to
a woman who lived in an
active religious commu-
nity, one that balanced
prayer with work outside
of or within the convent or
monastery.

Visitandine. A member of the
community known as Visi-
tation Sisters of Holy Mary.

BIBLIOGRAPHY

de Sales, Francis. *Select Salesian Subjects: Over 800 Passages by or about Francis de Sales and Jane de Chantal selected from fifty sources.* Compiled by Mary Grace Flynn, VHM. Stella Niagara, NY: DeSales Resources and Ministries, 2007.

Hampl, Patricia. *Virgin Time: In Search of the Contemplative.* New York: Farrar, Straus and Giroux, 1992.

The Holy Bible. Trans. Ronald Knox. New York: Sheed & Ward, 1956.

May, William E. "The Virtues and Vices of the Elderly." *What Does It Mean to Grow Old.* Thomas R. Cole and Sally A. Gadow, Editors. Durham, NC: Duke University Press, 1986.

McCarthy, Mary Paula. VHM. "…all the branches of a thorough education…" *Vision.* (Spring 2007): 10-11.

Pernin, Raphael. "Visitation Order." *The Catholic Encyclopedia.* 1912. 15 May 2008. http://www.newadvent.org/cathen/15481a.htm.

Reis, Sr. Mary Frances. *Visitation Monastery of Minneapolis.* Maple Grove, MN: Lifetouch Publishing, 2004.

Sisters of the Visitation *et. al. Mission and Spirit.* n.p.: n.p., n.d. [ca. 1979].

Stopp, Elisabeth. *Madame de Chantal.* Stella Niagara, NY: DeSales Resource Center, 2002.